A Taste of *life* on the *Gunflint* TRAIL

Written by Luana Brandt, Sharon Eliasen, Sue Kerfoot, Jo Ann Krause,
Kathy Lande, Bette McDonnell, Sue McDonnell, Margy Nelson,
Barb Tuttle, Jean Williamson and Lee Zopff

Adventure Publications, Inc.
Cambridge, Minnesota

Dedication

This book is dedicated to the women of the Gunflint Trail. They built homes, raised families and welcomed visitors.

A book like this is not simply the creation of its authors. It could only have happened through the willing cooperation of the entire Gunflint community. The authors wish to thank everyone who has written of their own life on the Trail or their parents' experiences on the Trail. We also appreciate those who have searched through old recipe boxes and piles of pictures. The uniqueness of this small area comes from the unique people who have always been a part of it. We hope that our readers will gain a new appreciation for the wonderful people who have lived and do live on the Gunflint Trail.

Thanks to the Cook County Historical Society for the following images: 38, 52 both, 53, 65, 124 (by Hertha Rempel), 154, 172 (by Doris Popham), 220, 219 (courtesy of Nancy Nunsted Bargen), 220 top, 221 bottom (courtesy of Nancy Nunsted Bargen), top center image on back cover

Photo on page 56 courtesy of Lee Nelson

The authors and publisher have attempted to find all copyright owners to obtain permission and usage rights for the images in this book. If there is an image that you feel may not be appropriately credited, please contact us so we may correct the credit on a future reprinting.

Cover Design by Lora Westberg
Book Design by Jonathan Norberg and Lora Westberg

10 9 8 7 6 5 4 3 2 1
Second Edition 2013
Copyright 2005 by Gunflint Trail Volunteer Fire Department

Published by Adventure Publications, Inc.
820 Cleveland Street South
Cambridge, MN 55008
1-800-678-7006
www.adventurepublications.net
Printed in the U.S.A.
ISBN: 978-1-59193-422-6

Table of Contents

Introduction

This book is the dream of a woman named Gail Skrien who lived on the Gunflint Trail. She first came here from Colorado to work at End of the Trail Lodge in 1952. Her husband-to-be, Rolf Skrien, was a guide at the lodge. By the end of the summer they had gotten to know each other. In 1954 Gail and Rolf married. They found a piece of property on Saganaga Lake and started Way of the Wilderness Outfitters. They raised a family. Gail juggled family and business. Eventually the children grew up and moved on. Gail and Rolf sold the outfitters and moved to Grand Marais in 1976. They both retained their love of the Trail and frequently fished and recreated there.

In the early 1990s Gail began to think about collecting recipes from the businesswomen on the Trail for a Gunflint Trail cookbook. The idea remained just an idea for a long time. So it wasn't until 2001 that she actually began to work on the book. At that time she also organized a committee of Trail women who were interested in helping.

Over the years Gail's idea of the cookbook changed. She felt that there should also be some stories and history about the businesses on the Trail. Gail compiled a list and was shocked to see that there had been over 60 businesses on the Trail.

Most of the time, stories about Trail businesses seemed to center on the men who owned them. For example, Dave Clark owned Rockwood Lodge for a time, but his wife Ann Clark was right there working with him. And Al Hedstrom owned End of the Trail Lodge, but Mary Hedstrom worked just as hard. Gail wanted to tell about the lives these women led.

Unfortunately about this same time Gail was diagnosed with cancer. It looked like she would not be able to finish the book. But Gail didn't quit. She organized a luncheon for many of the women who had owned businesses on the Gunflint Trail. It would be an opportunity to get together and renew old friendships. She talked with her committee and asked them to continue the project. Eventually time ran out and Gail died, but not before all her friends were impressed with Gail's grace and courage in facing a terrible illness.

So now we are a committee continuing the dream of one woman. What a wonderful story Gail left us to tell! We all knew that some pretty amazing women had lived on the Trail but their actual stories took our breath away. The hours of work and variety of things these women did is staggering. A second-generation resorter wrote about her mother:

"I remember one day waking up early, going downstairs, and there was my mom already up, dusting the lounge area, while everyone else slept. All day she'd juggle cooking, baking (because of course the guests had to have homemade pie and rolls with their dinner, and the canoeists had to have "Monster Bars" out on the trail), answering the phone, visiting with guests, making sure the cabins got clean, the laundry got done, and the next week's orders got placed, comforting her daughters when one of us got our finger stuck in the wringer of the old washing machine, checking on the little kids when the normally-babysitting-daughters were wrestling with that wringer on the washing machine, plus handling not only any extra staff we had for the summer but also the mail, bills, reservations and general bookwork, which she usually saved for the calmer hours of 10 or 11 at night.

"The isolation of Trail life called for lots of level-headed common sense and resourcefulness from men and women alike. Most often, there was not so much men's work or women's work but 'whoever's around and can get to it first' work. My mother can fix any slow or leaking flush box in the world, I am sure! You had to just figure it out and make it happen. You had to depend on yourself, each other, and your neighbors, and you could."

We invite you to join us and spend some time on the Gunflint Trail collecting stories and recipes. You'll get to know some interesting women and maybe a man or two. So sniff the air! You can already smell the baking bread! There are a lot of people to meet and each one has a story to tell you.

Luana Brandt, Sharon Eliasen, Sue Kerfoot, Jo Ann Krause, Kathy Lande, Bette McDonnell, Sue McDonnell, Margy Nelson, Barb Tuttle, Jean Williamson and Lee Zopff

The Gunflint Trail Volunteer Fire Department

It was Gail Skrien's wish that royalties from this book go to this local volunteer organization. Like all such groups, the Gunflint Trail Volunteer Fire Department owes its existence to a combination of dedicated volunteers and widespread local support.

In the mid-1970s, four residents, Dave and Barb Tuttle, Sue Weber and Jack McDonnell, took a Community Education course in Advanced First Aid taught by Chris McClure, RN. During the course, introductions were made to the Grand Marais ambulance squad: Vera Flavell and Darrell Smith. Vera and Darrell encouraged the four residents to organize a rescue squad to serve the Gunflint Trail. At the time, the nearest ambulance service was in Grand Marais, a one- to two-hour wait depending upon the location. Also the Gunflint Trail population was growing steadily, as was the number of visitors to the area.

Sue Weber sent out letters to the business owners on the Gunflint Trail, encouraging attendance at an organizational meeting for a rescue squad. The meeting was well attended, and the formation of a rescue squad began. The first president was Bruce Kerfoot, vice president was Gay Lynne Liebertz, Sue Weber was secretary, and the treasurer was Barb Tuttle. In addition to training, rescue members raised funds through mail campaigns. Loon Lake cabin owner Joe Grinnell assisted in filing for nonprofit status.

Vera Flavell and Darrell Smith served as the primary instructors for first aid and CPR courses. Both voluntarily traveled to Gunflint Trail locations so the maximum numbers of residents were able to attend the courses. Many of the classes were held in the lodge at Adventurous Christians. It was a mutual learning experience for the novice teachers and the novice first responders.

The first rescue squad call was an unusual road grader accident. The grader pinned a woman canoer in the water at the Clearwater Lake Landing. Squad members quickly assembled to extricate the woman from under the grader blade. Meanwhile, Vera Flavell was on the ambulance coming up from town. Vera later remarked that when she saw the green jackets of the rescue squad, her first thought was, "These are my students. Everything is under control." The second call involved a stroke victim and rescue squad members were quickly initiated into both the physical and emotional aspects of providing emergency service.

Fundraising was successful thanks to generous contributions of the Gunflint Trail residents. Equipment and a used ambulance were purchased. Russell and Eve Blankenburg donated funds to build an ambulance garage, Gunflint Lodge donated the land, Bob Cushman leveled the site, and other neighbors helped. An old-fashioned barn raiser put up the basic building. Mike Lande and Paul Baumann provided the building expertise and organization. Justine Kerfoot and Charlotte Merrick manned the table saw, cutting boards to length and bickering about how to cut best. This initial fundraising and building was the start of a partnership between the rescue squad and the community. Businesses, cabin owners and year-round residents would provide the financial support. Squad members would donate their time for training and operating the volunteer services. The partnership works to this day.

As the size of the rescue squad increased, it was clear that a better means of fundraising had to be found. Cabin owners on lakes in the area began to hold canoe races during the summers of the early 1980s. Eventually these races combined into two events: canoe races at Gunflint Lodge and a Mid-Trail Owners Auction, Flea Market and Boutique. Between the two events, raffles were held, baked goods were sold, races occurred, quilts were made and money was raised. Everyone in the community joined together to support the rescue squad. Besides, it was fun to meet your neighbors at one of these events and to catch up on all the latest gossip! To this day canoe races are held at Gunflint Lodge on a Wednesday night in late July. For over 25 years the neighbors have gathered for a night of fun and fundraising.

The next stage of development for the rescue squad was to add fire protection. George Carlson spearheaded this area of growth. New garages were built at mid-Trail and at Seagull Lake. Fire trucks were purchased. Another group of volunteers were trained in new skills. Soon the Trail had a fire department. A special tax district was created to help finance the additional expenses.

Today the ambulance responds to approximately 25 calls a year. About half the calls are for residents and the rest for tourists. The members have gone as close as their next-door neighbors and as far as Pencil Lake, one of the most remote areas in the BWCAW. They have experienced the emotional highs and lows of providing emergency services, but everyone on the Trail knows these dedicated people will be there when you need them.

The fire department has matured into a strong unit. In addition to responding to wild structural fires, they help the ambulance with vehicle accidents, work with the U.S. Forest Service on controlled fires and help educate residents about making their homes safer from fires. Today, the department is an established part of the Gunflint community. Its members donate hundreds of hours of their time each year to provide fire and ambulance services to every road, lake and cabin on the Gunflint Trail. Royalties from this book plus local support will give the department the means to provide its members with the best possible training and equipment. It's a winning combination for the Gunflint Trail.

The Gunflint Trail Association

In her book, *Woman of the Boundary Waters*, Justine Kerfoot describes the beginning of the Gunflint Trail Association: "The people who operated resorts on the Trail were independent, ingenious and self-sustaining. Each operator competed for the scattered tourists who took their cars over the rocky, hilly roads to reach the inland border lakes. Lodge signs were scattered along the Trail and concentrated, in assorted sizes, at each side road. The lodge entrances at the lower end of the Trail were burdened with signs from all the resorts beyond. Signs on the Trail began to look like roadside advertising approaching a honky-tonk city. Signs were sometimes taken down by one resort owner and thrown into the woods, but eventually retrieved and replaced by the sign owner.

"Into this atmosphere Bill [Kerfoot] offered the suggestion that we all get together to try to solve some of our joint problems. I thought he was wasting his time, but he persisted and a meeting was called at Gateway Lodge. Everyone came—the Gilbertsens from Greenwood, the Boostroms from Clearwater, the Gapens from Hungry Jack, the Brandts from Poplar Lake, the Kerfoots from Gunflint (us), and the Blankenburgs from Seagull. They came partly in a defensive mood with their hackles ready to rise, and partly to see what we newcomers were trying to do.

"First Bill presented our mutual problems, then we had an open discussion. We discovered we had been "had"—not by each other but by the public. The incoming guests were aware of our lack of cooperation. When one resort quoted a price of accommodations or boat rentals, the guests claimed a lower price was being offered at another resort. The first resort would match the lower price to get the business. We had all fallen for this maneuver, and the result was we all were barely eking out a living and making very little profit.

"We agreed to remove the unsightly signs along the Trail and post one sign for each resort at its spur entrance. We worked together to place groups of mileage signs along the road every 15 miles.

"This then in 1935 was the beginning of the Gunflint Trail Association, an organization that grew stronger and became a united and cooperative group. Our successes did not come without debate. We faced some controversial problems, and working out solutions to out mutual benefit often took time."

The Trail businesses soon discovered that solving problems and working together was easier when you were sharing a meal with your neighbor. The spring and fall potluck meals/meetings were known far and wide for delicious food. A bowl holding Charlet Kratoska's German Potato Salad was practically licked clean. Only crumbs were left from Alis Brandt's Trail Meeting Hot Cross

Buns. Eve Blankenburg personally saw to it that your dessert had a huge scoop of ice cream on it. Eve also made sure that the coffee grounds and leftover lettuce were collected for her compost pile.

An early step of the Gunflint Trail Association was to enter into some cooperative advertising for the region. Pooling their resources enabled the business to attend more sports shows, advertise in more publications and put out a joint brochure. For many years the Trail was represented at sports shows by George "Bud" Kratoska. Even though Bud owned Trout Lake Lodge, he impartially represented all the businesses on the Trail. An added bonus was Bud's wife, Charlet, who helped work the booth with him. When the Internet started to become a tool for advertising, the Gunflint Trail Association was there at the beginning. Sue Weber, the Executive Director at the time, spearheaded the development of the Gunflint Trail Association website. It was the envy of other regions in Minnesota and won a statewide award.

Businesses on the Trail recognized the need to educate Grand Marais businessmen about the recreational facilities on the Gunflint Trail. Motel owners in town would rather keep visitors renting their own beds than send them up the Trail. Eventually Bud Kratoska would man an information booth for the Gunflint Trail Association in Grand Marais. Reorganization of advertising groups closed the booth for some years, but in 2003 the information booth in town reopened. Executive Director Judie Johnson has an excellent staff of people dispensing information about the Trail

There have always been government agencies involved in the management of lands along the Trail. The Gunflint Trail Association helps express the views of its members to these bureaucrats. At its very first meeting the district ranger from the U.S. Forest Service was there to discuss the armyworm menace. At later spring and fall meetings, Trail members formulated united stands on the legislative and regulatory issues of the day.

Maintaining the beauty and cleanliness of the Trail has always been a high priority of its businesses because it is their home. The association has organized annual cleanup days on the main Trail and its side roads. Everyone helps—business owners, year-round residents and seasonal cabin owners.

Today the Gunflint Trail Association remains primarily an association of businesses. Its members include not only the traditional resorts and outfitters but also a gift shop, youth camps, a shuttle service and a taxidermist. Just like its members, the season for the association now runs year-round. Winter advertising promotes cross country skiing, snowmobiling, dog sledding, sleigh rides and ice fishing. No matter what the season Gunflint Trail Association members are there to welcome visitors to their much beloved home.

Originally a footpath used by Native Americans to reach Grand Marais, the Gunflint Trail has a long history. When settlers arrived, the trail served as a vital transportation hub, first as a wagon road, and then as a tote road that connected local mines to area railroads. The road was later paved and improved in order to make it easier for fire-fighting crews to battle wildfires in the area. Today the trail extends 57 miles from Grand Marais to the Minnesota-Canada border.

Note: The lakes shown on the map are just a handful of the nearly 600 in the Gunflint region.

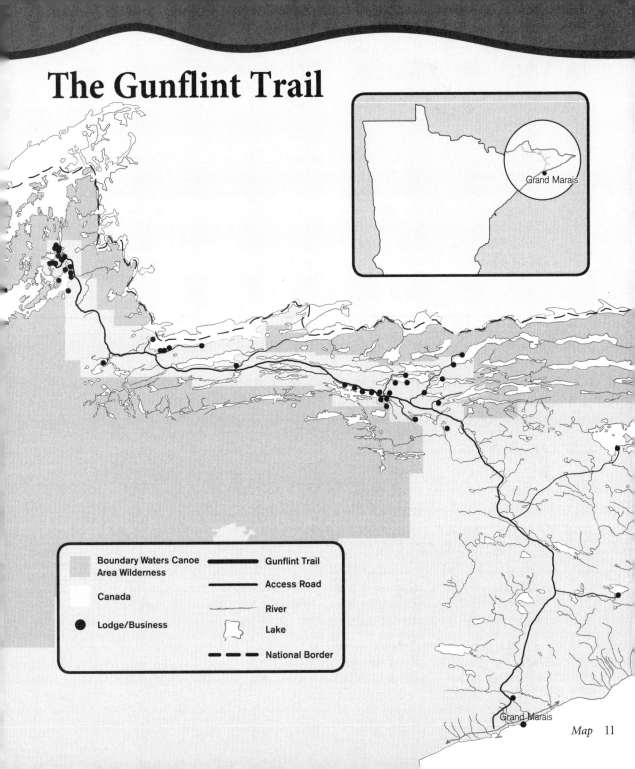

The Gunflint Trail

Grand Marais

Boundary Waters Canoe Area Wilderness — Gunflint Trail

Canada — Access Road

Lodge/Business — River

Lake

National Border

Grand Marais

Map 11

Trail HISTORY

Before talking about individual resorts, a little history of the Gunflint Trail would be helpful. Originally the Trail was a footpath used by Native Americans to get to Grand Marais. Prospectors and miners used an improved wagon road to search for the fabled mineral resources awaiting them in the north country. A tote road was built in the 1890s to meet up with the Duluth, Port Arthur, and Western Railroad coming in from Thunder Bay near the west end of Gunflint Lake. This was to build the Paulson Mine but the ore from the mine was taconite and could not be refined at that time. As dreams of mineral wealth faded, loggers tapped the forest of stately pines growing up the Trail.

One of the early boosters of an improved road was Charlie Johnson of Grand Marais. Charlie was a good friend of Jake Preus, then the governor of Minnesota. His son, Lloyd K. Johnson, related in an interview how Charlie convinced the governor to build the Gunflint Trail:

"My dad said to the Governor, 'you know you have a tremendous amount of timber in the state ownership. Why don't you walk down the old Gunflint Trail, walk down to Grand Marais and go through your forest?' When they got midway, about North Brule I guess, my dad said to the governor, 'What would you do about putting out a fire if you had a fire coming in here and no access for firefighters or anything?'"

It is important to realize that at the time the two men were just walking down the remains of the old tote road. Charlie was convincing enough that money from the conservation funds was soon dedicated to start building the Trail, which made it easier to fight fires and protect the valuable timber lands in the area. Because of the governor's help, the Trail was first known as the Jake Preus Highway.

Starting in Grand Marais on Highway 61, the official start of the Gunflint Trail was for many years a pair of entry markers built by the Civilian Conservation Corps in 1937 and 1938. You can see them now right by the library in town. From this point the road winds up the hill behind Grand Marais.

Just past Hedstrom's Lumber Company at what used to be known as Grandma Hedstrom's Corner, there is a straight easy drive past the George Washington Forest to The Pines. Today it gives no hint of what drivers faced in the winter during the early days of this section of road. The heavy forest generally protects the road from blowing winds and drifting snow but that wasn't true during the twenties and early thirties. In 1918 there was a forest fire here and for many years afterward the area was wide-open to the winds. In those years a driver would fight his way down the unplowed Trail on a winter day. Each uphill stretch needed two tracks shoveled by hand before the car went up. Every car had a full set of chains and baling wire to repair the chains when an inevitable break occurred. Once the driver passed The Pines going to Grand Marais, an impenetrable wall of snowdrifts lay ahead. There was no option but to dig to Grandma Hedstrom's Corner.

About 1830 a part of this Gunflint Trail was built into a tote road and led into Rove Lake at about the present East Bearskin turnoff, to a Hudson Bay Trading Post. This trading post fell into disuse and was later taken over by Henry Mayhew, a mining prospector, and the old tote road cleared so that a team of oxen could be driven over it.

In 1909 the Pigeon River lumber company through C. J. Johnson of Grand Marais was authorized to have a tote road constructed from East Bearskin to Gunflint Lake. It was built and completed in 1912.

In 1917 the tote road was improved to The Pines. A small portion of the Gunflint Trail was improved in 1918, but the real improvements started in the spring of 1919. That year Jim Smith came to work as the county engineer and the state granted an appropriation for $30,000 to improve the road for fire protection. Jim laid out the road to the North Brule by dead reckoning. Rough stakes or a broken tree limb marked the route. The hill just before Northern Light Lake was a badly burned-off knob and the ridge between the road and the lake was covered with grass.

In the summer of 1919 a crew of 24 men and seven horses headed by George Bayle built a mile of road a week. Wasps attacked the men and the horses as they made their way up the trail. Ditches through the swamps were dynamited out by John Issacson. He used a lot of dynamite but was so skillful that only a little shoveling was needed to smooth the road bed.

While the finished Gunflint Trail was officially a road, residents still walked a lot of places up the Trail to get to lakes and to explore the area. On May 7, 1925, the *Cook County News Herald* printed an article titled "Pedestrians As Well As Motorists" which read:

"Mr. & Mrs. A. M. Anderson and Ed Nunstedt walked 22 miles Sunday. They motored out the Gunflint Trail to the Greenwood Road, walked to Greenwood Lake, along the shore for several miles, and then walked back to the Gunflint Trail. Mrs. Anderson stood the extraordinary exertion without complaint and with no bad after effects, but the following day Mr. Anderson complained of being a little stiff in the joints. Mr. Nunstedt is accustomed to hikes in the woods and we presume the little jaunt gave him a good appetite for dinner."

Even today the part of the Gunflint Trail from the Greenwood Road to Swamper Lake has no homes or resorts. What it does have is feeding areas for moose. Longtime resident Luana Brandt of Nor'Wester Lodge is one of the Trail experts on Moose sightings. During her thirty-year teaching career she drove to town and back innumerable times and she has accumulated many interesting stories like this one:

"In the fall of 1995 I was coming home late one night from school. Alone in the car I was listening to a book on tape. Suddenly I realized that the shape in front of my windshield was the back end of a very large moose. He sped up and I stood on the brakes. Just as I thought we had made it, he fell and I rolled over his legs. When I got out of my van, the moose was lying on the Trail bellowing in pain, and I was vomiting by the side of the road.

I hurried home to call the DNR. My husband, Carl, and Tim Austin also volunteered to go down and help. When they got to the Lullaby Creek curve, they found where I had laid rubber trying to stop; they also found large amounts of moose hair, a bit of blood but no moose. They spent several hours searching and then gave up. The next day Carl went down again to try to find the animal and put it out of its pain. No luck.

Then two weeks later I came around the curve to see several moose on the road. Most stood and looked at me, but one high-tailed it to the woods. As he did, I took a closer look: all four legs were missing hair. I must have torn the hair off as my locked tires ran over the legs. For the rest of that winter, one moose made it a habit to give me plenty of space on the road."

In 1920 the road was extended from the North Brule to Milepost 23 at Swamper Lake. A state crew originally surveyed this portion and plotted the road. Their route ran straight into cliffs and down into spruce swamps. Frost would have heaved it in the winter and the swamps would have flooded it in the spring. County Engineer Smith referred to these types of surveys as "swamp crazy surveys." He ignored them and laid his own route over ridges and hogbacks where there was a chance to get enough dirt to cover the rocks.

In the beginning dog teams were widely used for travel, freight and trap lines. It took two days to travel by dog team from Grand Marais to Gunflint. The first stop was

"Swamper City" on Swamper Lake. Here Caribou Swamper shared his overnight facilities with anyone traveling through. From his home, he provided help to many stranded travelers. Swamper died in 1925 and is remembered for giving his name to the lake he lived on.

Even after he died, Swamper City was used by travelers as an emergency stop. In an interview, Justine Kerfoot told about such an occasion:

"One time it was cold. It was 45 or 50 below and the Gapens (of Gateway Hungry Jack Lodge) had started up in their city clothes and they broke down. Sue and Jesse Gapen hiked from their broken-down car in their clothes, she in silk stockings and slippers, to Swamper's old cabin which they remembered and which they knew of, of course, and camped out there at night."

About 1830 a part of this Gunflint Trail was built into a tote road and led into Rove Lake from about the present East Bearskin turn off, to a Hudson Bay Trading Post. This trading post fell into disuse and was later taken over by Henry Mayhew, a mining prospector, around 1875 and the old tote road cleared so that a team of oxen could be driven over it. The modern road into Bearskin Lake was cleared and built in a month by Jack Dewar during the '20s.

Like many roads up the Trail, past the resort there was a road with summer homes on it. Almost all of these roads were called the "private road." The Bearskin private road was one of the few to have a name from the beginning, as its summer home community came to be well known. Most of these seasonal residents on East Bearskin were either teachers or preachers, so the road is informally known to this day as Teacher/Preacher Row.

Just a short distance up the Trail is the Clearwater Road. The Clearwater Road was built in 1926 after Charlie Boostrom, the owner of Clearwater Lodge, petitioned the county board. The cost of the road was $5000. When it was completed, Charlie and Petra held a grand opening dance to celebrate the opening of the road.

The Clearwater Road was perhaps one of the worst side roads to drive in the winter. When the one-room schoolhouse was in operation during the late 1940s, parents would leave school with two major obstacles between them and the main Trail. The hill leading up from West Bearskin Lake sometimes required pushing and shoveling to get up. Even if you made it up this hill on the first try, the hill just before the main Trail regularly had the student driving while the parent (and anyone else around) was pushing the car.

Another lake off of the Clearwater Road was Flour Lake. The longtime resident, Billy Needham, gave this story to tell of the naming of Flour:

"They claim that when the surveyors were there the bear used to keep breaking into camp. You know a bear, what he'll do, he'll take a sack of flour and he'll pour it all over everything. He put it all over himself. They called it Flour Lake because they had so damn much trouble with bear and flour down there. Ain't it funny a bear does that though? They just bust a bag of flour and roll in it."

As you leave the Flour Lake Road today and continue up the Clearwater Road, there are some results from the cleanup of the Blowdown of July 4, 1999. The Blowdown was a straight-line windstorm that reached speeds of over 100 miles per hour. The wind swept through any given spot in 20–30 minutes, leaving thousands of fallen trees behind. The local residents, the U.S. Forest Service and the State of Minnesota spent years cleaning up the mess and replanting.

A little farther on the Clearwater Road, the young trees on the left were planted after a fire in 1967. There are also a few virgin pines still standing along the road. These pines were here when Clearwater Lodge was built.

The fame of the Gunflint Trail seemed to spread as quickly as the road moved north. Hungry Jack Lake is a typical example of this phenomenon. The August 31, 1922, *Cook County News Herald* reported that "work to the north is progressing and by next Saturday night it will be passable for cars clear through to Hungry Jack." By November of that year, an article appeared in the *Hutchinson Minnesota Leader* describing driving up to Hungry Jack Lake and taking a canoe trip into the border lakes.

On September 20, 1923, the *Cook County News Herald* reported that Jesse R. Gapen and Robert T. Wegg were in town to lease land on Hungry Jack for a resort. Years later Jesse Gapen said that they first arrived at the west end of Hungry Jack Lake just ten days after the road reached the lake. Gateway Lodge opened on Hungry Jack Lake the following summer. Road access also made building private cabins on the lake attractive. Resorts and summer homes sprang up regularly whenever a road connected a lake to the Trail.

The intersection of the Gunflint Trail and the Hungry Jack side road used to be one of the busiest spots on the Trail at mail time. Neighbors from all along the side road would gather to send their outgoing mail and wait for the incoming mail. Plenty of news was exchanged. Beginning in the late 1940s, Walter Bunn of Swanson's Lodge was a fixture of this daily conversation. For over fifty years, he knew more of what was going on than anyone else. Justine Kerfoot always talked with him before writing her weekly columns in the local paper. Walter had lots to say but much was prefaced by the dreadful words, "Now you can't put this is the paper but . . ." Needless to say it was always the most interesting story of the day. Today the mail is delivered to individual mailboxes down the road in the summer. One can't help but feel that the lost conversation with your neighbor might be worth more than the inconvenience of driving out to the main road.

From this point on for several miles, the Gunflint Trail runs along the north shore of Poplar Lake. Residents on the side roads of the Gunflint Trail may envy these people who have "Gunflint Trail" as their street. Yet the Gunflint Trail and all its side roads are really just streets in a 60-mile-long neighborhood. Perhaps the essence of the Gunflint Trail is found in the fact that it is a neighborhood.

From the beginning, people had to work together and help each other. They lent each other a spare part and picked up groceries for others on a trip to town. They knew their children could grow up with the illusion of freedom under the watchful eye of a caring, unseen neighbor. These neighbors bickered too. That's part of being a neighbor. But when push came to shove, they stood together. They supported their ambulance and their fire department. They cleaned up their road and their environment. They came without being asked when help was needed. For those who live on and love the Trail, this neighborliness is the icing on the cake of the Northwoods.

Today you can get a glimpse of what the early Trail was like by taking County Road 92 just past Poplar Lake on the left. This is actually a small loop from the original Gunflint Trail. A couple of miles further on it joins the main Trail again.

One of the more interesting spots on the loop is McGinty's Knob. This little hill starts on the south end with a sharp jog to the left before it plunges downward. At the bottom is a wet area where the road was once covered by logs laid across in a method known as corduroying. The old logs can still be seen. A small rock also pops up in the middle. If you come down the hill too fast, it is easy for your car to become momentarily airborne at the bottom and make a hard landing on this seemingly innocuous rock. The rock took out the gas tank on young Bruce Kerfoot's car some years ago. Explaining that to Mom, Justine Kerfoot, must have been fun.

Moving forward to a Sunday about thirty-three years later, an agitated sixteen-year-old Robert Kerfoot came into the lodge at Gunflint. He told his mother that he had to talk with his father right now. Sue's response was that Bruce was busy carving for the smorgasbord. Robert insisted that his mother take over the carving for a few minutes.

After a short conversation in back Bruce came out with a bemused expression on his face. It seems that Robert had been showing a young lady the old Gunflint Trail. A "new" rock had jumped up and taken the manifold out of the car. To Robert's surprise, Bruce immediately responded that Robert had come down McGinty's Knob too fast and hit the rock at the bottom. Robert's expression told Bruce the guess was right on target. Needless to say, Bruce did not explain how he knew what had happened. It was another lesson for Robert that whatever you do, your parents have either heard of it or done it. In a few years Robert's son Zach may meet that same rock.

In a couple miles the main Trail begins to follow the south shore of Loon Lake to Gunflint. There are many private homes along this shore. This area, however, did not get electric service from the local Rural Electrification Administration (REA) until the 1980s even though the rest of the Trail got power in the mid-1950s.

When the REA was starting to come up the Trail, Russell Blankenburg was on the original board. He recognized that everyone would want electricity. As hard as it is for us to believe it today, not all the people on the Trail agreed with him. Russell convinced the new REA board to run their main power line due north at the east end of Loon Lake. This would take the line up over the north ridge and down onto the east end of the road along the south shore of Gunflint Lake. A small spur could be run to Loon Lake Lodge. If the line followed the road along the south shore of Loon Lake, a much longer spur would have to be run down the south shore of Gunflint Lake. It is also worth mentioning that Russell owned some land on the north shore of Loon Lake, which was almost adjacent to the line going over the ridge between the two lakes. A very short spur off the main line would give power to Russell's property. With no one to speak for the south shore of Loon Lake, Russell's route suggestion was followed.

At the bottom of a large hill, the South Gunflint Lake Road meets the main Trail. The Gunflint Trail was completed to Gunflint Lake in 1924. On October 9, 1924, the newspaper reported:

"The Matt Lanktree road crew near Gunflint broke came yesterday morning. Fifteen men came to town. The road is now complete all the way to Gunflint Lake . . . Mr. Lanktree says the last few miles of the road are very good, though there are a few rough stretches this way, owing to the wet summer." The completion of the road to Gunflint is the beginning of a new epoch for Cook County.

The corner where these two roads meet looks rather innocent, but that's deceiving. As you come down the hill and slow down for the right turn, it is really easy to attempt the turn going too fast. Many of the local resident and visitors have gone too fast and ended up in the ditch."

Before four-wheel drive vehicles were so common, the next step was to call Mryl Heston, who lived at the end of the road and owned Heston's Border Lodge. Mryl owned an old Range Rover and would come and pull you out.

In the 1920s there was a lot of surveying work being done in the Gunflint Lake area for the international border with Canada. Bill Magie, who worked for the U.S. Corps of Engineers surveying the border from Pigeon River west through the canoe country, wrote about his experiences here. He talked about one of the problems they encountered on Gunflint Lake:

"We had a lot of trouble with the first line of levels we ran from the mouth of Pigeon River to Magnetic Bay (Gunflint Lake). We were off all the time. They kept writin' us letters from Washington and Crawford was sendin' 'em to me. Somethin' was wrong. So, then we found out that there was a variation between the east end and the west end of Gunflint Lake, if there was a northwest wind running. The water would raise up two inches at one end and would be two inches lower at the other end. We couldn't correlate 'em."

The Gunflint Trail always seemed to have out-of-the-way cabins where independent-minded men lived. Benny Ambrose, Billy Needham, Charlie Cook, Al Graykowski, Ollar Snevets and Harry Hummich are some of the better known of these men. One of the earliest of these men was George Wartner, who lived on Gunflint Lake. In 1917 a writer named Dietrich Lange spent the summer with his wife camping on North Lake. They met and visited with Wartner during their stay. Later Lange was to write about him in his 1923 book, *Stories from the Woodland Trail*. Here is what he had to say about Wartner:

"The largest and most gorgeous pansies I ever saw were not raised by some rich man's gardener, but by an old hermit, who lived in the wilderness north of Lake Superior. A beach of red shingle and pebbles on Gunflint Lake on the International Boundary, the old man had converted into beds of pansies. Pansies white, and yellow, blue and purple and very dark, pansies smiling and pansies laughing, pansies suggesting all human moods and faces. It was worth a journey of many miles to see the pansies of the Hermit of Gunflint Lake and the old man enjoyed bringing his finest pansies to the lady in camp."

On your way up the Trail from Gunflint Lake you go over the Cross River and then come to the Gunflint Narrows Road. Right around here is where the Duluth, Port

Arthur and Western Railroad came in on its way to the Paulson Mine. The mine was one of the major factors in opening up the area. Prospecting has always been part of life in the Gunflint country. In the late 1800s many people were convinced that there were large mineral deposits in this area.

In *Pioneers in the Wilderness*, Willis Raff talks about the Paulson Mine. Dr. J. G. Norwood made the first iron ore discovery in Minnesota at the west end of Gunflint Lake in 1850. In 1891 a group of investors was formed to pursue the Paulson Mine. Probably due to the possible economic benefit to the county, the Cook County Board of Commissioners built a "wagon road" from Grand Marais to the site of the Paulson Mine with a connection to the railroad. Unfortunately, the mine was only taconite, which could not be refined then.

Just after the Round Lake Road is the Kekekabic Trail. Walking in about one mile will bring you to the site of the Paulson Mine. Walking 42 miles will bring you to Ely.

The next parking lot up the Trail is for Magnetic Rock, a rectangular rock that stands about 30 feet tall. Before the road was built, it served as a landmark for people hiking down from Seagull and Saganaga Lakes. At some point in time its exact location was lost. Local Native Americans must have told Justine Kerfoot about the existence of Magnetic Rock. Justine hiked all through the area hunting for the rock. In July of 1936 the *Cook County News Herald* ran a front-page story announcing that she had discovered the location of Magnetic Rock. The CCC built a trail to the rock, and the trail has long been a favorite hiking trail for residents and tourists alike. After the Blowdown in 1999 and the Ham Lake Fire in 2009, the short trail is now surrounded by saplings reforesting the area.

The first view of Seagull Lake can be seen from the remains of the road that led to the original public landing on the lake. In 1974 Sue Weber of Hungry Jack Outfitters worked for Janet Hanson at the end of the road. Although she had worked on the Trail before, this summer she experienced the threat of a forest fire for the first time:

"It was 2:15 and we could hear another Beaver float plane approaching. Even in the heavy wind, it landed gracefully on Seagull Lake and began taxiing toward the dock. The men had all been called to fight forest fires, and the women were taking all the home base duties. It was our job to assist in loading the planes and bring supplies to the firefighters. We ran to the dock, grabbed the plane as it neared the platform and tied it off. Quickly, helping the pilot, we handed over boxes of food, Pulaski axes, fire hoses and other equipment that Forest Service staff had earlier stacked on the dock.

Fresh coffee and food was offered to the pilot, which he gratefully accepted. The plane was then untied and pushed away from the dock. We stood for a moment and watched it take flight. Two miles away, wind-driven flames and vast columns of smoke continued to rise in the west. We wondered if the fire would change its course and we would have to leave."

Continuing up the Trail from Seagull there is a sign noting that this was the location of the Nunstedt-Blankenburg Toll Road. The story of this road begins with Russell Blankenburg and Ed Nunstedt. In 1930 Russell and Ed wanted to extend the road to Saganaga Lake. Russell wanted the road to be built so fishermen caused less damage to his boats. Before the road was built anglers would take his rented boats up and down the rapids between Seagull and Saganaga Lakes. Both men also wanted to start resorts on the land they owned on Saganaga Lake. The Forest Service did not want to extend the road. The two men put together a patchwork quilt of private lands to build the road over, despite the objections of the Forest Service. To add insult to injury, they put a gate across it and charged a toll for its use. To the end of her life, Justine Kerfoot would talk about that toll. The county was quickly forced to take the road over.

Today this section of the road has a large dip. It is the result of one of the more interesting experiments in road building. At this point the road passes over a fairly deep wet spot. When this section was improved, the county engineer decided to try a new method called floating to cross the swamp. It should be been called sinking because that is all the road does. Every few years the county adds another layer of blacktop in an attempt to level the road. It has been about 30 years since this section was built so the blacktop must be pretty thick by now.

Saganaga Lake may be the end of the road but it is not the end of the Gunflint Trail. On the Canadian side of the lake there are a number of resorts and businesses that have always been part of the Trail community even though they are separated by water and an international border.

Most of the time the Canadian side of Saganaga Lake is of interest only to a few fishermen and cabin owners. But in 1934, everyone was anxious to explore that side of the lake. The August 9 issue of the *Cook County News Herald* reported that the Powell boys had found gold on the north shore of the lake. From newspaper accounts it appears that everyone started staking claims. Over 40 claims are said to have been registered including those to the Powell boys, Russell Blankenburg and Art Nunstedt. A later story says that the value of gold found in a quartz vein was about $17.50 per ton but no one knows how valuable ore beneath the surface could be. By the end of the summer, the Saganaga Gold Rush was over with no one finding any appreciable amount of gold.

Having talked briefly about the history of the Gunflint Trail, it is time to end. Eve Blankenburg, however, has one more thing for us to remember. It is her childhood blessing reminding us to give thanks for all that we have:

Dear Lord,

Our thanks we offer Thee for priceless gifts bestowed upon us.

We use them constantly and the Giver we sometimes forget.

So we thank thee Lord for our lives, our food and all the glories bestowed upon us.

And our friends.

Amen

Pincushion Bed & Breakfast

"The name Pincushion goes back to the Maple Hill fire of the early 1900s when most of the hills above Grand Marais were burned. The story is that a family was coming along the road and looked up to see a rounded hilltop with a few barren tree trunks poking skyward. One of the family members said it looked like a pincushion and the name stuck," says Scott Beattie, owner of Pincushion Bed & Breakfast.

Scott Beattie outside Pincushion B&B

Scott and Mary Beattie got to know each other in the warm southwestern United States. When Scott got a job teaching cross-country skiing at Bearskin Lodge in the early 1980s, he persuaded Mary to come along with him. Mary tells the story of her transition from Phoenix to the Gunflint Trail.

"For me, moving from sunny, warm Tempe, Arizona, was a challenge in itself. When I told my parents that I was planning to move to a remote corner of northeastern Minnesota they said, 'Scott must be the one. Why else would you move there?' Scott and I were not yet married. I left a fantastic job with an airline, said goodbye to dear friends and bid farewell to a climate most people would die for. When I drove north from Arizona to Minnesota that December of 1984, I remember people at gas stations saying, 'Little lady, you are going the wrong direction for December!'"

"I was not sure what I was getting myself into. After arriving at Bearskin Lodge I found that the cabin Scott and I were to live in was not winterized and just used as a summer cabin. Scott tried to explain having our own cabin was a real plus since staff never gets their own cabin to live in! We placed a port-a-potty in the shower because we didn't have running water in the winter, and we put several concrete blocks under the bed frame to raise it off the freezing cold floor. My Arizona car would not start for two months and interior parts of the car broke off from the cold. Barb and Dave Tuttle, owners of Bearskin Lodge, and other staff members had bets going on how long this gal from Arizona would last! Needless to say, I would never move back to Arizona for any amount of money to this very day."

Mary specializes in breakfast and has some outstanding get-out-of-bed recipes to share.

The Bed and Breakfast is now owned by Lynn Parish.

DREAMY CINNAMON BREAKFAST ROLLS

Mary got this recipe from her mother, Betty Miller.

1 package 2-layer French vanilla cake mix
5½–6 cups all-purpose flour, divided
2 packages active dry yeast
1 tsp. salt
2½ cups warm water
¼ cup butter, softened, divided
¾ cup granulated sugar
1 T ground cinnamon
1⅓ cups packed brown sugar
1 cup butter
2 T light-colored corn syrup
1½ cups chopped walnuts

In a large mixing bowl, combine the dry cake mix, 2 cups of the flour, yeast and salt. Add the water and beat with an electric mixer on low speed until combined. Beat on high speed for 3 minutes. Stir in as much remaining flour as you can with a wooden spoon. Turn dough out onto a floured surface. Knead in enough of the remaining floor to make a smooth dough. Dough will be slightly sticky. Place dough in a large greased bowl. Cover and let rise in a warm place till doubled in size (about 1 hour). Punch dough down. Turn dough out onto a well-floured surface and divide in half. Cover and let stand 10 minutes. Roll each portion to form a 16x9" rectangle. Spread each rectangle with half of the ¼ cup butter. Sprinkle with a mixture of granulated sugar and cinnamon. Starting from the long side, roll up dough into a spiral. Pinch to seal. Cut the dough into 1" slices. In a saucepan, combine the brown sugar, 1 cup butter and corn syrup. Bring to boiling. Remove from heat. Divide mixture between two 9x13x2" baking pans. Sprinkle walnuts evenly into the pans. Place half the rolls cut side down into each baking pan. Cover and refrigerate for 8 hours or overnight. Before baking remove the rolls from refrigerator and let stand at room temperature for 30 minutes. Bake in a 350° oven for about 25 minutes. Let cool for 10 minutes in pans on a wire rack. Turn out onto foil. Serve warm or cool. Cover and store at room temperature for 8 hours or wrap and freeze up to 3 months. Makes 32 cinnamon rolls.

PINCUSHION BAKED APPLE PANCAKES

Mary says, "When we were ready to open the B&B (New Year's Eve weekend in December, 1986), I hadn't even thought about breakfast! We were so busy trying to finish the rooms! A young neighbor girl, Kathy Patten, helped us that very first weekend. She served this baked apple pancake to our first guests. We've been serving it ever since."

1½ cups pancake mix
1 cup whole milk
3 eggs
2 T sugar
Dash of vanilla
½ stick butter

3 Red Delicious apples
1 cup finely chopped walnuts
2 tsp. nutmeg
2 tsp. cinnamon
3 T brown sugar

Preheat oven to 450°. Mix pancake mix, milk, eggs, sugar and vanilla. In another bowl mix walnuts, nutmeg, cinnamon, and brown sugar. Melt half a stick of butter in a 9" ovenproof skillet. Cut unpeeled apples in half and remove core. Slice apples thickly and put into the skillet and sauté until soft but not mushy (about 10 minutes on low). Sprinkle nut mixture over the top of the sautéed apples. Pour pancake batter over the top of the apples in the skillet. Add a little nut mixture over the top. Cover and bake in oven for 20 minutes. Take pancake out and cut into wedges. Serve warm with syrup. Makes 4 servings.

CHILE EGG PUFF

"This recipe came from one of our guests, Hildred Olson, from Louisiana. She comes with her husband and a friend every January," said Mary.

10 eggs
½ cup flour
1 tsp. baking powder
½ tsp. salt
½ tsp. dry mustard
½ tsp. dried basil

½ tsp. garlic powder
1 container (16 ounces) small curd cottage cheese
1 lb. Cojack cheese shredded (4 cups)
4 T (half a stick) butter, melted
2 cans (4 ounces each) mild green chilies, chopped
8 slices tomato

Spray a 9x13" baking dish with nonstick cooking spray. In a medium bowl, beat eggs until light. Add flour, baking powder, salt, mustard, basil, and garlic powder. Stir in cottage cheese, Cojack cheese, and butter and mix well. Add green chilies, stirring well. Pour mixture into prepared baking dish, cover and refrigerate overnight. Preheat oven to 375°. Bake uncovered for 40 minutes. Remove pan from oven and place tomato slices equally spaced apart for serving sizes over top of puff. Bake an additional 10 minutes. Let stand a few minutes before cutting into 8 servings. Top should be golden brown and the center firm.

Trout Lake Lodge

Grace and Bill Boissenin thought the Gunflint Trail area was just a place they'd pass through on their way further west. After camping for a few days at the West Bearskin public landing, Bill knew he had found "Heaven on earth." They never left and Trout Lake Lodge is still in the family. Bill's niece Nancy now runs the lodge.

Bill Jr., Grace and Bill Sr. with their dog Pooch

Grace and Bill Boissenin with Grace's parents came through Grand Marais on their way to fish in Canada. They all arrived in Grand Marais on a cool foggy day and asked where they could park their trailer near good fishing.

They were directed up the Gunflint Trail to the public landing at West Bearskin Lake. Bill and Grace had been told about the long hill going out of Grand Marais, but Grace's parents had not. Grace's parents became alarmed when their car started going slower as the fog had prevented them from noticing the hill. They honked and honked but Grace and Bill could not hear them. Finally realizing that they were on a hill, Grace's father shifted to a lower gear and had no further problems. But an enduring family joke was born.

Just around a couple corners from The Pines is the turnoff to Trout Lake Lodge. It's about four miles off the Trail. Nancy now operates it.

Nancy's family has lived in the area for years. "My aunt Grace Boissenin and her husband, Bill, came up here in 1938. They were on their way to meet some folks further west and stopped here on the way. Uncle Bill liked the country so well that he contacted the other folks and told them that he wasn't going any further. For the first years Uncle Bill and Aunt Grace didn't have any buildings but an icehouse. They lived in a trailer and rented boats. The first building they built was a boathouse. Over the next few years, they would add cabins with the help of family members during the summer months. My folks and grandparents all participated in the cabin building projects.

"Uncle Bill found a place up on Clearwater Lake that he wanted to buy and start another resort. In 1945 my dad, Bud, called to say that he and my mom were ready to leave Chicago and buy Trout

Lake. In the spring of 1946 we moved from Chicago to Trout Lake. At that time the resort had a boathouse and four cabins. During the winter we lived in one cabin but we moved into the boathouse in the summer so there would be an extra cabin to rent.

"Dad said that the only complaint they had about the outhouses was from the guest who wanted to make sure that the Sears & Roebuck catalog in the outhouse was changed yearly."

"The one major item that Dad brought with him was a 32-volt light plant he bought from an Indiana farmer. My folks immediately started improvements by running electricity to the cabins. Of course, there was no indoor plumbing or telephones. Dad said that the only complaint they had about the outhouses was from the guest who wanted to make sure that the Sears & Roebuck catalog in the outhouse was changed yearly."

As with any resort this size, all the improvements made to cabins were done by the owners. Charlet worked right along with Bud. She has a good story about remodeling Cabin #5.

"After the REA brought electricity to the resort in 1956, we were able to get a well and start to pump water. This meant that bathrooms and kitchens equipped for running water had to be added to all the cabins. For us and for most resorts on the Trail, this was accomplished by adding another room, a bathroom, to the existing cabins.

Charlet Kratoska

"Bud and I worked together on all the building projects around the resort. My specialty was cabinetry and finishing work. While adding the bathroom to Cabin #5, we decided to also add pine paneling to the walls. I wanted to also panel the front room but Bud was dead set against it. It was just a porch to him.

"Before we could settle the issue, Bud had to leave for his afternoon school bus run. With him gone, I decided that the front porch was going to have paneling. With the electric saw, I started to cut through the wall in preparation for paneling. In a very few minutes my saw blade ran through the hot 110-volt electric wire in the wall. The saw was ruined and I was a little shocked. When Bud got home and heard what happened, he was furious that I had done something like that while home alone. Who knows what could have happened to me? He didn't speak to me for two weeks but Cabin #5 had pine paneling in the front room.

"A couple years after that was our 25th wedding anniversary. Bud asked me what I would like for a present. My answer was that now that all the cabins had bathrooms, I wanted one too."

Nancy has also had some unusual experiences growing up in this area. "For a couple years I went to the Clearwater Lake School that my Aunt Grace taught," recalled Nancy. "As soon as the ice was safe we walked across the lake to school. Aunt Grace made us each carry a long birch sapling just in case the ice broke through. We also had to stay far apart. During the winter of 1948–49, I was helping my folks cut ice on the lake. As usual, we had a few lines out to fish while we worked. At dusk Mom and I cleaned up the project and prepared for the next day. I pulled the fish lines and gathered our catch. Walking back, I didn't quite clear the open water and went in. Aunt Grace's training must have clicked in because my arms immediately went out to catch myself, but I was still in the water up to my armpits. Mom panicked a little and tried to pull me out. I had so many clothes on that I couldn't feel the water. Mom settled down a bit and I was able to climb out of the water alone. We loaded the gear onto the toboggan and headed for home. By the time we got into the house all the zippers on the pants, knots on the boots and the outer layers were frozen solid. We had to thaw them out before I could take my clothes off. I was one cold gal but I was also safe!"

> "Aunt Grace's training must have clicked in because my arms immediately went out to catch myself but I was still in the water up to my armpits."

As far as cooking and recipes are concerned, the rumor is that even though Trout Lake Lodge doesn't serve meals, Nancy has experience baking for guests.

"I learned to bake bread when I was about 10," said Nancy. "We had a three-burner stove (like a propane camp stove, only it was fueled with kerosene), and to provide a baking facility, there was a metal oven that sat over two of the burners. It was a little tricky to get the proper temperature

Russ and Nancy Waver

for baking. During the summer, when there were guests in the cabins, I would bake six loaves of bread. When the guests would smell that bread baking, they would ask to buy a loaf. We would end up with one loaf for ourselves and the whole process would begin again the next day."

Did you know . . .

The first Lions Club winter Trout Derby was held on Trout Lake. Bud Kratoska estimated they had 2,000 people and 600–700 cars on the ice.

Venison with Gingersnap Gravy

Nancy says, "Dad's mother made this next family favorite for as many years as we can remember. Unfortunately we don't remember what the Bohemian name for it is, but it is probably one of the most requested meals by family and guests. Grandma started the entrée with round steak, but one of those Northwoods improvisations happened one day when the family requested beef with gingersnap gravy for dinner and there was no beef in the freezer. There was venison, however, so we decided to try it. We have never made this dish with beef since. So this is the Bohemian/Northwoods version of German sauerbraten."

½ cup butter
3 lbs. venison cut into 1½" cubes
salt and freshly ground pepper
2 or 3 large onions cut into 1" pieces
2 quarts water
3 T mixed pickling spices tied into a spice bag
1 pkg. Lipton Onion Soup Mix (for kick)
1 cup red wine (for more kick)
30 gingersnap cookies, plus a few more
¼ cup cider vinegar

Melt butter in a heavy duty Dutch oven. Add venison and generously salt and pepper. Saute until juices cook off and meat is nicely browned. Add onions and saute with meat. Add about 2 quarts of water, enough to cover meat. Also add pickling spices, soup mix and wine. Simmer for 1½–2 hours until meat is tender. Remove the spice bag.

Into a large mixing bowl, break gingersnaps and cover them with a little cold water. When they have softened, wire whip them a little to get a fairly smooth mixture. Ladle a few scoops of the juice from the simmering meat into the cookie mixture, stir to blend and then add the mixture to the simmering meat. This is going to thicken your gravy. Add cider vinegar.

Now the "skinny cook" must leave, because you have to taste. Add more vinegar or salt to adjust, and cookie mixture if your gravy isn't thick enough or a little water if it's too thick. If you put a little gravy in a sauce dish and add a little something, in time you will find the right combination.

This meat and gravy delight can be served over mashed potatoes, noodles or dumplings.

NEVER FAIL DUMPLINGS

2 eggs	1 cup Bisquick
½ cup milk	1 cup flour
pinch of salt	3 slices of day-old bread cut into ½" cubes

Mix eggs, milk and salt. Stir in Bisquick, flour and bread cubes.

Shape into two loaves. Drop into boiling water. Cover and boil 20 minutes, turning over after 10 minutes. These will double in size, so pot should be large enough to accommodate. Remove from water and slice into ½" slices. Cover with gingersnap gravy and enjoy.

GERMAN POTATO SALAD

We were hoping that Nancy's recipes included the most famous dish at any Gunflint Trail Association potluck dinner.

"I think I know which recipe you are referring to," said Nancy. "Dad was the executive secretary of the Gunflint Trail Association. For many years the social events of the Trail were the fall and spring meetings. The meal for these meetings was always a potluck. Mom never had to decide on what to bring to the potluck because everyone expected her famous German potato salad. This dish dates back to her childhood so there is no recipe. It's what we call a 'never trust a skinny cook' recipe, because the cook needs to taste it until it is just right."

5 lbs. potatoes	⅓ cup sugar
1 lb. bacon	⅓ cup vinegar
2 large onions, chopped	2–3 T cornstarch mixed with about ½ cup cold water
2 quarts of water (about)	1 bunch of green onions, chopped with tops, and/or
salt and freshly ground pepper	2 T parsley

Cook potatoes, cool and peel. Cut them into cubes and salt them a little as you set them aside. Cut bacon into bits and saute until crisp in a large Dutch oven. Pour off a little of the bacon grease, add onions and saute until tender. Add about 2 quarts of water and salt and freshly ground pepper. As it simmers, add sugar and vinegar. Stir cornstarch and cold water in a cup and add to mixture. Stir to thicken and add more if needed. This should be a gravy. Now this is where the skinny cook leaves the kitchen. Spoon a little sauce into a sauce dish. Cool it a little so you can taste it. Add a little salt, or sugar or vinegar, until it has the right combination of all of these. Add chopped green onions and/or parsley. Let your gravy simmer for half an hour or so until all the flavors blend. Add the cubed potatoes. Serve warm.

RAINBOW PIE

According to Nancy, "One of the very special things about Trout Lake is the wonderful fish and fishing. The rainbows are plentiful, and there is almost always some type of fly-fishing going on. The fly fishermen say you have to match the hatch, but trolling with spin gear is just as effective. Around the first of July the large hex mayfly hatch begins and the thrill is watching the hatch. The trout come to the surface to feed and the cedar waxwings get their share of mother nature's work. We have found that one limit of rainbows doesn't go far enough when you have a crowd to feed. So the recipe for rainbow pie evolved from an Alaskan cookbook that used canned salmon."

5 rainbow trout
salt and freshly ground pepper
orange juice
½–¾ cup diced celery
½ cup sliced onion
1 tsp. dill weed
1 lb. Swiss cheese, grated
2 cups mayonnaise
broccoli spears or broccoli Normandy, partly thawed
pastry for two 9" pies

Fillet 5 rainbows and arrange them in a glass dish. Sprinkle with a little salt and pepper and drizzle a little orange juice over them. Microwave on high for 5 to 7 minutes. (These are excellent as an entrée cooked with a little fresh chives, dotted with butter and served with orange slices as a garnish.) Break fish into bite-sized pieces and put into a bowl. Add celery, green onion, dill weed, a little more pepper, Swiss cheese and mayo. Fold ingredients together.

Arrange partially thawed broccoli spears or broccoli Normandy in the bottom of two uncooked 9" pie shells. Spoon fish mixture over broccoli. Bake at 375° for 30 minutes. Let it sit for 10 minutes before serving.

Memories of —
Greenwood Lodge

Greenwood Lodge was the first lodge built on the Gunflint Trail. The owners, Edith and Gilbert Gilbertsen, made accommodating their customers the first priority. Everyone from the family to the staff was eager to do what it took to please their customers. This attitude continues today at all the resorts on the Gunflint Trail.

In 1920 Gilbert and Edith Gilbertsen bought the Greenwood Hunting Lodge from the Yawkey Estate. Edna Gilbertsen Crossman wrote describing one of the first trips her parents made into the lodge.

Edith and Gilbert Gilbertsen, with their children Edna and John

"In May, 1921, Mother, Papa, John and I started off in a buckboard for Greenwood. John was one and I was three. The first night we stayed in a ranger cabin. The second night we stayed with an Indian family near the Brule River. It rained hard all night on a washtub outside. I thought it was Indian tom-toms.

"The next morning we headed for the Greenwood road. The bridge over the Brule had flooded out during the night so we had to ford the river. Soon after we got underway, the spokes fell out of the wagon wheels. Mother took John on one of the horses, as she was still breastfeeding him. I rode with Papa on the other horse.

"We arrived at Greenwood at about one o'clock in the morning. While Papa took care of the horses, Mother bundled John up and set him on the floor while she made a fire in the airtight stove. He uncovered himself and stood up. Holding onto a dining chair, he pushed himself over to where Mother was. She said, 'I guess he thought that if things were going to be this rough he had better take care of himself.' Those were his first steps."

Greenwood Lodge was quite small when the Gilbertsens bought it. There were four log cabins, a boathouse, an icehouse and a barn. The Gilbertsens slowly expanded, adding cabins, enlarging buildings, opening a store and increasing their business.

Guests came mostly from the Midwest for family vacations, fishing trips and fall hunting. In those early days there were also guests coming for their health. People with asthma came all summer before medicine was available to help them breathe.

Edith Gilbertsen with Margaret and June

Edna explained that Greenwood was truly a family owned and operated business. Everyone in the family knew how important it was to keep the guests happy so they would come back next year with their friends. If fishing was slow or the weather bad, the family worked to entertain guests in other ways. Sometimes all it took to keep people happy was popping popcorn in the kitchen. Edna said, "I remember many times when we didn't get to bed until 2 a.m. and had to get up at 4 for some guests that wanted to go fishing early."

Even the staff at Greenwood knew the importance of giving their guests good service. Margaret Johnson Ranum worked at Greenwood in the summer of 1925 just after she had graduated from high school. She told about the time she was at the lodge alone when a group of fathers and sons arrived. Margaret said, "The reason I was still there was that I was baking bread for supper. And here came these ten men and they had walked eight miles in and they were hungry and thirsty. I said, 'Well, the bread is just being baked.' They said, 'We'll have bread and jam and bring us all the water you can. We'll come and help you.' So they ate up all the bread with jam and water and coffee. And when the Gilbertsens got back, I almost cried. I said, 'There's no bread for supper.' Mrs. Gilbertsen said, 'Don't let that bother you. I'll make baking powder biscuits.' She didn't mind that a bit and this group gave me the biggest tip I ever had while I was up there."

Margaret also remembers how Mr. Gilbertsen took care of his guests and wanted them to learn safe canoeing habits. "When families with children would come, the first thing he taught the children was how to paddle a canoe. And before he let them out, he would tip the canoe so they would realize how easily they could fall overboard in a canoe. The parents thought this was kinda strong treatment but he said, 'They need to know that a canoe can be tipped that easily.'"

Edith Gilbertsen

Life at the resort was not all work. There was time for picnics, dances or wiener roasts. Although other resorters in later years made pets of deer or mink or fisher, the Gilbertsens were one of the few who had a pet moose. Edna was happy to share her story about the moose.

"The first year that we were at Greenwood we were all in a boat out on the lake and we saw a moose calf swimming across the lake. There was no sign of its mother so we put it in the boat and brought it home and put it in the barn with the cow and horses and chickens. It stayed as wild as can be so after two days Papa said, 'It's no use. We'll just turn him loose.' He let the moose out and it stayed right there and never went away.

"We used to have a root house where we kept potatoes, carrots, cabbages, onions and things like that. Once when my mother went out there to get things for supper the moose put his feet up over the door and wouldn't let her out as he wanted to get in and get at the potatoes."

"We had more fun with him. He was a real clown. One time my dad went to pick some sticks by the woodpile and didn't notice the moose and the moose kicked him. He picked up a stick and threw it at the moose. The moose ran around the end of the cabin and peeked out to see if my dad was after him.

"We used to have a root house where we kept potatoes, carrots, cabbages, onions and things like that. Once when my mother went out there to get things for supper the moose put his feet up over the door and wouldn't let her out as he wanted to get in and get at the potatoes. Mother threw one potato after another as far away as she could to get him down and away so she could scurry to the house. Sometimes he would stand on top of the root house and paw and dig with his hoofs because he could smell the vegetable smell coming out of the ventilator.

"One time Auntie Ella was trying to peel potatoes. There were big windows in the cabin and the moose would tap on the window and she would have to grab her pan and go to the other side of the room. The moose would run around and tap on that window but he wouldn't tap hard enough to break the glass."

Guests at Greenwood Lodge

In 1939 tragedy struck the Gilbertsen family. Gilbert was killed in a boating accident. Edith tried running the lodge by herself, but it was very difficult. One of her children, Ethelmae, had rheumatoid arthritis and needed a drier climate. Also World War II made it almost impossible to find men for guiding and running the resort. Gas rationing made access difficult.

When Edith's son John enlisted in the Army in 1943, she was forced to sell the resort to Mr. Carlson of the Carlson Funeral Home in St. Paul. Shortly afterward he sold it to H. P. Skoglund.

In 1956, Andy Anhorn and his mother, Marie Anhorn, purchased Greenwood from H. P. Skoglund. The lodge on the point had burned prior to their ownership, so they built an Esther Williams swimming pool on the spot. The seven-bedroom cabin was used as the main lodge with other cabins available to rent.

Winter at Greenwood; note the stumps left from building the lodge

Anhorns maintained eight miles of road from the Gunflint Trail and the same measure of telephone line. Andy soon found out that it helped to be a Witte generator mechanic, a small engine mechanic, a lineman, a gravel hauler, an electrician, a plumber and a handyman when owning a resort.

They arrived for their first season to find snow drifts in April. The cabin was inaccessible but Marie solved the problem by filling a huge dishpan with goods and pushing it ahead of her up the hill.

Marie had an artistic flair and was always gathering decorative weeds, flowers, cones and, of course, berries for jam. Because the Anhorns came from Austin, Minnesota, the Hormel city, there was often a large ham simmering. Their dainty Italian greyhound, Sugar, was always alert for a bear invasion. By 1965, most of the cabins and property had been sold off individually.

Did you know . . .

A root house is a storage building that is totally surrounded by a foot or more of dirt. The entrance is through a set of double doors. The dirt acts as insulation that keeps food cool in the summer and above freezing in the winter. Before refrigerators and winterized buildings, every business had a root house.

We like to think that winter business is a recent development, but Gilbert Gilbertsen led the way here too. The *Cook County News Herald* reported on January 7, 1931, that "Greenwood Lake Lodge started the new year with several guests from Minneapolis it was reported this week. Some of these Gunflint resorts are becoming winter resorts as well as summer retreats."

Barbecued Meat Balls

The Gilbertsen children live in Arizona and Colorado now but they did send a couple of Mrs. Gilbertsen's recipes to be included with the other Gunflint Trail recipes.

½ lb. ground beef
½ lb. ground pork
2 or 3 strips of bacon, cut fine
½ cup bread crumbs
½ cup milk
1 tsp. salt
1 egg

2 T finely chopped onion
Mix and shape into small meatballs.
Cover with the following sauce:
½ cup ketchup
½ cup vinegar
1 T Worcestershire sauce
1 tsp. chili power

Heat sauce and pour over meatballs. Bake at 350° for about an hour.

Fruit Cake

Surprisingly, fruit cake has always been a favorite of people in the Northwoods. It's like an early energy bar with high caloric content, Vitamin C, and a sweet taste, and it keeps well for long periods. Early trappers used to take it out on the trail during the winter months.

BOIL:
2 cups water
2 cups sugar
2 cups raisins
1 cup shortening
2 tsp. cloves
2 tsp. cinnamon
Add when cool:
3 cups flour
2 tsp. soda

ADD:
¾ cup dates
¾ cup nuts
½ lb. candied fruit

Bake in two pans at 350° for 15 minutes and then 300° for 45 minutes.

Bearskin Lodge

Sometimes the way a business starts is not how it ends up. The *Cook County News Herald* reported on May 7, 1925, that "Harley Jackson is building a place on East Bearskin Lake and will have boats and canoes for rent to pleasure seekers and fishermen. He and his family will make that their home for the summer season, being there at all times to care for visitors. It will not be a regular summer resort but only a place to rent boats."

The next side road leads to East Bearskin Lake. Jack Dewar built the side road in 1923 in one month by hand. The road leads to Bearskin Lodge. In 2007 Bob and Sue McCloughan bought Bearskin Lodge from Heidi and Mike Pazlar.

Harley Jackson, an early mail carrier for the Gunflint Trail, started Bearskin Lodge in the early 1920s. It was known as "Camp Jackson" and guests were reported to have stayed in tents. It was Mr. Jackson who built the first lodge building that served the resort until 1980.

In the early 1930s A. J. Allen and his wife purchased the lodge. The children's book *White Tail, King of the Forest* was dedicated to the Allens. After the Allens, a fellow by the name of Mr. Pine owned Bearskin for a couple of years.

Myrtle and Ed Cavanaugh owned Bearskin for about 28 years. Ed was a very interesting man. He had skated in the Ice Capades, been a professional glass blower, tournament sharp shooter, and billiard and horseshoe player.

> "It was early on that I began to understand how close knit the trail residents were."

Barb Tuttle, previous owner of Bearskin, continues the story. "They sold the lodge and eight cabins about 1971 to Frank and Mary Lou Rizzo from Kentucky who in turn sold to Dave and I in the fall of 1973. Dave had worked for the Rizzos while attending college. We built a new winterized lodge building in 1980 along with more cabins and then sold the lodge to Heidi and Mike Pazlar in May 2001."

Barb also has a few stories about her adjustment to living on the Trail. "It was early on that I began to understand how close knit the trail residents were. I was a good cook, not a great cook, but Dave and I were newlyweds starting a new venture in a fascinating area. There were many challenges along the way, some big and some just seemed big at the time. We were living in Cabin #8 because every season we moved, depending on what cabin was vacant. I was raised in a large southern city and new to this northwoods life.

"I remember a neighbor man by the name of Al Graykowski. He lived in a small cabin next to Helen Hoover on Gunflint Lake. When asked if he had ever married, he said he played hard to

Lobby at Bearskin Lodge

get and overplayed his role. Al was notorious for arriving just at lunch or dinner or sometimes hitting both meals. He always asked if he could help around the cabins. He'd do some chores, take care of his dogs who went everywhere with him and take a seat at the table. It was just expected if you were around during mealtime, you'd be at the table. You didn't wait for an invitation.

"It was grouse season and Dave and Al presented me with two birds. What do I do with this fine-feathered pair? I had no idea how to take the feathers off these birds. Well, the fearless hunters plucked them and then I took over. I prepared the grouse and we sat down to the table and I was so proud of my wild game dinner. It looked and smelled wonderful. But, no one told me about the shot. You know, the BBs that were used to kill the birds. You have to pick the shot out of the birds before cooking. Dave bit down on one of those and

nearly broke a tooth. Al laughed so hard he almost fell off his chair and I proceeded to cry over my dinner. Al felt sorry for me and assured me that the grouse was delicious despite the shot. Well, it must not have been too bad because about noon the next day, Al arrived just in time to get a seat at the table."

Did you know . . .

Barb Tuttle recalls that kids traveling up and down the Trail to trick-or-treat on Halloween had to cover about 75 miles to visit a dozen homes and businesses. She also adds that there always seemed to be a snowstorm on Halloween too.

In 1938 Nell Stolp Smock wrote a children's book set on Bearskin Lake and dedicated to the Allens who owned the resort then. The book is called *White Tail, King of the Forest* and is still available from used book dealers.

Ed Cavanaugh, past owner of Bearskin Lodge, was a semi-pro marksman and horseshoe player.

GROUSE with BLACKBERRY SAUCE

This is Barb's grouse recipe.

4 grouse
4 slices bacon
¼ cup butter or margarine, divided
½ cup diced shallots

⅔ cup dry white wine
3 T seedless blackberry fruit spread
fresh blackberries

Clean and rinse grouse; pat dry. Wrap one slice of bacon around each bird tucking it under the bird. Place the birds in shallow pan and roast, uncovered in a 375° oven for about one hour or till no longer pink. Remove from oven and let stand for about 10 minutes. Remove bacon from each bird.

SAUCE: Melt 2 tablespoons butter in a small saucepan over medium-high heat while grouse stands. Add shallots and saute 5 minutes or until tender. Add wine; cook 10 minutes or until liquid is reduced by half. Reduce heat to low; whisk in fruit spread and remaining 2 tablespoons butter. Cook 2 minutes or until slightly thickened.

Drizzle blackberry sauce over each grouse. Garnish with blackberries.

SALLY'S HERB BUBBLE BREAD

This easy recipe can be served warm from the oven. It's guaranteed to impress dinner guests in your home just as it did at Bearskin Lodge.

2-loaf recipe of white bread or 2 loaves of frozen white bread dough, thawed
⅓ cup butter or margarine, melted and cooled
½ tsp. dried basil, crumbled
2 T chopped parsley
¼ tsp. onion powder
4 cloves garlic, minced

Prepare dough from your favorite white bread recipe or use frozen unbaked loaves. Grease 2 loaf pans. Snip dough into walnut-size pieces, arrange in loaf pans. Combine the remaining ingredients; pour over dough. Cover, let rise until double, about 1½ hours. Preheat oven to 375° and bake until honey brown, 30–35 minutes. Cool in pan 10 minutes. Take from pans and serve. This bread also freezes well.

Acorn Squash Soup

When Barb and Dave Tuttle built the new lodge at Bearskin, it was time to hire a cook for the resort. Their choice was Sally Bresnahan, who remained at the resort until 2003, cooking scrumptious meals enjoyed by Bearskin's guests and Gunflint Trail neighbors. Sally gave us the following recipes to share with everyone.

4 acorn squash	1 14½-oz. can ready to serve chicken broth
3 carrots, sliced	½ tsp. ground nutmeg
1 onion, sliced	⅛ tsp. paprika
½ cup sherry	dash of ground allspice
1 T butter	½–1 tsp. pepper paprika
1 T all-purpose flour	1 cup half and half
1 tsp. salt	1½ T sherry
dash of red pepper	kale leaves

Cut squash in half lengthwise and remove seeds. Place squash, cut-side down, in a broiler pan. Add enough hot water to cover with ½" of liquid. Bake at 350° for 30 minutes. Spoon pulp from squash to create a serving bowl. Set aside bowls and reserve pulp.

Place carrots, onions and ½ cup sherry in a saucepan. Add enough water to cover vegetables. Bring to a boil, cover, reduce heat and simmer for15 minutes or until vegetables are tender. Drain. Combine vegetables with reserved pulp and ⅓ cup of water in the container of an electric blender or food processor. Process for 30 seconds or until mixture is smooth. Set aside.

Melt butter in a large Dutch oven over low heat. Add flour, salt and pepper, stirring until smooth. Cook 1 minute, stirring constantly. Gradually add pureed vegetables, chicken broth, nutmeg, paprika, allspice, and pepper paprika. Bring to a boil. Cover, reduce heat and simmer 1 hour, stirring occasionally. Stir in half and half and 1½ T sherry. Cook until heated. Serve in squash shells on a bed of kale. Garnish with paprika just before serving.

Hot Spiced Wine

Nothing warms you quicker than a hot drink on cold winter nights.

4 quarts of Burgundy wine	15 cloves
juice of 1 lemon	5 cinnamon sticks
juice of 1 orange	1 tsp. grated nutmeg
2 cups sugar	2 cups water

Mix all ingredients in a large kettle. Heat but do not boil. Serve in a mug with a thin slice of orange and a cinnamon stick. Makes 5 quarts.

Okontoe Family Campground

This campground was started in the 1970s by Dimnock Stevens who had previously run a campground in Ocontoe, Wisconsin. Dim, as he was known, ran the campground up here for several years.

About the same time, Bill and Willie (Wilma) Barr were looking for a place to buy. Bill Barr had spent his life in the ministry. He started preaching in four small towns in Minnesota. Later, the Barr family spent 10 years in the mission fields in Punjab, India. After preaching for a few years back in the States at a church in Dayton, Ohio, Bill started looking for a location to fulfill his dream of a family campground.

The first place the Barrs started looking was in this area. Nancy Patten, daughter of Bill and Willie, tells how they finally bought Okontoe Campgrounds: "They knew that Cook County had one of the few remaining wilderness areas in the lower forty-eight states. So with two other couples from their church, they came up to explore. They had been directed up the Trail by suggestions from people whom they talked with along the way. The Okontoe sign advertising hot showers and flush toilets appealed to the one woman in their group who hated camping. Using Okontoe as a base, the three couples explored the county looking for a suitable place to buy. Each evening they would come back in here and say, 'If only we could find a place like this.' Well, it was on the last day when they were checking out that Dad got to talking with Dim and kind of told Dim his dream. Dad discovered that Dim had the same dream for a campground that he did. Dim said, 'We're putting the campgrounds up for sale in a few weeks because my wife has leukemia.' They had to sell and were moving to Florida for her health. So, my folks arranged to buy Okontoe."

Shortly after buying Okontoe, the Barrs arranged to lease part of the land to Adventurous Christians. One of the people working for Adventurous Christians was a man named Mark Patten. During the summer of 1972 when Adventurous Christians was building their lodge, Nancy Barr and her sisters cooked for the builders in an outdoor kitchen. As the summer progressed, she and Mark got to know each other better.

Nancy continued, "I should tell this story. We had a little Styrofoam sailboat. Mark had some free time and he came over and asked me if I knew how to sail it because he was interested in doing that. And I said sure. We went out on Little Bow Lake and we sailed for probably three or four hours. When we came back in he said, 'I think I'm meant to marry you.' And I said, 'I think you are too.' It was just like that. We were hit over the head with a two-by-four. A little later Mark officially asked me to marry him and we got married the following year."

One of Nancy's most interesting challenges during her years at Okontoe has been learning to cook on a wood-fired stove. "It has been a challenge learning. The main thing is just figuring out the type of wood to use and how to maintain temperatures. I'm still learning how to get the oven right. The best wood is ash but that's hard to get up here. I use birch. It needs to be good and dry and split into small pieces. The split pieces give you a little bit more control because you don't want it to burn too fast. You need to maintain a bed of coals for heat. On a cookstove, that is hard to do because they sit on a grate and you lose them quickly. To get the top of the stove hot enough to cook on takes probably half an hour because the stove is all cast iron and it absorbs a lot of heat to start. In terms of the oven, to get a good consistent heat, it might take close to an hour. You read stories of older days and they tell about banking fires and trying to never let the fire go out. I think it's because it just took so long to get the stoves fired up."

> One of Nancy's most interesting challenges during her years at Okontoe has been learning to cook on a wood-fired stove. "I asked one lady what to do after just trying to bake bread. The bread was black on top and totally raw on the bottom. Her response was, 'Honey, just take the rack out and put the bread right on the bottom.'"

One of Nancy's greatest sources of information has been some of the women who have stayed at the campground. "Ladies would come in and say, 'I had a stove just like that!' So I would sit them right down and I'd say, 'Tell me how to do this.' I always use a thermometer but they would just put their hand in the oven and they would know whether it was the right temperature or not. Just by how it felt. My hat goes off to those gals. All these ladies canned on their wood stoves and baked tons of pies and breads. I asked one lady what to do after just trying to bake bread. The bread was black on top and totally raw on the bottom. There was only one rack in the over so I couldn't change that. Unlike a regular stove, there is no heat on the bottom or on one side of the oven so you have to turn the bread all the time. Her response was, 'Honey, just take the rack out and put the bread right on the bottom.' I wish I could have picked her brain for a long time. She was really fun!"

Homeschooling her four children was another challenge Nancy faced. In the early 1980s, home-schooling was not that common. They started for several reasons. One reason was that Mark traveled

Nancy Patten and her wood stove

doing mission work in Canada and didn't want to be separated from the family so long. Also they felt that their children needed to learn to get along better rather than arguing all the time.

But Nancy explained that it was a long process just to get started. "We worked through a school in Illinois called Christian Liberty Academy. They walked us through the whole process of how to take your kids out of school, how to do it legally, properly, the right way. They tested our kids to find out what level they worked at and then developed the curriculum for them at that age. I had total support from the school system in town. I was amazed. Each year I had to present the whole curriculum that I would do for each of the kids and my schedule and how we were going to accomplish everything and I was just really impressed with our school system in town because this was a volatile thing at that time. Homeschooling is a lot more prevalent in our whole culture right now."

Their classes had a daily routine to follow. "We start in the morning with the curriculum I had planned out. I had figured out how much we had to cover in each day for each subject. We had to have so many days a year that the kids were in school just to meet the legal requirements in Minnesota. I actually had a schoolroom and we had desks and we had bookshelves. It was in our basement for a while and then it was upstairs because our basement was too cold. We said the pledge to the flag every morning. We did exercises in the winter when we couldn't do much outside; we'd run around the house. The kids would have their list of what they had to do each day. We'd sit down and work together and most of the time they would be able to finish everything by about noon or one. And then that gave us time to do other things. We did a lot of baking. We baked bread and donuts and bagels and pies, the boys and girls alike and it was just neat. We'd also do a lot of nature stuff. You know, go out and identify stuff."

Nancy tells this story about teaching her children. "Because of having four kids in school, I wasn't able to pre-read everything that each child studied. When Chrissy was in ninth grade we were down at the Coast Guard Station one day as a family just hiking around. There was a gadget of some kind behind the Coast Guard Station and part of this thing was turning. One of the kids said, 'Mom, what's that?' I looked up and I didn't have any idea what it was. I said, 'Oh, it's probably to measure something. I don't really know.' I just gave it a shot in the dark. And so we went on our walk. About two days later when I was helping Chrissy review for a science test, right there in her science book was a picture of this gadget. It was an anemometer and I said, 'That's what that thing was!' Chrissy said, 'I know, Mom. When I saw it, I knew what it was but I didn't want to make you feel bad.' So, I thought, I'm probably learning more than my kids."

School days have passed for the Patten children but Nancy is still busy. The winter days that were spent teaching her children are now spent helping Mark run sleigh rides. That's right—good, old-fashioned sleigh rides with huge Belgian horses.

The Patten's adventures with Belgian horses began after Mark was asked to speak at a gathering of youth groups that was held at a business just west of Thunder Bay. The man who hosted the gathering had twelve Belgians and gave sleigh rides to the group. "Through the years we've always thought that it would be neat to have some horses and do something with horses. All the way home we were talking about it, thinking 'Wouldn't it be great?' So Mark called up the host and told him who we were. It turns out that he had a lot of things in common with us. He'd been a pastor himself. Mark said, 'Do you know of anybody that might have a team for sale?' He said, 'Well, I have one that I'm going to sell this spring.' So we talked to our board of directors and one of the board members gave a donation to buy the first team. Mark and one other guy went up to Thunder Bay and they spent three days with him. He taught them everything. He videotaped things and taught them how to take care of their feet, mentored them in how to drive the team, how to harness, everything. Then we brought the team down. We had to go through International Falls because that's the only place where there's a vet check by an international vet. It was a huge long drive to get them back here.

"Through the years, we've had young people come and live with us who have been troubled. It hasn't just been kids. We've had adults come too. Lots of times they don't have any money to help out for being here so we thought it would be good if we had something that would generate some income to help support them. The horses give them an opportunity to participate in something. Helping out with the sleigh rides and hosting people gives them an opportunity to relate to the public. It's a tool to work with these people but it also helps generate funds to help support them. It's just been tremendous." The sleigh rides have also been tremendous for the hundreds of people who take them each winter.

Did you know . . .

Some of the wood-heated cookstoves in resorts on the Gunflint Trail were modified by running water pipes through them to provide hot water for the kitchen.

One of the best treats for horses is fresh carrots. Every year when Nancy digs out the last of the carrots, all the tiny carrots and carrot tops are fed to their Belgian horses as a special treat.

Sleigh Ride Hot Chocolate

It seems appropriate to start Nancy's recipes with this beverage that warms the hearts and stomachs at the end of each sleigh ride. The recipe is for 30 10-oz. cups.

   11 cups powdered milk
   11 heaping T unsweetened cocoa
   1 T salt
   3 cups sugar

Combine all the ingredients and bring up to temperature.

Rose Hip Jam

This jam is made from the fruit that develops from wild prickly roses, which are found all over the Northwoods. The fruit is usually harvested in September when it is red and firm. To prepare the fruit, slit the side and remove the seeds.

   1 cup prepared rose hips
   ¾ cup water
   2 T lemon juice (about 1 lemon's worth)
   2 cups sugar
   1 85-ml. package Certo

In a food processor combine prepared hips, water and lemon juice. Process until smooth. Gradually add the sugar while constantly running the processor. Blend for 5 minutes until the sugar is dissolved. Add the Certo and blend for 1 minute. Pour into scalded jars and store in the refrigerator. If you wish to keep it more than 1 month, store the jars in the freezer. One tablespoon of this jam provides the minimum daily requirement of vitamin C for adults.

— Memories of —
Aspen Lodge

Aspen Lodge is typical of many small resorts that used to exist on the Gunflint Trail. It was a tiny family operation that never grew beyond that size. When the owner retired, new owners operated for a short time and then turned it into a private summer home.

This quiet log cabin was once a jumping place. During the era of Saturday night dances on the Trail, their dances literally shook the building. Fred and Annie Haffner were the owners. On October 6, 1949, Fred walked the mile to the main Gunflint Trail to get the mail and never returned. Willard Waters, a local bush pilot, joined the search, but Fred was never found. Annie continued the business and it soon came to be known as Aspen Annie's. When Annie retired in 1971, Ione Tofte bought the resort with her son, Jack. Their dining room specialized in fast food meals and homemade pies. In 1974 the Toftes sold to Dan Melander and Dave Westby. The two men ran a small canoe outfitting business until the property was paid for. Now their families use it privately.

> "Annie continued the business and it soon came to be known as Aspen Annie's."

CARAMEL BARS

Bars like these are a quick and easy way to satisfy our cravings for sweets.

1 14-oz. package of caramels	¼ tsp. salt
¾ cup whipping cream	6 T brown sugar
1½ cups flour	1½ cups oatmeal
¾ cup butter	½ cup broken nuts
¾ tsp. soda	

Melt caramels and whipping cream in a double boiler.

Mix flour, butter, soda, salt, brown sugar and oatmeal as for pie crust. Add 3 tablespoons cream and mix. Reserve 1 cup mixture and put remainder in a greased 9x13" pan. Bake for 10 minutes at 350°.

Pour caramel over baked portion. Add nuts to reserved mixture and spread over caramel layer. Bake 15 minutes at 350°.

Two-Layer Brownie

Follow the directions exactly for a rich creamy dessert.

FIRST LAYER:

½ cup margarine	3 eggs
1½ cup sugar	1 cup flour
3 T cocoa	1 cup chopped walnuts

Mix together and bake in a 9x13" pan at 350° for 25 minutes. Cool before adding second layer.

SECOND LAYER:

1 can Eagle brand condensed milk
2 cups coconut

Mix and pour over brownie layer and bake 15 minutes or until golden brown.

FROSTING:

1 cup sugar	6 T milk
6 T margarine	½ cup chocolate chips

Boil the sugar, margarine and milk for one minute and add chocolate chips. Beat until spreading consistency, then frost brownies.

Company Vegetable Casserole

When there are unexpected guests for dinner, Trail women appreciate recipes like this that are tasty and can be made from ingredients commonly found in their pantries. It is a long way to the nearest grocery store.

1 15-oz. can cut green beans or	½ cup shredded cheddar cheese
2 cups frozen cut green beans	½ cup chopped onion
1 15-oz. can whole kernel corn	¼ cup melted butter or margarine
1 can cream of celery soup, undiluted	¾ cup saltine crumbs
½ cup sour cream	¼ cup toasted sliced almonds

In a bowl combine beans, corn, soup, sour cream, cheese and onion. Pour into ungreased 2-quart baking dish. Combine butter, crumbs and almonds and sprinkle over vegetables. Bake uncovered at 350° for 35–40 minutes. Makes 6–8 servings.

Golden Eagle Lodge

This is the only lodge on the Gunflint Trail that was run as a "men only" business by its original builders, who happened to be two men. Subsequent owners happily accepted any guests who wanted to come. When Irene and John Baumann and their lively sons bought the business, families were always welcome.

The lodge was started by two brothers-in-law, Mr. Bell and Mr. Scruggs, in 1945. They were from Ohio and ran the place as a "men's only" camp. They built a main lodge and four cabins before selling to the Oxleys. The Oxleys ran it for a number of years before selling to Jack and Joan Underwood in the late 1960s.

Joan, Jack and Joan's parents owned Golden Eagle for about ten years. Coming from Chicago, they had to do a bit of adjusting to the Northwoods. One New Year's Eve, the Underwoods had some couples up for the weekend. During the night the lodge cooled down as only happens during a New Year's Eve cold spell. Everyone knew it was mighty cold outside but one couple found out it was also very cold inside. When the husband went to put on his boots in the morning, he found that they had frozen to the floor.

Exterior of the old Golden Eagle Lodge

"During the night the lodge cooled down as only happens during a New Year's Eve cold spell. Everyone knew it was mighty cold outside but one couple found out it was also very cold inside. When the husband went to put on his boots in the morning, he found that they had frozen to the floor."

During the last couple of summers at Golden Eagle, Joan Underwood ran the lodge alone. Jack had found year-round work roofing in the Chicago area. In 1976 they sold to John and Irene Baumann of Duluth.

The Baumanns had been camping in the area ever since John first came up as a district manager for Holiday Station stores. In fact for the last nine years before buying, their family had camped at the federal campground on Flour Lake. Every year after their two-week camping trip, Irene would cry because they had to leave and go back to Duluth. When they bought Golden Eagle, her children told her she didn't have to cry anymore because they would be staying.

For the first three years the lodge was open only during the summers. The family would come up during the winter weekends. Upon arriving at Golden Eagle on Friday night, the first project would be to light the fireplace and gas stove in the lodge building. Since this building sat unheated all week long, it took a bit to warm it up. The family would gauge the increasing warmth in the room by the level of frost on the outside doors. As the rooms got warmer, the frost line went down. When it reached the bottom of the door, it was time to take boots off and put on tennis shoes. During a later remodeling project on the lodge, Irene and John discovered that the only insulation in the building was ½" of felt.

Irene recalls a story from their early years at Golden Eagle. "At this time all of the businesses hauled their garbage to the Aspen Lake dump. When we first bought the lodge, there were only four summer cabins. We opened for the fishing opener and closed around September 15. Well, even though we were closed we would still come up for a weekend to enjoy the peace and quiet. Living in Duluth made this possible.

"Every Sunday we would pile into the station wagon and take our garbage and dirty clothes in plastic bags. As we passed the dump we'd drop off the garbage. One Sunday as we neared Silver Bay we noticed a terrible smell and it wasn't the two dogs. We had thrown

"I had grown up in Colorado and spent a lot of time in the mountains and woods, but basically I was a city girl. On the way back driving down the Trail by myself in a stranger's car, there was a beautiful rainbow. It began on one side of the trail and ended on the other."

our clothes in the dump and kept the garbage! We made a quick stop and called Dave Tuttle at Bearskin Lodge to please go get our clothes at the dump before the bears got to them. Calling Dave was really embarrassing because we didn't know him very well at that time."

In 1980 the Baumann's two youngest sons, Dan and Kelly, graduated from high school. The two boys and Irene moved permanently up to Golden Eagle. John commuted from Duluth until he got a job in town in 1981 at the liquor store. He managed the liquor store until his retirement in 1994 and Irene managed the lodge with the boys as her assistants. In 1981 and 1982 they added six additional cabins. Later years would see more cabins added, a couple cabins replaced and a campground added.

The second generation of Baumanns took over Golden Eagle Lodge in 1995 when Dan and his wife, Teresa, bought the business. Like many wives on the Trail, Teresa was raised in another part of the country. Getting married and moving up here was a big change in her life. She remembers one event from the first year.

"Right after Dan and I got married, we had some guests who wanted their car brought back from the Gunflint Lake access and parked at the Lodge as they were beginning their canoe trip on Gunflint and coming out on Flour Lake. No one else was available to drive up with them and then bring their car back so I had to go.

Teresa and Irene Baumann

"I had grown up in Colorado and spent a lot of time in the mountains and woods, but basically I was a city girl. I hadn't driven through the woods by myself, much less gotten in a car with four strangers. It was pretty interesting though, listening to them tell of their upcoming canoe trip (something totally new to me) and also how they envied me being able to live up here. I was feeling a little homesick about that time and was not so sure if I agreed with them. On the way back driving down the Trail by myself in a stranger's car, there was a beautiful rainbow. It began on one side of the trail and ended on the other. I guess I took it as a sign that I would be fine here in the Northwoods."

In another memory, Teresa speaks about a feeling common to most mothers with small children on the Trail, especially in the winter. "I remember when the kids were small, all preschoolers (we had three kids in 2½ years), that to get out a bit and see something besides the inside of the house or Lodge, we would all go cross-country ski trail grooming with Dan. Oftentimes this occurred in the evening. Dan would drive the groomer. I had two kids in my lap and one on the floor on a cushion. After 2–3 hours they were all asleep. When we got home, Dan would take them in one at a time and then come get me as my legs and arms were asleep. It was great being out at night, driving through the woods on the trails, knowing you were the only ones out there. The lights from the snowcat were illuminating the woods and bouncing off the snow. So many twinkling lights shining back from the snow hanging on the trees. It was a special time for all of us to be together." Anyone who has ever been out in the snow-covered woods at night knows exactly what Teresa is talking about.

Did you know . . .

Years ago garbage dumps used to be the best place for seeing bears. The garbage was literally dumped off the back of a pickup down a hill. Bears soon learned it was a great place to find food. If the dock boy whose job it was to the empty garbage wasn't fast enough getting it off the truck, one of the bolder bears would jump unto the truck and start eating. Dock boys usually took dogs with them on trips to the dump.

The road into Golden Eagle Lodge is unusually flat and level for side roads on the Gunflint because it was originally the roadbed for a logging railroad.

My Favorite Doughnuts

Like all the other women on the Trail, Irene has a few favorite recipes to share.

When looking at this recipe, the question arose about what temperature to fry the doughnuts at. Irene answered, "I just use an old Club aluminum frying pan. I put the grease in and when the temperature seems right, I test it with a chunk of white bread. If the bread browns too fast, I turn down the heat. If it takes too long, I turn up the heat. I never have used a thermometer. So if you have a temperature gauge, just use a standard doughnut frying temperature of 350–370°."

2 cups sugar	pinch of salt
2 eggs	2 tsp. nutmeg
4 T oil	1 T cinnamon
5 tsp. baking powder	8 cups flour
2 cups milk	

Mix all ingredients together. Knead 10 times. Cut out and fry in deep fat. Turn as soon as they come to the top of the grease. Turn again to brown. Remove and drain on brown paper. The doughnuts will darken as they cool.

Carrot Cake

This is a delicious recipe from Teresa.

3 beaten eggs	1 cup crushed pineapple, drained
2 cups sugar	2 tsp. vanilla
1⅓ cups oil	
2 cups flour	FROSTING:
1 tsp. salt	3 oz. cream cheese
2 tsp. baking soda	¼ cup butter
2 tsp. cinnamon	2 cups powdered sugar
2 cups grated carrots	2 tsp. vanilla
1 cup chopped walnuts	a little milk

Blend eggs, sugar and oil. In a separate bowl sift flour, salt, soda and cinnamon together. Add to the flour mixture the grated carrots, nuts, pineapple and vanilla. Combine with the egg and sugar mixture. Pour batter into a greased and floured 9x13" pan. Bake at 345° for 50–55 minutes. Thoroughly cool the cake. Blend together all frosting ingredients and spread on cooled cake.

Clearwater Lodge

Clearwater Lodge is the only lodge on the Gunflint Trail that is listed on the National Register of Historic Places. It is the oldest log lodge in Minnesota and a fitting memorial to its first owners, Charley and Petra Boostrom. Charley was a master builder and Petra was a master cook for their ten children and hundreds of guests.

The Boostroms outside their cabin

The first owners and builders were Charley and Petra Boostrom. They came to Clearwater Lake in 1912, lived in a tent for a few years and had a cabin for rent in 1915. Petra served meals in their small living room. In 1926 the current lodge was finished and Petra had a large kitchen to prepare meals and tend to her growing family. She always cooked on a wood burning stove and made fresh bread daily, except for Sunday. The coffee pot was always on, and she would serve food according to the time that was convenient for the fishermen. Her daughter, Harriet, quotes Petra, "Now, how would you like it if you came all this way up here and couldn't get a meal or at least a sandwich?"

Petra was a mother first and foremost, having ten children who all helped with the running of the lodge. She made sure they had time to swim and relax in the afternoons. After dishes were done in the evening the kitchen table became a poker table with Petra always in the game. Charley believed in getting up with the sun and going to bed early. They both lived long lives and live on in the memories of many.

In 1946 Art and Lavern Schliep purchased Clearwater Lodge and eight of the thirteen cabins. Lavern continued the hospitality and wonderful meals. They added kitchens to the cabins and electricity. Their four sons were guides for fishing and helped with the running of the resort. During the winter, around 4,500 blocks of ice were cut and stored in the icehouse for next season.

Potlucks and socials were held each weekend for the guests as well as square dances for the public. Lavern always greeted the arriving guests

Petra and Charley snowshoeing the trapline

with homemade bread or rolls that she baked daily. Can't you just smell that yeast aroma? She also made many batches of cookies.

The Eliasen Family were the owners of Clearwater from April, 1959, through January, 1964. Hank and Sharon were young with one daughter when they started, and had four children when they sold. Hank would cook breakfasts and Sharon or the cook would fix lunches and serve a family style dinner. The American plan at that time was $11.00 per person. What a bargain! One fall, Sharon made a huge pot of moose soup for the kitchen crew. A party of fishermen had been lost and hungry so they got the soup, too. The Eliasens raised chickens, had Golden Retriever puppies and one summer a horse named Mr. Ed.

"My Grampa Harold kept the tool shop organized with rows of neatly labeled jars of nails and also things like old pieces of faucet neatly labeled 'broke' (you never know when they might come in handy)."

In the summer of 1963 Jocko Nelson, Hank's football coach from Grand Marais High School, stopped in to see Hank and Sharon. They mentioned they would be interested in selling the resort. Jocko Nelson had always dreamed of owning a lodge and although his wife, Lee, was a reluctant partner, the wheels of change started. Soon Lee was making curtains and sharing plans for the 1964 season. The opening weekend with a full house of American plan men was a rude awakening! Lee went back to Ann Arbor, Michigan, for the children to finish the school year, crying all the way to the Duluth airport, wondering what in the world they had gotten themselves into.

Hank and Sharon Eliasen with children

Lee did the cooking and their four children helped out. She claims cooking for a crowd isn't so bad when you have someone else setting the table and doing the dishes. The Nelsons operated the resort only in the summer months and lived the rest of the year where Jocko's coaching duties were. Jocko died in 1978, but Lee continued on her own with the help of her son, Dan. In 1984 her oldest daughter, Margy, returned from France to help out. During Lee's time at Clearwater, the Lodge was placed on the National Register of Historic Places and is now the oldest remaining log lodge in Minnesota. Margy bought the resort in 1986.

Margy adds her share of the story of Clearwater Lodge. "When my parents, Jocko and Lee, owned Clearwater in the 1960s and 1970s, most lodges were summer hobby farms for teachers or others who ran them as a way of life and a means to keep the family together. We kids all helped out, and the extra staff was made up of neat old guys with names like Jan, Ralph and Helmer who lived nearby and came over to do carpentry and other odd jobs; neighbor women like Mattie, who taught me more about hospital corners than I ever needed to know, and one or two college kids for whom we were their "summer family."

"Our legendary neighbor, Neil Hall (son of Emil, master repairman for the entire Trail at one time), could jury-rig just about anything, magically fixing things everyone else thought were shot for sure. My Grampa Harold kept the tool shop organized with rows of neatly labeled jars of nails and also things like old pieces of faucet neatly labeled 'broke' (you never know when they might come in handy). We all ate meals together, took coffee breaks and worked until the day's work was done.

Lee and Margy Nelson

"By the time I returned from living in France for 11 years and bought the family resort in the mid-1980s, resorting had become a full time, year-round business, and government regulations had us carefully counting and respecting the total number of hours that 'staff' worked. We also needed to provide regular days off, room and board allowances, and a separate area for staff to make their own meals and hang out on their time off. We had six or seven workers beside ourselves and still felt way too busy most of the time. I would often wonder how my mother ever did it all with just a few helpers in her day. And she had four young kids, while I had but one!

"Being a child of the 1960s, I did try a bit of 'social experimenting' with my staff, getting the guys to clean cabins and the girls (oops! women) to mow lawns and flip canoes, but in the end the traditional roles were not abandoned that easily by either side. We also were one of the first in the county to hire foreign exchange workers, and several of my French friends' sons or daughters were also sent, over the years, to grow up under my summer tutelage so perhaps I was a bit of a summer mom, after all!

"But as a single, 33-year-old macrobiotic vegetarian when I took over Clearwater Lodge in 1984, I was terrified I could never be such a good "summer mom" to the staff, nor cook those comforting family-style meals like my own mother did before me. I lucked out in hiring as cooks first a nutritionist friend, Ann Ganey, and then Doreen and Neil Hall's daughter, Gloria (Petra's granddaughter, now Johnson, who is still baking those pies her mother made famous). Both fed staff—wonderfully—for years, with an eclectic mix of vegetarian experimentation and tater tot hot dish to keep everyone happy!

"Running a resort is truly a way of life. The days never end, and you feel you must always be on call. It was a quiet revolution at Clearwater when Jim and I rebuilt a one-room log home at the edge of the Lodge property and became the first owners to not sleep in the lodge itself. We could see it from our window, though!

"And I look at it from that same window yet today, although I am no longer the owner. The odd thing is that the resort still feels like it's mine. I bet every ex-resort owner secretly feels the same about theirs. And then there are all the guests who come back year after year, owner after owner, because the resort feels like it's theirs, too."

Bob and Marti Marchino

Finally, it's Marti's turn to tell us about her time at Clearwater Lodge. "Clearwater Lodge is a beautiful log building that is over 75 years old. When it was built, it had 13 sleeping rooms, no electricity and no running water.

"People lived here and guests stayed here year-round. In the early 1950s it was modernized with running water and electricity. In the 1960s some of the rooms were combined to create more modern suites with private baths and kitchens. Except for routine upkeep, it remains unchanged since that time. It still has the look and feel of days gone by.

"It's hard to believe we have been here close to ten years! My previous life as a health information administrator is all but forgotten. Now, I rattle off accounting stats and trip menus like I used to talk about hospital infection rates. My husband, Bob, and I began this adventure as 50-year-olds and a month from now I turn 60! Over the years lots of things have happened that I should have written down, but never did. How many times has that been said before?

"One of the funniest memories I have happened the first year we were here. It was a busy Saturday morning in August and the lodge and cabins were full. There was a lot of cleaning as we were expecting an almost full house again that night. A young couple that were obviously in love, evident from the shared kisses and intimate glances, barely made last call for breakfast at 9 a.m.

After they finished eating, they returned to their room. Check out was at 10:00 a.m. and the other guests had already departed, but there was no sign of the lovebirds. After breakfast, most of the staff went to clean cabins. One of the staff girls and I began to clean the lodge, stripping the beds, dusting and vacuuming in the Bed and Breakfast rooms. Even with all the noise, no one appeared from the couple's room. It was getting late and I was in a quandary. I thought, 'Perhaps they didn't know the check out time.' I decided to knock and see if there was a problem. It took a few minutes for the door to be answered. Just as I was turning to leave, an unclothed young man stuck his upper body through the crack of the door and sang, 'We're young. We're in love. Give us 20 minutes.' I was speechless, but gave them the 20 minutes they asked for! When they came downstairs they wanted to know if we had any rooms available for the coming evening. We did have one small room so they stayed with us another night. They even returned the following year but not since.

Lee and Jocko Nelson

"Another memory that I will not forget happened on July 4, 1999, also known as the 'storm of a century.' Again, it was a busy day, as are most holidays in the resort business. Sundays are always a busy check-out and cleaning day. It was hot and humid. The day kept getting darker and the air more pregnant with moisture. It felt like something ominous was going to happen. Suddenly, it began to rain heavily and the winds picked up. It was really blowing. I looked out the office window and saw canoes blowing across the parking area. Being an Indiana girl, I thought, 'This must be a tornado.' I thought it best to get the guests who were milling about the lodge down into the root cellar. I went around collecting people and directing them to the basement stairs. We got settled, seven guests, three staff kids, three dogs, two children and a baby who was crying. The baby's mother said she needed to nurse, so we found a bath towel to afford her some privacy as she sat on a cooler in the basement, nursing. After about 15 or 20 minutes, the wind was still blowing but beginning to let up. I didn't think it could have been a tornado as it had lasted too long. It must have been a strong thunderstorm. Everyone started to file out of the basement to look around. Trees and branches were littered all over the ground. Power lines were everywhere. Our cars were buried. I couldn't get to the front door of my cabin because trees blocked the walkway. I went around to the back and when I got inside I noticed the front door had blown open. I called for Bob. I couldn't find him and I was frightened. Then I saw some of the staff kids gathered near the garage, which was buried by trees. I discovered Bob had been in the garage during the storm. He rode out the storm with a porcupine that was seeking shelter. They had agreed to a truce and just stared at each other during the turmoil. Afterwards the porcupine just waddled off, hidden by all the debris.

"As guests were walking around surveying the damage, the realization struck. This had been a truly devastating incident. I still had no idea how widespread an area had been touched. We were cut off from everyone. It began to sink in that we were going to have to house and feed people without electricity, running water or flush toilets. Thank goodness for outhouses! One couple had just dropped by to see the old lodge before the storm hit and now could not leave. People began coming off the lake and couldn't get to their cars. That night we filled all our rooms and put people in cabins that had been reserved by guests who couldn't get through the disaster area that had been the Gunflint Trail. We housed some folks in the extra room in our cabin. Others asked to set up tents around the lodge. We started planning to feed people with food from our freezers, which weren't going to stay cold for very long, and people weren't going anywhere. It took two days to get the Clearwater Road cleared and another five days to get power and telephone back. Our guests stayed and we provided oil lamps, buckets to flush the toilets, ice from town and water from our 1000-gallon storage tank. We called it luxury camping! It is a memory I'll never forget and never want to relive.

"I only wish I had come here when I was 20 or 30 years old. This place has such a rich history and I feel like a custodian and curator, not an owner. It is a history to be touched and relived from the stories and pictures left by those who went before us."

In 2003, Clearwater Lodge was sold to Mike and Peggy Trace. After a really busy summer, Peggy found a moment to share an experience from the summer and some recipes.

"Our first summer at Clearwater Canoe Outfitters and Lodge has come to a close. It was an experience and we made some great new friends and it was a great season. Of special note, we had a visiting lynx all summer. Our Clearwater Lynx was seen every few weeks and was great for posing for pictures. She didn't seem intimidated by us at all. She would sit perfectly still for photo opportunities for up to 30 minutes. University of Minnesota Extension set several humane traps as they wanted to tag her for research. However, she was smarter than us all. Although we still saw her, she never was tagged. We did catch several skunks, a red fox and a German Shepherd in the traps."

In 2011, Adam and Kasey Van Tassell bought Clearwater Lodge from Mike and Peggy Trace.

Did you know . . .

The palisades that are visible from the lodge are the start of the eastern section of the Boundary Waters Canoe Area Wilderness.

The side road ended at Clearwater Lodge until Grace and Bill Boissenin started Forest Lodge one mile further along.

Perfect White Bread

Petra's Perfect White Bread is a winner. Her granddaughter, Gloria Hall Johnson recalls "I used to make this bread every Saturday when I was 12 and 13. I'm sure that Grandma tripled this recipe over and over. When I first started making bread Grandma said, 'Knead in enough flour to make a smooth satin ball.' Well, what did that mean? I found out that it is in the feel and the more bread you make the more you get the feel of it."

It is interesting to note that this recipe calls for canned milk because it was always available. Bruce Kerfoot (Gunflint Lodge) remembers that as a child he thought everyone ate their cold cereal with half canned milk and half water.

2 tsp. yeast
½ cup warm water
4 cups heated canned Carnation Evaporated Milk
¼ cup sugar

2 tsp. salt
2 T cooking oil
8–9 cups flour

Dissolve yeast in water. Cool milk slightly; add sugar, salt and oil. Stir in yeast. Add flour one cup at a time, stirring until a smooth ball forms. Knead on floured surface. Let rise once, then make loaves and let rise until double in size. Bake for 45 min in a 350° oven.

Au Gratin Potatoes

Hank's mother, Ellen Eliasen, was famous for her Au Gratin Potatoes. Her easy recipe follows.

8 medium potatoes
2 T butter
1 T cornstarch
1 T flour
2 cups milk

1 egg yolk
1 cup cheddar cheese, cubed or shredded
1 T yellow mustard
salt and pepper
grated onion

Peel and boil the potatoes. Let them cool slightly, then cube into a baking dish. Heat the remaining ingredients in a medium saucepan. Pour over potatoes and bake at 375° for half an hour or until bubbly.

KRINGLE

Lavern's Kringle never lasted long around the resort.

4 cups flour	½ cup water
3 T sugar	1 cake yeast
pinch of salt	3 egg whites
1 cup lard	brown sugar
1 cup lukewarm milk	

Mix flour, sugar, salt, lard and milk as for a pie crust. Add water and yeast to flour mixture and put in a cool place to rise overnight. Next morning roll out ¼" thick, keeping it longer than wide. Spread beaten egg whites over dough and sprinkle brown sugar on top. Fold in toward center and let rise. Bake at 350° for 20 minutes.

CUPCAKE BROWNIES

After the BWCAW legislation in 1978, canoe outfitting became a larger part of the business at Clearwater Lodge. The canoeists welcomed these cupcake brownies because they were easy to pack and kept a long time.

1 cup margarine or butter	4 eggs, slightly beaten
3 oz. unsweetened baking chocolate	1½ cups flour
2 cups sugar	½ tsp. vanilla

Melt butter and chocolate over low heat. Cool slightly. Stir in sugar and eggs. Add flour and vanilla. Add chopped nuts, if desired, and pour into 24 cupcake holders. Bake for 20 minutes at 350°.

COOK COUNTY PARTRIDGE

Partridge hunting is one of the most popular sports among Cook County residents. It is their best excuse to get out in the woods at this glorious time of year. Sharon included her recipe for this local favorite.

Brown in butter using a Dutch oven, using one bird per person. Add one onion, sliced. Sprinkle with thyme, parsley, salt and pepper and ¼ cup water or white wine. Cover and cook slowly, about one hour, turning after the first half hour. Thicken juices to make a gravy.

Monster Bars

We sent these out on canoe trips and invariably were met with recipe requests when the campers came back in from the woods. They must be cut in hearty portions. They will be way too rich, but haven't you just portaged your canoe 165 rods? You deserve it! Makes two pans.

1½ lbs. shortening (3 cups)	½ T vanilla
3 cups peanut butter	1 T + 1 tsp. baking soda
6 eggs	9 cups raw oats
2 cups brown sugar	2 cups chocolate chips
2 cups white sugar	1 lb. candy M&Ms (2 cups)

Soften shortening and peanut butter in microwave. Add ingredients together in order given. Press into greased 9x13" pans and bake 20 minutes at 350°. The middle of the pan will still wobble when you remove from the oven, but will firm up as it cools. Don't overcook!

Gloria's Blueberry Pie Filling   HERITAGE

4 cups blueberries, fresh or frozen (not canned)	and (the secret ingredients):
1½ cups sugar	⅛ tsp. cinnamon
3 heaping T flour	⅛ tsp. nutmeg

Gloria's Buttermilk Pancakes

Marti says that this pancake recipe for six is another favorite with guests. She explained, "Gloria Hall Johnson is the granddaughter of Charlie and Petra Boostrom, builders of the lodge. Gloria was also our cook for several years. It was really neat to have a 'real' Boostrom in the kitchen, shades of Petra."

3 eggs	1 tsp. salt
2½ cups buttermilk	1 tsp. baking soda
2 cups bread flour	½ cup melted margarine
2 tsp. baking powder	

Beat eggs lightly. Stir in buttermilk and set aside. Sift flour, baking powder, salt and soda. Stir egg mixture into dry ingredients, just enough to mix. Add margarine. Pour ¼ cup of batter on hot, greased griddle. When edges look dry and bubbles are popping on the top of each pancake, flip to other side. Serve warm with maple syrup.

ANNE GANEY'S SPINACH RICOTTA PIE

According to Margy, this recipe is deceptively simple to make. "It holds its shape once cut into, freezes well and has such a fresh, clean taste you just keep on eating. Anne used to make and freeze several of these for us in the fall before she left, so we had something to eat once she was gone!"

1 15-oz. tub low-fat ricotta cheese
1 10-oz. pkg. chopped frozen spinach
1 cup chopped onion

2 T lemon juice
1 cup grated Parmesan cheese
2 pie shells

Thaw spinach and squeeze out water so it's dry. Mix all together and put into pie shells. Bake 45 minutes at 350°.

BREAKFAST CASSEROLE

Marti says that they regularly used this recipe for their guests.

1 lb. bulk pork sausage
6 slices bread
1½ cups shredded Cheddar cheese
8 eggs, lightly beaten

2 cups milk
1 tsp. dry mustard
¼ cup (half a stick) unsalted butter, melted

In a skillet, fry the sausage until browned, stirring well to crumble. Drain. While the sausage is draining, cut the bread into 1" squares. Cover the bottom of a 9x11x2" pan. Cover the bread with sausage and cheese. Mix together the beaten eggs, milk and dry mustard. Pour over the casserole mixture and drizzle on the melted butter.

Cover the casserole with plastic wrap and place in the refrigerator to chill overnight.

Preheat the oven to 350° for 20 minutes before baking.

Remove the casserole from the refrigerator and let stand for 15 minutes while the oven preheats. Bake for 45 minutes, or until set. Serves 9–12.

Serve hot, or cool to wrap later and freeze.

MARTI'S SPAGHETTI DINNER for the TRAIL

One of the philosophies Bob and I have as canoe outfitters is that you work hard on the trail, therefore eating should be a rewarding experience. This is something we take along when we canoe camp. It takes a little preparation, but it is well worth the effort.

SAUCE:
3 T olive oil
1 T finely chopped parsley
1 T finely chopped onion
1 clove garlic, crushed

1 16-oz. can stewed tomatoes
2 8-oz. cans tomato sauce
¼ tsp. salt
2 bay leaves, crumbled
½ tsp. dried basil leaves
1 tsp. oregano

Slowly heat oil in large skillet. Over medium heat, saute parsley, onion and garlic until onion is translucent. Add tomatoes, sauce and salt. Over medium heat, bring to boil, stirring frequently. Remove from heat. Add bay leaves, basil and oregano. Mix well. Cook, covered, over low heat, stirring occasionally, for 1 hour.

Let stand until cool. While cooling, set up food dehydrator. Cut freezer wrap to fit dehydrator trays. Place cut freezer wrap, shiny side up, on the tray surface. When cooled, put sauce in a food processor and puree. Ladle by serving size to the trays of the dehydrator. It should form a thin layer about ¼" thick. Dehydrate several hours until the sauce has become leathery and dry to the touch. Peel the spaghetti leather from the freezer wrap and roll.

Place in plastic zipper bag. Store in refrigerator or freezer. Although the leather will last several months, the flavor is better the sooner it's used.

MEAT:
1 lb. lean ground beef
1 tsp. garlic

1 tsp. salt
pepper, to taste

Fry ground beef, garlic, salt and pepper in medium skillet until well browned. Stir frequently to crumble. When the meat is browned put in strainer to drain the grease. Allow to cool slightly. Then rinse under cool water until grease is no longer evident. The culprit in spoilage is retained grease so really rinse well. Pat dry with paper towels. Spread meat in small crumbles (break larger ones apart) in the trays of a dehydrator. Allow enough room for air to circulate. Process according to manufacturer's directions. When dehydrated, place in plastic zipper bag. Store in refrigerator or freezer. Although it will keep for several months, the sooner used the better.

To reconstitute on the trail (serves 4–5 hungry campers): Bring 5 cups of water to boil, add dehydrated hamburger, turn off heat and let stand about 10 minutes. Bring to boil again; add pieces of leather to mixture and simmer until resembles sauce. Add a little more water if needed. Serve over noodles with garlic bread, carrots and celery sticks, and a chocolate brownie.

BAKED SWEET POTATO CASSEROLE

Peggy may be new to the Gunflint Trail, but this recipe shows that she is not new to cooking.

3 cups mashed sweet potatoes (cooked)
½ cup sugar
2 beaten eggs
¼ tsp. salt

½ stick melted margarine or butter
½ cup milk
½ tsp. vanilla

Mix all ingredients together. Put into greased 1½-quart shallow baking dish.

TOPPING:
¼ cup brown sugar
½ cup plain flour
1 cup chopped pecans
½ stick melted butter

Mix topping and spread over potatoes. Bake uncovered at 325° for 30 minutes. This can be mixed the day before and refrigerated overnight. If you do make it the day before, then bake for 40 minutes.

VENISON MINCEMEAT

4 lbs. cooked ground venison
2 lbs. ground suet
8 lbs. apples, cored but not peeled
½ lb. lemon peel
1 qt. apple cider
1 cup vinegar
2 lbs. brown sugar
3 lbs. white sugar
½ cup molasses (optional)
4 tsp. salt

½ lb. citron
3 lbs. raisins
2 lbs. currants
4 tsp. cinnamon
2 tsp. mace
2 tsp. nutmeg
2 tsp. cloves
½ lb. margarine
juice from meat

Grind meat, suet, apples and lemon peel together. Add rest of ingredients and cook 1 hour. Seal while hot.

DOREEN'S PIE CRUST

When Gloria was cooking at Clearwater and her mother, Doreen Boostrom Hall, was still alive, we would buy pies from Doreen once or twice a week and serve them in our dining area. As did many cooks, Doreen had been trying for some years to reduce the amount of fat in her wonderful home-style cooking, and she had taken to making her pies with margarine. One day, as Gloria was tasting a piece of her mother's pie (surely just a little leftover morsel, as they always sold out, to the great dismay of the staff), she got a very funny look on her face. Gloria slowly turned to her mother and said, "Mother, are you using lard in your pie crusts again?" Doreen looked down at the floor, sheepishly, and then she raised her head and replied, a bit defiantly, "Well, you just can't make a good pie crust without lard."

I was telling that story one day to a very hip-looking family of four who were eagerly biting into their pieces of pie after a full day's paddling around the lake. As I served the punch line, their forks froze in mid-air, and they all looked at each other, aghast. Turns out all four of them were vegetarians! The father made some calm remark about good learning experiences, and I slunk out of the room, mortified that I had ruined their treat with my need to entertain. Later, when I went out to clear the plates, I saw that each of them had dealt with the situation differently. One had left the rest untouched, one had eaten out all of the filling, one had cleaned the plate completely, and one had picked at the pie so much as to make it unrecognizable.

On an unrelated but equally memorable note, I remember a young child gazing in awe at one of the moose heads in that same dining room and then asking, timidly but insistently, if she could please go around to the other side of the wall to see the rest of the moose.

> 2½ cups unbleached flour
> 1 tsp. salt
> 1 cup lard, cut into the salted flour until fine
> ½ cup really cold water

Mix not much. Form into 4 equal balls, roll out on a lightly floured surface

Gloria Johnson says, "The less amount of messing around you do, the better. To get a pie crust that is tender and flaky, the dough will be difficult and yucky to work with; but if you gather it all up and try over again with all that extra flour in there, it gets too tough."

Yield: 4 pie crusts or 2 full pies

— Memories of —
Forest Lodge

After founding and running Trout Lake Lodge from 1938 to 1946, Grace and Bill Boissinen moved up the Trail to Clearwater Lodge. They built a new lodge named after the massive pine forest surrounding the cabins. For several years during the winter, Grace was the Clearwater School teacher with children in eight grades.

The Boissenins are another pioneer family who helped open up this country. Bill and Grace Boissenin started Trout Lake Lodge in 1938 and then sold it to Grace's sister and brother-in-law, Charlet and Bud Kratoska in 1946. After selling, Bill and Grace moved up the Trail and extended the road from Clearwater Lodge to land they purchased from Chet Holden.

"When we walked across the ice, we each carried a pole to test safety and also hopefully to put across a hole in the ice if we went through."

Grace wrote in 1956, "Chet had an old fashioned waterless cooker that he used often. He liked stews, so would start them cooking and at the same time heat the stones that kept the cooker hot. He would put the kettle of food in the cooker and close it up and be gone all day on a fishing or exploration trip. When he arrived home tired and hungry, his meal would be waiting for him." Might be a forerunner of our crock pots.

While at Trout Lake Lodge, the Boissenins spent the winters in a small cabin by Hedstrom Lumber Co. Bill worked for them during the winter. Grace taught 1st grade and grades 5–8 at the Maple Hill School. After Grace and Bill moved to Forest Lodge, the Schlieps, who had four school-aged boys, asked her to teach them. They converted an old cabin to a schoolhouse. She would have six or seven students, more in the fall: Bruce Kerfoot from Gunflint, the three Brandt boys from Poplar, two from Swanson's Lodge on Hungry Jack, her sister's daughter Nancy from Trout Lake, Ravina, the daughter of a logger on Greenwood Road and the four Schliep boys were her students. Nancy and Ravina would stay with Grace and Bill during the week.

Students at the Clearwater School

Grace wrote in 1986, "We walked the mile over the hill in the fall and spring until the ice got thick enough to be safe. When we walked across the ice, we each carried a pole to test safety and also hopefully to put across a hole in the ice if we went through. I warned each of them to stay a distance apart from each other. Ravina always followed me and soon she would be hitting my heels. I would warn her but soon I'd feel her hitting my heels again. I always had a packsack with books I needed at home for lesson assignments. We didn't have enough copies so I could leave one at home." In the Trout Lake Lodge section (pg. 26) Nancy Kratoska Waver related how much of an impression these ice safety rules made on her.

Grace continued, "I'll never forget at Forest Lodge a chimney fire in the middle of the night. I had never experienced anything like that before and Bill was at the lumber camp so it was up to me. You had to go outside and use a ladder to climb up to a window to get to the attic. I went up with a flashlight, then made several trips with a bucket of snow, which I packed around the chimney to cool it down. Needless to say, I didn't sleep much the rest of the night. That never happened again as I learned that the pitch should be cleaned out every so often before it built up."

Bill and Grace cutting and moving ice blocks

Boissenins sold Forest Lodge, consisting of a house and six cabins, to Ray and Alice Kulick in 1966. Ray and Alice had been on many canoe trips in the area and had stayed at Loon Lake Lodge. They built a recreation building and always had plenty of popcorn on hand. Alice had a pet squirrel.

Alice could see Clearwater Lodge from her window, and one morning after an electrical storm, she called Jocko and Lee Nelson at Clearwater Lodge. Alice wanted them to look around as she could see smoke. One of the cabins had been hit and with her timely call the damage was minimal. The Kulicks sold the individual cabins to private parties and in a few years the resort was closed.

Did you know . . .

Forest Lodge got its name from all the beautiful Norway pines that grew on the point of land on which the lodge was located.

Shipwreck: A One-Dish Meal

Slice 1 onion into a buttered casserole. Over onion, arrange thin slices of raw potato. Over this place a thick layer of chopped beef. Cover with a layer of uncooked rice. Next a layer of chopped celery, then 2 cups of kidney beans. Season each layer lightly with salt, pepper and paprika. Top all with 2 cups of tomatoes rubbed through a sieve. Cover and bake in a moderate oven for 2 hours. If necessary, add water during the cooking period. You may have to add as much as 2½ cups of water. Serve in casserole with sliced green pickles as garnish.

Golden Cheddar Broccoli Bake

4 T margarine, divided
2 T flour
¼ tsp. salt
1½ cups milk
1½ cups cheddar cheese

¾ cup cracker crumbs, divided
1 12-oz. can whole kernel corn (drained)
2 10-oz. package frozen broccoli spears
 (cooked and drained)

Melt 2 tablespoons margarine. Stir in flour and salt. Add milk gradually, mixing until smooth. Cook until mixture boils, stirring constantly. Add cheese; stir until melted. Mix in ¼ cup cracker crumbs and corn.

Arrange broccoli in 11¾x7½" baking dish. Pour cheese mixture over broccoli. Toss remaining crumbs with remaining 2 tablespoons melted margarine. Sprinkle over casserole. Bake at 350° for 30 minutes.

Calico Bean Bake

½ lb. bacon, diced, fried and drained
½ lb. ground beef, fried and drained
1 cup finely chopped onion, fried
1 tsp. mustard
½ cup ketchup

¾ cup brown sugar
1 can pork and beans
1 can lima beans
1 can kidney beans

Mix all together and bake on high for 1 hour in crock pot or bake 1 hour in a 350° oven.

Note: 1 can Brook's chili beans may be substituted for kidney beans and green beans for lima beans.

Rice Krispies Bars

1 cup (6-oz. package) butterscotch morsels
½ cup peanut butter
4 cups Rice Krispies (half of a 7.2-ounce box)
1 cup (6-oz. package) chocolate chips
½ cup powdered sugar
2 T butter or margarine
½ tsp. vanilla
1–2 T hot water

Melt butterscotch morsels and peanut butter together in a heavy pan over low heat. Add the Rice Krispies and mix well. Put half the mixture in a 9x9" pan and pat down well.

In another pan, melt chocolate chips; add powdered sugar, butter, vanilla and enough hot water to spread over first mixture. Spread rest of Rice Krispies mixture over chocolate mixture and press down. Chill and cut into squares.

Old Fort William Scones

Alice did share this scone recipe with one of the new cabin owners.

2 cups flour
¼ cup sugar
½ tsp. salt
2½ tsp. baking powder
½ tsp. baking soda
¼ cup shortening
¼ cup currants or raisins
1 cup buttermilk

Sift dry ingredients, cut in shortening, add currants or raisins and milk. It will be sticky. Turn onto a floured board. Knead 1 minute. Divide into 2 rounds. Bake on an ungreased pan for 12–15 minutes at 450°.

Poplar Creek Guesthouse Bed & Breakfast

For more than 30 years Barbara and Ted Young have operated a bed and breakfast on the Trail. The location changed from an island on Poplar Lake to the present forest hideaway. Their guests can experience a bit of everything from rustic yurts to cozy rooms. Most of all they keep coming back for the quiet of a smaller place and for Barbara's meals.

Owned by Barbara and Ted Young, this guesthouse is the culmination of many years' work on the Trail. Along the way Barbara developed the most unusual meal for guests staying on the Gunflint Trail: Mongolian Firepot Dinner. Barbara tells the story of this meal.

Barbara and Ted Young at a yurt with guests

"How did I ever come up with this idea? First things first. I arrived in 1974 with my husband, Ted, to his family's island summer home on Poplar Lake. We were only going to stay a few months, but are still here. A few years later we had a team of dogs and wanted to earn money with them. Ted started giving rides and then overnight camping trips were scheduled. People needed a place to sleep and eat before their trips. We used a room in our small log cabin, first as winter guest lodging and later added breakfast and lodging in the summer. With no restaurants nearby at that time in the winter, I started baking and cooking for our guests.

"By the early 1980s, we realized that a wall tent for sleeping during a dog sled trip was not adding that special touch. I read a story in Cross Country Skier magazine about a yurt system in Sun Valley, Idaho. I liked the idea and showed it to Ted. He did not think it would work up here. Then a local resorter mentioned the same story and Ted gave it another look.

"At about the same time and at the insistence of the Gunflint ski lodges, the U.S. Forest Service opened a ski trail though the BWCAW to connect the Central and Upper Ski Trail Systems. The trail was to be used for the Gunflint ski lodges' new Lodge-to-Lodge Skiing Program, which had just been introduced. However, the 29-kilometer trail was a bit long for most skiers. We felt the need for an overnight stop along the trail.

"Necessity being the mother of invention, in 1982, we leased land from the U.S. Forest Service along the trail and our first yurt, the E.J. Croft Memorial Yurt, was opened to skiers as an overnight stop.

"It was at this time that we incorporated our dog sledding, island bed and breakfast and new yurt business under the name of Boundary Country Trekking.

"I arrived in 1974 with my husband, Ted, to his family's island summer home on Poplar Lake. We were only going to stay a few months, but are still here."

"The trail up to this time was called, depending upon who you talked to, the Ski-Thru Trail, the Artery Trail, and the Tucker Lake Ski Trail. Finally at a meeting of the Gunflint ski lodges, in an effort to end the confusion over the trail name, we proposed naming the trail the Banadad Ski Trail after a lake of the same name midway along the trail. Incidentally *Banadad* in Ojibwe means lost. The name stuck.

"Since we were planning to serve meals at the yurt, I had to have a meal that would add to the yurt experience. Looking over my Asian cookbooks, I found the photo of a Mongolian firepot. Then I started searching for the recipes using a firepot. Of course I could not use mutton, so I adapted the meal to American tastes. Tried lamb. Loved it, but no one else did. Eventually I came up with the recipe.

"Although the recipe is very time-consuming to prepare, in the overnight hut it solved a big problem for us: entertainment. When guests skied into the hut, they were met by a hut host who spent the night with them, cooked the meals, kept the wood stove going, and generally answered questions. The firepot meal is one that is best enjoyed over a period of time and accompanied with conversation. Evenings in the hut were a perfect setting. Also the variety of vegetables, meats and condiments meant that almost everyone could find a combination of foods that they liked.

"In 1986, we purchased land on Little Ollie Lake, a small lake south east of Poplar Lake and at the eastern end of the Banadad Trail. Little Ollie Lake rental cabin was added a year later. Our plan was to build a Bed and Breakfast on this land also. Construction finally began in the late summer of 2000. Christened the Poplar Creek Guesthouse Bed and Breakfast, after the creek that flowed through the property, the new B&B opened September 14, 2001.

"Currently, I continue to prepare meals for the yurts and now the new Guesthouse. We still operate Boundary Country Trekking that encompasses the many adventures we offer. I put together trips for the yurts, Lodge-to-Lodge skiing, dog sledding, hiking, biking, canoe trips and more."

Mongolian Firepot Dinner

(A Yurt Fondue For 4 Persons)

A medley of artfully arranged vegetables and meats, cooked in a savory charcoal-heated broth and topped with Oriental condiments, this meal is an event. Read the recipe completely before starting preparations.

VEGETABLES:

Vegetables are listed in the order they are arranged on the platter, from the outer edge into the center.

1 bag green loose-leaf lettuce

1 bag red loose-leaf lettuce

carrots, peeled baby, slice in half at a slant

broccoli, broken into bite-size florets

cauliflower, broken into bite-size florets

bok choy, slice stems at a slant; save leaves for decoration

kale, slice stems at a slant; save leaves for decoration

½ lb. firm tofu, drain for one hour and cut into large cubes

pea pods, whole flat (substitute whole sugar snap pea pods)

whole mushrooms, sliced into four to six pieces

whole baby corn, in can

green and red pepper, slice at an angle to make a ring and cut this ring in half

radishes

MEATS:

small pork tenderloin roast without bone

small beef roast, bottom round

two turkey breast halves, boned

1 lb. shrimp, 12–15-per-pound bag

8 oz. package of Surimi sticks, these are prepared Alaskan Pollack made into 1-oz. lobster flavored sticks

OTHER INGREDIENTS:

1 or two oranges

1 lemon

2 quarts chicken broth— as this boils down in the firepot, it makes a great soup

Preparation of meat at least 24 hours ahead of preparing platters: After trimming off excess fat, cut the beef and pork roasts into 6–8" lengths that are 2" in diameter. Place each cut of meat onto plastic wrap and roll up tightly to make a cylinder and tie the ends. Place in freezer. Roll up the turkey breast into a lengthwise cylinder after cutting off the tail end and place onto plastic wrap and roll up tightly and tie the ends of the wrap. Place in freezer. Slice the cylinders into thin slices.

Preparation of platters that hold the meats and vegetables: Clean and drain all the vegetables. Arrange the green leaf lettuce on one platter that holds the vegetables. Arrange the red leaf lettuce on one platter that holds the meats. Arrange the vegetables and meats on the platters and decorate with leftover kale or bok choy leaves and lemon and orange wedges.

Readying the Firepot: Place the firepot in the center of the table on a ceramic tile. Prepare ½ cup of raw white rice (jasmine rice is good) per person. (Sticky rice is the best.) Light 15 charcoal briquettes in a pail. In the meantime keep the chicken broth very hot. When the briquettes are covered with a fine coat of ash, pour the broth into the bowl of the firepot; carefully drop the briquettes down the firepot chimney. Put the lid on the firepot bowl.

Put out the condiments, the platters and place settings: Condiments should include hoisin sauce; hot & sweet mustard; tamari or soy sauce; Szechwan sauce; chili hot sauce; a bowl of 4 chopped garlic cloves; 4 chopped scallions and as much ginger as there is garlic, all mixed together, and homemade sweet and sour sauce. Then, place the meat and vegetable platters on the table. At each place setting there is a rice bowl with a scoop of cooked rice, chopsticks and a small brass basket seine.

A few pieces at a time, each person takes their choice of meats and vegetables and puts it in the chicken broth. Then the lid is put back on and the food is cooked in two minutes or so. Each person takes their seine and scoops out the cooked meats and vegetables and puts it on their rice. Then they choose among the condiments and put that over the rice. Eat with chopsticks. When everyone is finished, all remaining meats and vegetables are cooked in the chicken broth and served as soup. Serve iced fruit as a dessert.

Stuffed French Toast

This recipe is a mainstay at Poplar Creek Guesthouse Bed and Breakfast.

STUFFING:
8 oz. cream cheese	⅓ cup apricot preserves
8 oz. ricotta cheese	½ tsp. rum flavoring
½ cup ground pecans	½ tsp. maple flavoring

In a mixer on slow speed, combine the cheeses until blended together. Then, add the pecans; then the preserves; finally the flavorings. (This keeps in a refrigerator for no longer than two weeks.)

Cut a loaf of French bread in diagonal slices no more than 1½" thick. Then slice a pocket in the center along the top, but do not slice to the bottom. Spoon about 1 tablespoon of the stuffing into each pocket.

Make an egg wash using one egg and ⅛ cup milk for each person for coating the bread slices. This should make enough for 2 slices of bread.

Heat the grill on medium heat. Put butter down right before you set the stuffed bread slice down to grill. That way the butter will not burn. Turn over the French toast when golden on one side. Add more butter and grill until the French toast is golden on the second side. Serve with a sprinkle of powdered sugar and Cook County-produced maple syrup.

Loon's Nest Gift Shop

For many years Herb and Lou White lived in a cabin on Road Lake just off the Hungry Jack Road. Lou White started a rock shop there. She also made jewelry from agates and Tomsonites. Her husband, Herb, sold animal skins that he trapped in the area. He was especially known for his success in trapping wolves which are one of the most difficult of all animals to capture. In the mid-1970s, Herb built the present building on this location. A master mason, Herb did all the rock work on the building along with many fireplaces on the Gunflint Trail. Darlene and Dennis Katajamaki spotted this place while vacationing in the area. They had a wholesale craft business in Michigan's Upper Peninsula called Sweitzer Valley Crafts. In the summer of 1999 they opened the Loon's Nest Gifts utilizing their own handiwork. Both of them like to cook and their Finnish heritage is reflected in their favorite recipes.

Ugly Baby Bait Shop

On the right is a small building that was almost hidden by trees for many years. Its first use as a business was as the Loon House Gift Shop. Jennifer Walsh, one of the gift shop's original owners, tells about the beginnings of this store:

"The Loon House was the brainchild of Bruce and Sue Kerfoot, my husband Kevin Walsh and myself. By 1992 Kevin and I had worked for the Kerfoots at Gunflint Lodge for about twelve years when they suggested that we form a partnership to purchase a "warehouse" on Road Lake across the Gunflint Trail from Trail Center. The Liebertz family owned the property and building that served as a storage facility for their small resort, gift shop and restaurant . . . Although the structure was sound, it needed a lot of work, primarily consisting of getting it cleaned out. Bruce's packrat tendencies were in full evidence as we struggled to dispose of an enormous accumulation of junk, but there were definitely treasures unearthed, including some neat old bar signs and a wood stove. After sifting through the inventory we decided to hire outside help to complete the renovations. In short order a handsome counter and display case was constructed, a unique porch with a natural birch-branch railing was added to the front and blue shutters adorned the windows. We decided to concentrate on Minnesota-made wares and fill in with other "northwoodsy" things. By early summer of 1993 we opened the Loon House for business . . . We operated The Loon House for five summers before selling to another couple."

Scott and Diane Stahnke, the new owners of the Loon House Gift Shop, renamed it Ugly Baby Bait Shop. They started their lives on the Trail by spending many summers of vacationing at Trail's End Camp Ground. Scott was a union laborer and Diane had a cleaning business in Minneapolis. Both were ready to try something new and in 1998 they found this spot. Their business will trailer a boat and motor to any of the lakes in the area and sell the equipment needed to fish. The mid-Trail area has lots of smaller lakes that don't get fished much. They and their youngest daughter live here year-round and their small but very productive garden feeds them well.

Hungry Jack Outfitters

The original name of Hungry Jack Outfitters was Sunset Point, a name that came from the spectacular views of the setting sun. Even though the name has changed, the sunsets are still just as beautiful here. In fact, Dave and Nancy Seaton's home sits on the peninsula that Margaret and Harry Nolan chose for their home.

The outfitters was started by the Nolans as Sunset Point, a small resort with a couple of housekeeping cabins to rent. Harry was an accomplished carpenter and built the cabins himself. He worked on the Trail at his carpentry while Margaret took care of renting the cabins.

In those days, Nolans did not have indoor plumbing and used the two-holer behind their cabin. In an August, 1959, newspaper column, Justine Kerfoot related the story of a rather unusual day for Margaret. "Margaret Nolan of Sunset Lodge on Hungry Jack made a short sortie to the 'chick sales' behind their cabin. Upon emerging from the two-holer, Margaret was confronted by a large bear that calmly stretched across the path in a reclining position. Margaret was trapped and retreated to her shelter. The bear watched with interest every move she made. Hours later Harry came

Sue and her son Andy McDonnell with guests

home for his supper. After many shouts for his wife, he heard a desperate call: 'Out back!' He ran for his gun and scared off the bear. They wondered if the bear had been waiting his turn to use the biffy. Margaret was relieved to be freed from her confining quarters."

Margaret Nolan was one of several women interviewed by Catherine R. Peterson for her master's thesis. This is how Catherine relates Margaret's early years on the Trail starting in 1950: "She was a young bride from Minneapolis who had fallen in love with an avid and able-bodied woodman named Harry Nolan. Together they traveled up and down the Trail and into the BWCAW. She mined silver on the Duncan portage, carried meals for the loggers, guided canoes and fisherman. A vast number of homes on lakes near mid-Trail were built by Harry and Margaret. She held her own as beams were raised."

The Nolans sold to Jack McDonnell and Sue Weber in the early 1980s. After their marriage, Sue and Jack worked at several resorts on the Trail, but Hungry Jack Lake was where they would settle. Sue related some stories about living at the resort and on the Trail.

"Jack and I had been searching for a resort or canoe outfitters to purchase for several years when Nolan's Sunset Point came up for sale in 1983. We had been married for eleven years. I was working for an insurance agency in Grand Marais, and Jack was building vacation homes and resort buildings. Both of us desperately wanted to get back to the resort business. Jack grew up at Gateway Lodge on Hungry Jack Lake, and for him, this was 'going home.'

"In November of 1983 we moved into the home built by Harry and Margaret Nolan on Hungry Jack Lake. It had two bedrooms, and in the winter, when the uninsulated part of the home had to be shut down, the square footage was less than 600 feet. But, the home was only about 15 feet from the lake, and it felt like a castle to me. In warm weather we could listen to the waves lapping. True to its name, the sunsets were always spectacular.

"The 'resort' had two rental cabins, and we quickly set out to add canoe outfitting to the business. Our first step was to change the name to Hungry Jack Outfitters because Jack felt Sunset Point did not fully describe the nature of outfitting. We cleaned out the garage and attached shop, which had a dirt floor, remodeled and fixed up things as best we could. We hauled in an old shower house from Tuscarora Outfitters, which they were discarding. (Several years later we were able to build a large, fancy shower house with 'men' and 'women' sides and a laundry.) A bunkhouse was built on the hill for the outfitting guests to sleep in the night prior to their trips. Canoes, packs, equipment and freeze-dried food were ordered, and we began our career as outfitters.

"At the same time we also decided to have a child. By 1984 I was pregnant with Andy. He was due in late November, but high blood pressure had sent me home for a month. Novembers on the Gunflint Trail often bring early snows, and that year was no exception. Our two-mile driveway was icy due to mix of snow and freezing rain.

"In mid-November Jack had a Tip of the Arrowhead board meeting to attend in Grand Marais. The fog was so bad that evening that he stayed in town at his mother's house overnight. I settled in that evening with a cup of hot apple cider, which then gave me a queer bit of indigestion that lasted all night and into the next morning. Jack made it home early in the morning of November 15, and began to work on the driveway. Our large plow truck, Snort, had questionable traction on ice and ended up crossways in the driveway, in a place where it completely blocked the road.

"Around 10 a.m. I realized my indigestion had evolved into labor pains. By noon the labor pains were caving in my knees, and I knew it was time to begin the 30-mile trip to the hospital, but Snort was still blocking the road. I started to think about preparing for emergency home birth or attempting to get across the semi-frozen lake. Somewhere around noon Jack also realized we might be in a pickle, when a saving figure appeared in the form of Oscar Everson. Oscar was a heavy equipment operator and did roadwork all over Grand Marais and the Gunflint Trail. Jack told him of the predicament, and Oscar quickly went to work. Luckily, Oscar's equipment was nearby. With Jack assisting, Oscar's TD 9 Cat moved Snort out of the way, and by 3 p.m., Jack and I were headed down the Trail. A little before 8 p.m. Andy was born. To this day I have a hard time drinking apple cider.

"Before we bought Sunset Point, we worked for Gunflint Lodge and Gunflint Northwoods Outfitters in the mid-1970s and lived at the Soderberg cabin on Birch Lake in the winter. Gene and Rita Doody were our neighbors. Jack, Harry Nolan, Gene Doody, and Mike Lande (Jack's brother-in-law) won a moose-hunting license through the lottery in the mid-1970s. The moose-hunting season was divided into two time periods, one in September and one later in the fall.

"A large bull moose was finally taken in the latter period, hauled out and butchered. We looked forward to a winter of reduced grocery bills and a freezer full of meat. But that must have been the oldest, toughest moose in the Gunflint Trail area. A few attempts at cooking it fast proved that another means of cooking would be necessary. Crock pots had just come out and we purchased one. The moose meat stewed all day and came out fairly edible. We could not waste that meat and so were determined to use every bit of it. One day I decided to fix barbecued moose ribs in the crock pot. The ingredients were put together early in the morning, and it cooked and cooked. It smelled wonderfully by suppertime. We eagerly filled our plates and began dinner, but something was very wrong with that rib meat. The meat had somehow turned to rubber, like a rubber ball, and one's teeth literally bounced when chewing it. Plus, the rubbery stuff was impossible to bite through. It was more like gum than meat. I gave up, and I think my portion went to our dog. Jack partially ate his meal, but Jack's brother, Tim, who was visiting, politely ate his entire portion and said it was a great meal!"

Nancy and Dave Seaton bought Hungry Jack Outfitters from the McDonnells in 1991. This young couple met while working on the Gunflint Trail. Nancy says, "We grew up a mile apart in the Twin Cities. We've said over and over, it was good we didn't meet until we moved up here because we were still trying to figure out who we were." Nancy and Dave are reliving an evolution that couples often go through on the Trail: from casual residents to permanent residents, from single adults to a married couple, from summer employees to business owners, and from no children to a full family.

Nancy first came up to this area with her parents on a weekend getaway around 1975. Soon after, her family built a cabin on Gunflint Lake. In the early1980s she spent her summers working on the Gunflint Trail. Nancy says, "After that, I spent several summers on Gunflint, painting and not working. I knew all the retirees and got a sense of history, that sense of what they saw when they came to the area. It was fun seeing it through their eyes." Why did Nancy keep coming back? She says, "It was a sense of feeling at home. I felt connected to this place and the land in a special way."

For two years Nancy ran Trail Center, and met Dave Seaton while he was spending his first summer on the Trail. The connection they felt to this place soon led to a wedding and a commitment to the Trail. During the early years of their marriage, they worked for others on the Trail. Then Hungry Jack Outfitters came up for sale and they jumped at the opportunity. But there was a difference between being the owner and being an employee. Nancy says, "I like this side better. There is always something that needs to be done and it's hard for me to make the time for myself. The difference is having the choice to walk out the door and leave work behind when it's possible, being able to go for a walk or go to dinner and not feel like you are supposed to be doing something else. It's good to have that option."

The next step was children. The Seaton boys, Ben and Will, are very much a part of Hungry Jack Outfitters. Dave and Nancy work together at raising the boys. "Definitely kids are fifty-fifty. That's what's great about this business, we are here together and the boys are part of it." Are they a helpful part right now? "Not much, but I do hear those words. 'Can I help?' Ben peeled all the potatoes last night. You know we're going in the right direction."

During the winter, Hungry Jack Outfitters is closed. It gives Dave and Nancy more time to be part of their children's lives. When Ben was in school and Will was in preschool, Nancy says, "We volunteered in Ben's class and really enjoyed knowing all of the kids, knowing that we were filling a void some of them have. Mostly I listened to kids read, those were the early years and they just needed practice reading, having somebody help them on a word when they were stuck, somebody telling them they were doing a good job. It was just real basic things that you didn't need teaching skills to do. This year we each did two five-week courses with some of the kids, eight kids at a time.

Having both children in school gives Dave and Nancy some time for their own interests. Dave makes guitars and Nancy is an accomplished artist. Nancy says, "Painting is a winter thing at this point. Art for me is not something where I can sit down and paint for fifteen minutes before picking up the boys from the bus. I need bigger blocks of time to shut out the rest of what's going on. I don't actually shut the door, but Dave gets the phone on painting days. You really have to work at not being distracted because even in the winter there's some business issue that needs to be dealt with. I really haven't painted much for nine years. With my youngest, Will, going off to kindergarten, I thought there would be bigger blocks than there were. Work and other things kept creeping in. But somehow, I got some painting done."

As an artist, Nancy looks at the forest around her with different eyes. "Not always but sometimes. About twenty years ago when I was in college, I took a botany class. Part of the class was a canoe trip in the Boundary Waters, exploring. We were paddling. I was the duffer and just kind of looking around. One girl who was in the canoe with me said, 'I always wondered. Do artists look at things differently?' And I said, 'Well, as a matter of fact, right now I'm looking at the reflection in the water and how the small wave pattern is breaking it up.' The girl said, 'Well, I didn't see that.' So that was when I really did realize that I do observe differently. I focus in different planes. Sometimes. I definitely know my focus is different when I watch my boys stepping on flowers."

As far as living permanently on the Trail, Nancy says, "Dave and I knew we would be permanent residents on the Trail because we can't imagine being anyplace else. At this point, it's the view out this window and watching that season change. It's a sense of place and that place becomes your identity. I don't even have any clothes that don't say Hungry Jack. I always tell people that I rarely have that 100% day-off feel, which the people who go out on their trip get. But I get 50% some days or even more in the off-season. It's a good trade-off to be able to live here."

Hot Dish or Stuffed Pepper

Mother Bunn's famous cookbook yielded this recipe from Margaret Nolan. Except for parboiling the peppers and the cooking time, the recipe assumed the cook could assemble the hot dish with the proper proportion of ingredients.

4 green peppers
1 lb. ground beef
½ cup uncooked rice
celery
salt and pepper
1 can diced tomatoes
onion, diced

Clean and core the peppers. Parboil them for a few minutes. Combine the raw ground beef with the uncooked rice, celery, salt, pepper, tomatoes and onion. Fill the prepared green peppers with hot dish mixture and bake at 350° for 1 hour.

Moose Jerky

"We found turning the moose meat into jerky made it considerably easier to eat. Here's is my mother Dixie's recipe for making jerky," said Sue McDonnell.

1½ lbs. moose steak (round or flank cut good)
¼ cup soy sauce
¼ cup Worcestershire sauce
1 tsp. liquid smoke

½ tsp. garlic powder
1 tsp. onion powder.
⅓ tsp. pepper, fresh ground
⅓ tsp. salt

Trim off all fat and sinew. Cut the meat into wide strips across grain. The strips should be about ¼" thick. (Chill for easier slicing.) Put strips of meat sideways in a quart jar. Mix all the remaining ingredients for a marinade. Pour sauce into jar and cover tightly. Place sideways in refrigerator for 24 hours.

Turn occasionally so meat absorbs through. Place meat strips on paper towels to absorb excess sauce. Put strips on racks over pans. Do not bake, but dry out in oven by having oven as low as possible. Leave oven door slightly open. Let dry for 10 hours or until consistency you desire.

MOTHER BUNN'S ANGEL COOKIES

Margaret Nolan sent a recipe for Mother Bunn's Angel Cookies, which are truly heavenly.

- 1 cup shortening
- 1 egg
- 1 tsp. vanilla
- ½ cup white sugar
- ½ cup brown sugar
- 2 cups flour sifted with 1 tsp. cream of tartar, ½ tsp. baking soda and ½ tsp. salt
- 1 cup coconut

Form in balls the size of walnuts and flatten with glass bottom dipped in sugar (patterned glass bottom looks nice).

No shortening needed on pan. Bake at 350–375° for 10 minutes. They burn easily. Good luck.

TOMATO BASIL SOUP

Nancy finds this homemade variation of tomato soup is a big hit with the Seaton boys. Another plus is that this soup is quick and easy to assemble.

- 2 T olive oil
- 1 large onion, chopped
- 1½ tsp. minced garlic
- 3 cup tomato juice
- 1 28-oz can diced tomatoes with juice
- 3 cups shredded carrots
- ¼ tsp. black pepper
- 1 tsp. coarse salt
- 1 T dried basil
- 2 T maple syrup
- 2 cups heavy cream

Saute onion and garlic in oil until soft. Add all ingredients, saving the cream until last. Heat to temperature and serve.

Swanson's Lodge

Today we don't know much about the Swansons but Mother Bunn and her son, Walt, are Trail legends. When the two of them were running the lodge, Mother Bunn was a taskmaster while Walt was more easygoing. Mother Bunn's cookbook has provided a wealth of recipes for this book and for women all along the Trail.

Swanson's Lodge was home to two of the Trail's enigmatic residents: Walter Bunn and his mother, who was known by all as Mother Bunn.

At the public landing to Hungry Jack Lake is the start of Bunn Road off to the right. For many years, Swanson's Lodge was a favorite resort here. It was started by Marvin and Sybil Swanson. Although we don't know much about the Swansons, Bev Denyes from Grand Marais worked for the Swansons in 1948 and describes what that summer was like.

"In June I went to Swanson's Hungry Jack Lodge to work as a cabin girl and a waitress. I was 16 years old. My mother, Helen Kreiner, was hired to cook. My stepfather, Frank Kreiner, was hired as a guide and my 13-year-old sister, Barbara, was hired to wash dishes and help out in the kitchen.

"A young couple, Ruth and Leo Hovland, were also working there that summer. I believe they were caretakers but also did many other jobs. Ruth and Leo were a newlywed couple from Albert Lea, Minnesota.

"One of the employees was a young woman about 18 who was hired to do the laundry. She was unmarried and very pregnant. She stayed a few weeks and left in the middle of the night when her boyfriend came for her. That meant more work for the rest of us. Another woman whose name was Lucille Burauger helped out at the resort as a day worker. As I recall she had a place on the Trail and hired out to different resorts.

"Emerson Morris had a float plane and would come around to give guests rides. I had my first plane ride that summer in his plane.

"The owners were the Swansons. They had two pre-teen children, a boy and a girl. There was also a Grandfather Swanson who was there that summer.

"We were provided with room and board and my wages were $60.00 per month plus tips. My sister and I stayed in a dormitory-type building. My folks had their own quarters. We were all hired for the entire season. My job was to clean the cabins and wait on the tables of the guests from the cabins that I was assigned to clean. We also housecleaned the cabins before the guests arrived. This included washing down the log walls, floors, windows, furniture, etc. I also helped in the laundry as it seemed to me they were short of help.

"Mrs. Swanson had a number of special items on the menu. The one I recall the most was Swedish pancakes and, oh, how my mother hated making those pancakes for a dining room full of guests.

"The meals were served at set times. Breakfast was 8:00 to 9:00 a.m., lunch was 12:00 to 1:00 and dinner was 6:00 to 7:00. Of course, for the fishermen, the kitchen crew put together lunch to take along. If the fishing was good, the guides would prepare a shore lunch for the guests, and they were always a hit.

"It was a busy time as Ruth and I had to serve the guests breakfast. After we cleaned up the dining room, we'd get busy on cleaning up the cabins. Ruth and I had to wear white uniforms in the dining room, so we'd hurry and change after each meal into cleaning clothes and then back into uniforms for the meal serving. These tasks included making the beds, putting in clean towels, emptying the 'Thunder Mugs' or 'slop jars,' (there was no inside plumbing), bringing in pails of fresh water and also cleaning up and freshening the outhouses and shower rooms. Then time for lunch duties. After

Sybil and Marvin Swanson with lodge staff

lunch if there was a lull, we'd have a little time for ourselves before the dinner bell rang. Often there wouldn't be help to do the laundry so we'd help out with that.

"When my first guests left after one week, they left me a $10 tip and I was pleased and surprised. I'd worked mostly at babysitting up until this time, and that paid 25 cents an hour. A $10 tip was big money in those days.

"There was friction between my folks and the Swansons over a number of matters and my folks decided to quit. They packed themselves and my younger sister Barbara up in the middle of the night and left without any notice. I knew they were going to leave, but I wanted to stay and work out the summer. I didn't like the idea of leaving like that so I stayed. You can imagine the mess the next morning when the Swansons discovered they had no cook, no guide and no kitchen girl. Somehow we made it through until they were able to get more help. I stayed until late August just before school started again.

"Although it was hard work, I have fond memories of that summer. I made many friends and kept in touch with Ruth Hovland off and on until her death a few years back."

The next owners at Swanson's were Walt Bunn and his mother. They bought in the late 1940s and both would remain at Swanson's for the rest of their lives. Young Luana Brandt (then Burns) was one of their many employees over the years and shares this glimpse of life at Swanson's.

Swanson's Lodge

"It was the summer of 1965 and I was headed north to work on the Trail. My family had vacationed there many times, but little did I know that this summer would change my life, for I would not only meet my future husband, but also one of the trail legends, Mother Bunn. I am sure she had a given Christian name, but I never knew it and I doubt if anyone else did either.

"The summer of 1965 spent at Swanson's Lodge on Hungry Jack Lake was an education in itself. Early that year Mother Bunn had gone to Rochester to have surgery, for what I now presume was cancer of the mouth. Major portions of her mouth were removed along with portions of her tongue. This did not prevent her from making the long journey from Rochester by bus to Grand Marais following surgery.

"The next morning she was in the kitchen supervising everything. The dock boy lasted a week, followed by the cook ten days later. It was now me in the kitchen alone with her. I learned a lot, and not only about cooking. One of her favorite rituals was checking the paper each morning to see the previous day's stock report. She would then consult her little black book and frequently place a call to her broker to buy or sell. For this teenager, even knowing someone who had stock was an eye opener, but a woman older than my grandma! There would then follow spirited exchanges with her son Walt as they compared each of their portfolio results. Within weeks they had me hooked. They taught me how to read the stock pages and to glean from the business pages of the paper pertinent information. Of course, I was a college student with no money to invest, but the lessons I learned from the two of them have stayed with me.

"Mother Bunn may have been a demanding boss, but she left me with a wealth of memories and a standard for being a businesswoman. I had come north to earn the money for the next school year, but left with far more than money."

As Mother Bunn aged, she and Walt cut down the services offered at the resort. Soon they just offered housekeeping cabins. After she died, Walt continued to rent a few cabins to old-time guests. He became one of the many characters who lived on the Gunflint Trail. Gay Lynne Liebertz, who with her parents owned Trail Center, recalls some of her favorite stories about Walt.

"Walt was a bit of an eccentric, to say the least. He would never shake anyone's hand, citing arthritis pain, and he was always very much concerned with everyone else's business. He would arrive at the mailboxes at the intersection of the Hungry Jack Road and the Gunflint Trail at 10:30 a.m., Monday through Saturday, ready to get caught up on any scuttlebutt from his neighbors as they, too, arrived to wait for the mailman (who showed up promptly at 11:00 a.m.—or explain exactly why he was late, thank you very much!). Walt also kept up with all the "outside" news via Duluth, Minneapolis and St. Paul newspapers, and managed to pick up information from the telephone party lines.

"In those days, the late 1960s and early 1970s, everyone on the Gunflint Trail was on an 8-party line, split in half with four phone numbers per half, so that each of the four parties had his or her own number of rings. For instance, my ring was two, so that if the phone rang once, or three short rings, or four short rings, I wouldn't answer—no one was calling for me. Of course, if any of the other three parties on my party line were using the phone, I could listen in on, or even take part in, their conversations!

"My first official encounter with Walt Bunn was shortly after my family and I arrived at Trail Center in the late spring of 1966. It had been a long winter, very cold, with lots of snow—not a particularly unusual winter, but spring was a bit later than normal. We arrived near the end of April to a couple of feet of snow on the ground,

The dining area at Swanson's Lodge

drifts several feet higher, and thick ice on Poplar Lake. Our caretaker had our house (a two-bedroom cabin) ready for us, but we had to chip away at the ice and snow blocking the doors of the main store building to get inside to begin preparing for the upcoming summer season. Also at that time, no one had year-round indoor plumbing, so drinking water had to be carried up from a hole kept open in the lake ice. It happened that I had measured the thickness of the ice in the water hole (having come from Detroit, Michigan, carrying my own water from a hole in the ice was enough of a novelty that I wanted to tell my friends back home all the details).

"Later that day, the phone rang (two short rings—aha!—someone's calling me!). It was a reporter with the *Duluth News Tribune* inquiring about snow depth and ice thickness. I dutifully reported the couple of feet of snow, and then told him that I had just that morning measured two feet of blue ice on the lake, topped off with six inches of snow and slush. After giving him my name, and answering his questions about my location on the Gunflint Trail and where I had come from, I thought nothing further about it.

"Come that Sunday, in the Outdoors sections of the *Duluth News Tribune*, there was an article about all the wintry conditions on the Gunflint Trail, quoting me, and giving my name and the name of my family's business, Trail Center. Seeing as how there was no Sunday newspaper delivery up the Trail and Grand Marais was thirty miles away, no one on the Trail saw the paper until after the mail arrived on Monday.

"Neighborhood socializing generally consisted of driving several miles down snow-covered roads (always with blankets, snowshoes, axe and chainsaw in the vehicle in case someone ran off the road, or hit a moose, or otherwise got stuck somehow) to get together with other Trail folk for dinner or to watch a favorite TV show."

"At 11:30 Monday morning, my phone rang. It was Walter Bunn, in his very-recognizable, high-pitched voice, 'Gay Lynne, I just want you to know that I have been on the Trail for nearly twenty years and no one from the Duluth paper has EVER called me to ask me anything about how much snow or ice we have up here, and here you haven't even been here a week, and you're famous already!' Click! I thought I'd broken some rule of Gunflint Trail etiquette!

"Another Walt Bunn anecdote dealt with Walt's high ideals, and thoughts of propriety. In the 1970s, winter on the Trail was still pretty quiet; there weren't that many year-round residents, and only a handful of resorts were attempting to do any winter business. Neighborhood socializing generally consisted of driving several miles down snow-covered roads (always with blankets, snowshoes, axe and chainsaw in the vehicle in case someone ran off the road, or hit a moose, or otherwise got stuck somehow) to get together with other Trail folk for dinner or to watch a favorite TV show.

"One of those favorite TV shows was "Laugh-In." Walt was the first one in the mid-Trail area to get a color television, and wanted to invite some neighbors over to watch "Laugh-In" in color, a special treat! One weekday afternoon, I received a phone call from Margaret Nolan (from Sunset Point). Margaret asked if I would like to go with her and Harry on Friday evening to Walt's, to watch "Laugh-In." I replied that I'd love to. Sounding rather amused, Margaret said she and Harry would pick me up on Friday.

"Sure enough, that Friday evening, the Nolans pulled in to the drive, and when I got in the car, Margaret and Harry just couldn't stop chuckling and smiling to each other. As I looked at each of them rather quizzically, Harry said, 'Are you going to tell her, or should I?' Margaret, still laughing, told me that when Walt invited them to come over that evening, he hadn't called them on the phone—he had gone over to their place to personally issue the invitation. And then he told them, 'You know, Gay Lynne is over there at Trail Center all by herself, and she might like to come over, too, but I can't call and invite her because one of those busybodies on her party line would hear me, a bachelor, asking a young single woman to come over to my place, and might get the wrong idea! So you call her and ask her, and then pick her up, so no one will see her drive in here all alone!'

"Dear Walter, who at that time was in his 70s, was so very concerned about protecting the reputation of a 30-something single girl and keeping her out of the rumor mills that he drove several miles, round-trip, to issue those personal invitations for his friends to join him for an evening of television. And why didn't Walt just drive up to Trail Center and invite me himself? In Walt's mind, that wouldn't have been proper either for him, an older bachelor living alone, to go to the home of a younger woman, who also happened to live alone. Even up in the woods, in the border country of northern Minnesota, there were certain unwritten rules of propriety and neighborliness and being considerate of others.

"As mentioned previously, Walt refused to shake hands with anyone, making his untouchability very obvious. Several years after I sold Trail Center and left the Gunflint Trail, I made a return trip up the Trail and stopped in at Trail Center to have lunch. While there, in the door came Walt. I was glad to see him, and unthinkingly and automatically stretched out my hand to greet him. To my complete surprise and delight, and to the shock of nearly everyone in the room (there happened to be several Trail folk there), he gripped my hand in his, giving me a very firm handshake! We had a brief visit; then he abruptly turned on his heel and left. I had the feeling that he had so surprised himself, and had exhibited in front of several friends and neighbors that he wasn't quite the eccentric curmudgeon that he would have all of us believe, that he had to save face and leave!"

Swanson's Lodge is now owned by Tom and Linda Hendrickson. They have restored the lodge building for their private use with many artifacts of the 1930s preserved.

Did you know . . .

Waitresses at early American plan resorts did more than just wait tables. After breakfast they helped clean cabins before lunch. Between lunch and dinner there might be time for a quick swim in the lake. The days were long and they were paid very little by today's standards, yet many young women came up for a summer and stayed for a lifetime.

Walt Bunn was an avid reader and had a good collection of books in the main lodge. Even after he closed the lodge, neighbors would stop by with a grocery bag full of books to exchange with him.

Swedish Pancakes

Mother Bunn kept a recipe book; it is now owned by Luana Brandt at Nor'Wester Lodge who carefully preserves this bit of Gunflint Trail history. This is one of the recipes.

3 eggs, beaten
1 13-oz. can evaporated milk
1½ cans water
2 cups sifted flour (just enough to make light batter)

3 tsp. baking powder
salt
1 T or so of sugar
3 T of melted shortening
(more if desired)

Fry pancakes in a hot frying pan similar to making crepes.

Danish Pastry Dough

This recipe and the three variations came from Swanson's Lodge on Hungry Jack Lake. To make pastry dough:

1 cup hot milk
4 T salted butter
½ cup granulated sugar
4 eggs, well beaten
1 tsp. vanilla

¼ tsp. salt
juice and rind of half a lemon
2 oz. yeast combined with 2 T sugar
4 cup bread flour
1 cup sweet butter, cut into thirds

Pour hot milk over the salted butter and sugar. Add well-beaten eggs, vanilla, salt, juice and rind of lemon. When lukewarm, add yeast, which has been combined with 2 T sugar. Add flour gradually, forming very soft dough. Turn out onto a covered board and knead only until smooth, several minutes. Place in greased bowl, brush top of dough with melted butter and allow to rise until double in bulk in cool place or icebox. When the dough is ready, roll into an oblong to about ¼" thick. Cut 1 piece (⅓ cup) of sweet butter into small pieces and distribute it over two-thirds of the dough. Fold the unbuttered portion of the dough onto half of the buttered portion. Then fold the other half of the buttered portion onto the first two layers so that you have three thicknesses of dough. Press the edges together and refrigerate for half an hour. Remove the dough from the refrigerator and roll into an oblong. Repeat the above process. Refrigerate the dough for another half hour. Roll the dough out again into an oblong and repeat the process for a third time. Refrigerate the dough for half an hour before using it for one of the following recipes.

VARIATIONS FOR USING PASTRY DOUGH:

Danish Butterfly Rolls

Roll portion of dough into an oblong about ¼" thick. Brush with melted butter, spread with mixture made of 1 yolk of egg, 1 cup scalded raisins, ½ cup finely chopped nuts, ¼ tsp. cinnamon, and enough confectioner's sugar to form right consistency to spread. Roll like jelly roll. Cut this in about 2" pieces. Through the center of each piece, parallel with the cut sides, make a deep crease with the handle of a knife. Brush with melted butter and place on cookie tin that has been covered with 2 thicknesses of brown paper. Allow to rise until double in size and bake in a moderate oven (350–375°) for about 30 minutes. When cold, brush with Karo syrup, frost and sprinkle with nuts.

Danish Alligators

Roll portion of dough into an oblong about ¼" thick. Brush with melted butter. Spread center with prune mixture, made of stewed prunes that have been through a sieve and to which chopped nuts, rind and little lemon juice has been added. Add confectioner's sugar, if necessary to make right consistency to spread. Fold lengthwise into thirds and cut into 4" pieces and cut ends. Brush with melted butter and place on cookie tin that has been covered with brown paper. Bake in a 350–375° oven about 30 minutes. When cold, glaze with syrup, frost, etc.

Danish Pastry Horns

Roll portion of dough into a round. Brush with softened or melted butter. Cut like pie. Place a tablespoon of filling on each and roll like butter horns. Brush top with melted butter. Place on cookie sheet that has been covered with brown paper and bake in 350–375° oven about 30 minutes. When cold, glaze, frost, etc.

Hungry Jack Lodge

Hungry Jack Lodge is one of the remaining Grand Old Dames of the Gunflint Trail. Its history is typical of many resorts in the area. The builders, Jesse and Sue Gapen, came in immediately after the road. They built their resort using materials supplied by the land around them. They were tough enough to survive the setbacks but gentle enough to cherish the land.

Hungry Jack Lodge, originally called Gateway Lodge, was built on a lake with a funny name. Many visitors have wondered where that name came from. Here is the story: Late in the fall sometime in the early 1870s, a small crew of government surveyors guided by a colorful local named Jack Scott set up their winter camp along the shores of a beautiful lake deep into the woods north of Grand Marais. About two months into their winter work, it became obvious they would need further provisions to carry them through the winter. The government men decided to snowshoe the 32 miles to Grand Marais to replenish their supplies, leaving Jack alone to care for the camp. While in the town, it seems a lot of their provisions became liquid in nature and along with a snow-storm, Christmas festivities, etc., they were delayed much longer than had been planned. Jack ran out of staples and spirits early on, but as an experienced hunter and trapper, he was in no real danger. Finally as the overdue surveyors came tromping through the snowdrifts, they cried out, "Are you hungry, Jack?" He answered, "Wow, wow! Am I hungry, Jack! I'm damned near starved to death!" So came the name of Hungry Jack Lake.

Finally as the overdue surveyors came tromping through the snowdrifts, they cried out, "Are you hungry, Jack?" He answered, "Wow, wow! Am I hungry, Jack! I'm damned near starved to death!" So came the name of Hungry Jack Lake.

It was at this spot in 1923 Jesse Gapen from Monroe, Wisconsin, built his first cabin of what was to become Gateway-Hungry Jack Lodge. The hay fever Jesse Gapen suffered from in the southern Wisconsin summers drove him in his search for a refuge. He found this relief in a newly opened area in northern Minnesota called the Gunflint Trail. As an added bonus, it was a fisherman's paradise, and Jesse was indeed a fisherman. The daily limit for trout was 25 and he could easily fill his limit. This was the place he had been looking for. He would build a resort and his future here. He would call it Gateway Lodge, as this lovely spot on Hungry Jack Lake was the gateway to the wilderness.

That first summer Jesse and his original partner, Robert Wegg, secured a lease from the U.S. Forest Service for the selected spot. They built two log cabins and an "annex" building, which housed a temporary kitchen, dining room and eight guest rooms. The main lodge was to be built the following year. While the cabins contained a sitting room and bedrooms, they had no bathrooms or kitchens. The resort was to be American plan with all meals taken in the lodge. By 1924, Mr. Wegg had withdrawn from the partnership and Jesse became sole owner. This was also the first summer of actual operation. The log lodge had been built, other cabins started and the whole family moved from Wisconsin for the summer.

Guests outside the second lodge

Jesse's wife, Sue, became an important part of the actual running of the resort. She was in charge of the day-to-day operation, planning meals and activities, overseeing the kitchen, dining room and cabin staff, keeping the books, and keeping the ladies entertained while the men went fishing. She also designed much of the handmade furniture. The Gapens also depended on their two teenage sons, Don and Bob, to help with the myriad of camp chores. It proved to be a wonderful life for the whole family.

Gateway, which early on added Hungry Jack to its name, became a very well known resort during the late 1920s, the 1930s and even early 1940s. The concept of "splendor in a woods setting" was very appealing to a lot of higher income people.

Fred Salisbury, a former employee and longtime friend wrote about the beginning years at Gateway. "In those days you didn't have hot and cold running water and flush toilets. This was a rustic atmosphere, yet Sue and Jesse had people coming from all over the country: the Mayos, Bellfores, and Pipers from Rochester, the Mars candy people from Chicago, the great restaurant people, the Fred Harveys who would come to Duluth by train and a flotilla of taxi cabs would drive them up the north shore to spend a week at Gateway Lodge, living in log cabins and enjoying a total change of pace from the normal way of life.

"Everything about the service was incredible. To start the day, Jesse would blow the bugle, blow reveille at perhaps 7:30 in the morning and at that point, the cabin boys would start out from the main lodge with pails of hot water to deliver to each cabin so that people could pour pitchers into the bowls and perform their toilet with hot water delivered. It wasn't turning on a faucet. These people didn't expect it. It would have spoiled the experience if it had been done differently. Service in the dining room was often delayed. Meal time would arrive and people would be expecting to hear the bugle call, but Sue would hold up the whole performance while somebody ran out and plucked green leaves from the thimbleberry bushes to use as doilies under the fruit cocktail glasses that were going on the table. Sometimes it was little blossoms of ferns or some little touch that you wouldn't expect anywhere else.

"Sue Gapen was a real artist at heart. She had just magnificent taste, restrained, but beautiful. It used to be kind of a pain in the neck to some of us who worked around there to meet the standards that she demanded. But this was the secret of the success of their operation. She and Jesse wouldn't compromise on anything. They had the ability, particularly Sue, of creating things from the woods and from the natural environment and adapting them to serving the purpose of a resort.

"Another thing that used to drive some of us right up a tree was the picnics that she would stage for the guests. Very few resort owners would go to these lengths but the Gapens did! They had a cabin up on an island on Sag and about once every two or three weeks they would have a Saganaga picnic for all of the guests. This meant transporting all the guests up to Saganaga, getting them in the motor boats and getting them across to this island, together with great baskets—they were really laundry baskets—filled with all the food, all the things to be served for a picnic, including tablecloths and napkins and cushions to sit on the rocks—just everything imaginable.

Sue and Jesse Gapen

"This took a crew of a dozen people just to lug and climb over the rocks and haul all of these things up there for a noon's outing. This was a great experience for people from the city who didn't often have a chance to get bitten by the black flies and enjoy all the glories of the great out-of-doors.

"She would do the same thing for picnics at Caribou Rock. Caribou Rock is a nice hike and a nice climb if you've got a walking stick and you want to see a beautiful view over West Bearskin Lake, but to tote all this food and climb up this rock, that's a different story! I would say it probably was three-quarters of a mile, straight up and through woods and over rocks and rills but when you got there, this great beautiful view. There was a stone fireplace to build a fire to heat the coffee and there were even picnic tables up there, which have long since disintegrated and gone back to mother earth, but there were tables and they were spread with cloths and you had a helluva outdoor picnic. Where else, but Gateway Lodge? It was the sort of thing that made it unique, at least in these parts."

Fire has always been the biggest threat to all resorts in the woods. The original lodge burned in September 1932. During those depression years there was a lot of local help available, especially for a winter project. The Rudolph Weyerhausers were guests and friends of the Gapens. They offered their tall pines on adjacent West Bearskin Lake for a new lodge. The hired craftsmen were paid $1.00 a day plus room and board. Part of the crew worked on the building. The rest made furnishings. When the resort opened the following summer, it was a showplace. The massive structure with its 80-foot timbers was reported to be the largest log building in the state of Minnesota. Spindle-backed chairs made from aspen had seats upholstered in buckskin with fringed edges. Servers and chests were covered in birch bark and had handles from deer horn. The great grandfather clock with its split spruce limb numerals overlooked the lounge area where sofas, easy chairs and tables were all crafted from local wood. This was the epitome of using the bounty of the woods.

> "We had been dreaming of finding a new area to raise our young family. What better place than a resort in the woods? Our oldest son, seven-year-old Jack, was always hungry. It must be an omen."

The 1940s, World War II and the age and health of the Gapens were turning points in the history of Gateway. The clientele was aging and dying off. Younger people were not very interested in "going out back." The public started to travel with better cars and roads. People brought with them boats, motors, fishing gear, even food and lodging. It was a new age in the resort industry. Very few improvements had been made at Gateway over the years. The Gapens' sons and grandchildren had lives of their own and were not interested. Gateway Hungry Jack Lodge was for sale.

Bette McDonnell tells about the years she and her husband, Pat, spent at Hungry Jack Lodge. "On a Sunday morning in early 1958, Pat and I were reading the resort ads in the Chicago Tribune. We had been dreaming of finding a new area to raise our young family—three boys and one girl. What better place than a resort in the woods? Our oldest son, seven-year-old Jack, was always hungry. It must be an omen. So with stars in our eyes, we purchased the resort, made the big move from the city and opened for business in May of 1958.

Bette McDonnell

"I had been promised the existence of one bathroom as I was pregnant again with boy #4. It really was a 'bath room.' It had a bathtub and sink. Period. So the improvements began immediately. Building a common bathhouse and a bathroom in our cabin were first on the list. Then one by one over the next few years, ten cabins each had a makeover. There was a nucleus of a few of the second generation of Gapen's guests who had fond memories of a vacation spent at Gateway Hungry Jack Lodge when they were young. From here the business grew, as did our family, adding two more boys. We all loved our wonderful life. We worked very hard for very little money as everything went back into the resort. But the people we met and the proximity of all natural things made it a very memorable experience.

"Even though we were off the Gunflint Trail 2½ miles, one of the daily rituals was showing the lodge to people who passed by. They had heard of it, or possibly stayed there years before. It was rather like living in a museum. I remember one woman asking the whereabouts of Caribou Rock, a favorite lookout over West Bearskin Lake and about a 20-minute hike. We showed her the path but she was incensed! Pointing down the shore of Hungry Jack, she spouted, 'Well, it used to be right down there!' Yes, we loved the people."

During the McDonnell years, the "happening" during the summer was on Saturday nights, when mid-trail residents and friends would gather for Gateway's weekly Chuck Wagon dinners. These were all-you-can-eat buffets with the menu alternating between oven fried chicken one Saturday night and roast beef the next. The chicken buffet was probably the most popular, especially with the younger generation. It always included the special fried rice, chuck wagon beans, and assorted side dishes, salads, homemade bread and desserts. The beef buffet was a similar spread with oven-browned potatoes replacing the rice.

"The wheels fell off our lives in 1970 when Pat had a severe stroke and became completely disabled. We, too, had to sell the resort." Dick Williams in partnership with his mother, Bonnie, bought Gateway Hungry Jack Lodge in 1971. After a short time, Dick sold his partnership to Jerry Parsons.

Fire struck again in December 1972 and the showplace lodge with its handmade furniture burned to the ground. As luck would have it, the Forestry was building a new headquarters in Grand Marais and their old log building was for sale. It was dismantled log by log, and rebuilt as the new lodge. It stands today as Hungry Jack Lodge. Very shortly after the fire, Jerry Parsons became the sole owner.

Many changes have been made over these years. Kitchens have been added to all the cabins and it is no longer all American plan, but has the option to have all, part or no meals. It is now open year-round with popular winter activities. A campground has been added. In 2003 Forrest Parsons took over running the lodge from his father, and so the legacy of Sue and Jesse Gapen lives on.

Did you know . . .

The vast majority of furniture and decorations in the first two main buildings at Hungry Jack Lodge were built at the lake from locally available woods, barks, hides, etc.

SARA'S DATE COOKIES

Not many recipes have come down to us from the Gapen years at Hungry Jack. Mother Bunn's cookbook includes this recipe with the note that Sara was Gapen's cook. The cooking directions were added because Mother Bunn didn't have any. Just as with the Swedish Pancakes recipe, she assumed that everyone knew how to make cookies.

1 cup water to 2 cups dates, boil until thick
1 cup shortening
2 cups sugar
3 eggs
vanilla
4 cups flour

1 tsp. baking powder
1 tsp. soda
1 tsp. salt
1½ tsp. cinnamon
¼ tsp. nutmeg
1 cup chopped nuts

Combine all the ingredients. Drop from teaspoon onto cookie sheet. Bake in a moderate oven for 8–10 minutes.

DATE APPLESAUCE CAKE

This is another recipe from Mother Bunn's cookbook. She attributed the recipe to Gapen's cook, Sara. Down at the bottom of the same page is the identical recipe, but it was attributed to Margaret Nolan from Sunset Lodge. Who knows where it came from!

½ cup shortening
1½ cup sugar
1½ cup hot applesauce
1 cup raisins, with ½ cup hot water
    poured over the top
2 cups regular flour
2 tsp. baking soda

½ tsp. salt
1 tsp. cinnamon
1 tsp. cocoa
¼ tsp. cloves
1 cup chopped nuts
1 cup dates, cut into small pieces

Cream together shortening and sugar. Add applesauce and raisins to the shortening and sugar.

Combine flour, soda, salt, cinnamon, cocoa and cloves with raisin mixture; stir in chopped nuts and dates.

Bake about one hour in a 350° oven. If you should use sweetened applesauce, use less sugar. Grease and flour your pan.

Trail Center

There has been activity on this property since 1938. That was the year Sam and Mayme Seppala moved up to start a logging business. Sam had been in business with his brother at Pike Lake in Cook County when the two decided to split.

According to Gladys Seppala, daughter of Sam and Mayme, the mill at Poplar Lake was quite large. It operated 24 hours a day and employed 100 men. Gladys offered some insights into life around the mill:

Mayme and Sam Seppala with their daughter Gladys

"My mom and aunts were cooks . . . always homemade bread and pies. They even made their own soap out of grease and lye. I remember all the crates of dried raisins, prunes, apricots and coconut (my favorite!). There was a Cook, Cookie (helper) and Bull Cook, a man that did the heavy work —wood, water, and dishes. There was a screen house where they kept meat, so they had trouble with bear. My mother used to can bear meat. When she served it, a lot of people thought it was beef. They also cut their own ice from the lake. The men played a lot of cards in the evenings. Poker mostly. Or they would read or mend their clothes. Sometimes they would have dances in the Cook Shack. Someone would play an accordion. Of course, on pay day many went to town."

Near the camp the Seppalas had a small store. The store had supplies, a bar and two nickel slot machines. Sam and Mayme slept in a back bedroom and Gladys slept in the loft. This store was the beginning of what is now the lodge building at Trail Center.

As the Depression worsened, the mill was forced to close in the fall of 1940. Sam and some friends planned to earn their living by trapping. Unfortunately, Sam Seppela drowned that same year while canoeing and ownership of Trail Center passed on.

In 1948 Bill and Carrie Flavell bought Trail Center. The Flavells learned of Cook County when they bought a house from an Illinois family who was moving to run a resort on Pike Lake. They came up to vacation at the resort and fell in love with the country. During the late winter of 1948 the Flavells came up to Grand Marais to look for property. Realtor Bev Johnson took them up the trail to look at an available piece of land. The snow was up to the rooftops. In fact, there was so much snow that they couldn't see much at all. They bought the property anyway.

In 1948 Trail Center was a small store, a gas station and 2 cabins. Over the next few years they added on to the store and built several other cabins and the motel unit across the road. Some of the first customers for the motel unit were the men who originally paved the Gunflint Trail.

The next owners of Trail Center were George and Eva Cleaver. Eva was the sister of Carl Soderberg. Carl and his wife, Elinor, owned Soderberg Cabins located just a few miles further along the north shore of Poplar Lake. George and Eva's daughter, Joyce Leddy, tells how her parents bought Trail Center.

Eva and George Cleaver

"In 1962 (the year I was married) my father took an early retirement from Lehman Brothers where he had been a Bond Trader. At that time he and my mother purchased Trail Center and moved to the woods. Our household furniture now filled the motel and cabins.

"I think my parents may have been the first owners of Trail Center to offer some restaurant fare. In 1963 my husband and I remember visiting them en route to El Paso, Texas, where my husband was to be stationed as a new 2nd Lieutenant. During our visit, we were often relegated to the kitchen to help fry hamburgers and French fries for the patrons. In fact, hamburgers and French fries may have been the only item on the menu. In the store, my parents also offered a deli with freshly sliced cold cuts, etc. They lived in a lakeside cabin, next to Trail Center, which is now gone."

Joyce also recalled one very unusual experience her mother had in June of 1964. A young couple had driven up the Trail to take a boat trip out to Jock Richardson's place on Saganaga Lake. As the very pregnant wife got into the boat, she felt beginning labor pains. The couple immediately turned around and set out for Grand Marais. The baby was born en route and the couple turned into the first place they came to for help: Trail Service Center. Eva Cleaver and Mary Joe Retzer, one of their employees, were quickly summoned to the parking lot. The two women helped the new mother and baby get organized for a trip to the hospital in Grand Marais. Justine Kerfoot summed up the women's work by writing in her column, "The Cleavers of Trail Service Center are noted for their ability to meet all challenges and take care of all customers."

"In the early 1960s Trail Center was only open from May to October and my parents found it difficult to find enough help. Unfortunately the strenuous work required to handle a bar, restaurant, store, motel, cabins, boat rentals, gas, etc., proved to be too much for this older, retired couple. Within a few years my parents sold Trail Center to the Liebertz family."

After the Cleavers sold, the new owners of Trail Service Center were Thelma and Fred Liebertz and their daughter, Gay Lynne. Gay Lynne gives an idea of their first arrival at Trail Center as the new owners:

"In April of 1966, we arrived at Trail Service Center, midway up the Gunflint Trail from Grand Marais. We had driven from Birmingham, Michigan (a suburb of Detroit), to begin operating the business that we had purchased the previous fall from George and Eva Cleaver. It had been a "normal" hard winter—lots of snow, lots of cold. The ice on Poplar Lake was still several feet thick, and the snow was still 12–18 inches deep, on the level, with deeper drifts and higher snowbanks. We had a caretaker staying in the cabin where we would be living. Floyd Soderberg, Eva Cleaver's brother, had his own cabin on Birch Lake (farther up the Trail), but always stayed along the Gunflint Trail in winter for ease of getting to and from Grand Marais and Duluth for supplies, appointments, etc. Floyd had our cabin all warm and cozy, and had the parking area and walkway to the cabin cleared of snow. What with arriving in late afternoon, getting the cars and truck partially unpacked, and taking care of our two Siberian Huskies, Nordic and Taiga, my first night at Trail Service Center is a dim memory.

Gay Lynne, Thelma and Fred Liebertz

"The next morning, however, brought activities I have always remembered. First of all, I got a feel for just how much snow there was! And how much ice! In those days, most folks did not have indoor plumbing in the winter months—no hot-and-cold running water, no indoor toilets. Water was carried from a hole chopped through the lake ice, and down a path from the cabin was an outdoor biffy. I recall going after water that first day—it was cold enough that the water hole in the lake was always frozen over, and it was necessary to take a small hatchet along to open up the hole so fresh water could be dipped from the lake into a pail.

"Then there was the problem of getting into the main resort building, which housed the store and restaurant. Snow and ice had to be shoveled and chopped away from the doors, so that we could unload the remainder of the gear we had brought with us, and also so we could get inside to start preparing the place for the upcoming summer season. Needless to say, our first Gunflint Trail spring was memorable!"

After that, the seasons became predictable. Summers were busy with preparing and cooking meals for the restaurant; renting out cabins and boats and canoes; making regular trips to Duluth and Grand Marais for supplies. Autumns were slow-down times; customers were

Gay Lynne and Thelma Liebertz

fewer and further between, and get-ready-for-winter times. Winterizing consisted of end-of-season cleaning: building and grounds maintenance that couldn't be taken care of in the summer; and draining cabin and main building water pipes.

Gay Lynne continues, "Winters were fun! Sure, it snowed a lot, and it got cold, but there was time to enjoy being in the north country—there was snowshoeing and cross-country skiing, some snowmobiling and dogsledding. There were evening get-togethers with neighbors."

Winter chores were snowblowing the drive, parking area and the pathways to the cabin, the biffy, and even down to the lake; keeping the water hole open in the lake ice; filling all the birdfeeders and putting out corn for the deer. Then came the spring, the time to wrap-up from winter and begin getting ready for the summers all over again. Farther south spring was heralded by robins and daffodils, but along the Gunflint Trail, the first pungent smell of fresh mud was one of nature's signs that winter was over.

"When our family first moved to the Gunflint Trail, we decided that we could fill a niche that other resorts hadn't up to that time. Several of the Trail resorts had very good kitchens, but mostly they served meals only to their lodge or resort guests, or to the general public (private cabin owners or other vacationers) by reservation only, or only at specific meal times if there was available seating. We had come from a restaurant and food-service background, and felt that we could offer food all day. So by our second year, we had enlarged the kitchen and restocked it with all-new commercial refrigeration, cooking and food-preparation equipment; with

The original building at Trail Center, around 1939

commercially approved cooking utensils; and new dinnerware, flatware and glassware. For the nineteen years that we were on the Trail, we served a full menu of meals and "in-betweens" twelve hours a day, seven days a week, from Memorial Day through September 30.

"Dad took care of regular trips to Duluth for supplies for both the kitchen and the store (groceries and other items for resale). Dad grew up in a butcher shop—his dad had been a meat-cutter and sausage-maker—so all of our meat items were cut and prepared by us. We cut our own steaks and chops; made our own hamburger and breakfast sausage; prepared our own boneless chicken breasts, legs and thighs; made our own corned beef; filleted fresh fish; cut and rolled our own roasts.

"Mom and I shared the cooking duties—Mom baked the pies, sweet rolls and dinner rolls, and made the soups (lentil was the all-time favorite), while I handled the meal-cooking and grillwork. Every item on our menu was prepared from scratch. We made our own sauces and cut French fries.

"Mom's special expertise was in the baking department, what with preparing breakfast sweet rolls and dinner crescent rolls daily. But her specialty was pies. She baked between 2000 and 2500 pies every summer—18 different varieties, from apple, blueberry and cherry to lemon meringue, pecan and rhubarb. Folks would come to Trail Center for dinner, and order pie first just to make sure their favorite wouldn't be gone when they were finished with their meal. And quite often, half of a customer's meal would go along in a doggy bag so that diner would have room for pie! In the afternoon, customers would stop in for a piece of pie as a midday snack. Twenty years after leaving the Trail, former customers will still say to Thelma, 'I sure miss your pies!'"

By 1984, it was time for the Liebertzes to move on from Trail Center. They sold it to Bill and Nancy Edwards-France. After a couple of years the property resold to Bruce and Sue Kerfoot from Gunflint Lodge.

Bruce and Sue asked Nancy Hemstad, a longtime summer employee, to take over the job as manager down at Trail Center. They also renamed the place Poplar Lake Lodge but basically it was still the same gift shop, convenience store and restaurant it had been under the Liebertzes.

This was Nancy's first management position and she really turned it into a busy, humming operation. The number of meals that they served surprised both the Kerfoots and Nancy. Apparently there was quite a demand for what Bruce called "good roadhouse cooking."

After running Poplar Lake Lodge for a couple of years, the Kerfoots sold the operation to Larry and Ginny Backstrom. The Backstroms continued the traditional operation of this general store and restaurant. In fact, their breakfasts were so good that they impressed a visiting producer of "Good Morning, America." After the first visit, the producer returned with a film crew. Not long after that viewers across America were greeted by a Poplar Lake Lodge waitress saying, "Good Morning, America, from the Boundary Waters Canoe Area in Minnesota."

In the early 1990s, Larry and Ginny Backstrom hired a new kitchen helper named Sarah Hamilton. Sarah had learned the restaurant business from her mother. "My mom trained me, but it was a lot of family style and she really worked me through. It was never line cooking. It was never my creative cooking, thank goodness. We had little cafes and two of us would run it. So we'd do a couple daily specials. I would be in the kitchen throughout the day and at lunch we'd come out and serve it kind of cafeteria style."

In 1995 Sarah bought Trail Center. One of the first changes locals noticed was new decorations appearing on the walls and ceilings. As Sarah said, "My mother once again. We've been going to dumps since I was a little kid getting stuff. An awful lot of it came out of dumps all over Iowa: most of the bottles, most of the jars. She had a restaurant in 1968 that looked just like this in Des Moines, Iowa. Not so woodsy, but a lot like it. Just covered with, I think, it was called primitives. She always collected tools and bottles and she got us all started on it."

Part of Sarah's new collection of decorations at Trail Center

Sarah brought all this stuff up north and "arranged" it in the restaurant. But she doesn't think of it as arranging, "That's the beauty of it. You don't need to arrange it. Really. Antiques you tend to put in an order. These I can just keep putting stuff on top of them and next to them and the clutter actually looks good. Clutter and I get along really well."

Another thing that Sarah gets along well with is work and projects. When explaining the purchase of Trail Center, she said, "It definitely gave me something to do all of the time. I was no longer bored, but I like to work. I always have. But every job I have had, I always worked too much. I've been there 60, 70 hours a week when we had a project because I really enjoyed doing it. I'm not a person that has any hobbies of any kind. I don't have a passion for walking, hiking, biking, fishing, anything. I like all of it a little tiny bit. But I just loved having projects so it was actually great because there was so much to do and there still is. It was just kind of nonstop."

One of the first projects was making taffy. One day she was watching "City Confidential" on television and the story was about a town that thrived on making taffy. "It was a big tourist destination because of their taffy. And, of course, when we're closed in December and April, all I think of is different ways to make money 'cause the money stops and I start getting scared. So I decided we can make taffy. And making taffy was awful. We didn't have a machine so we pulled it all by hand and it was a nightmare. But it kept everybody employed for a whole winter, which is really what it was about. We figured if we started something new that we

Sarah Hamilton

could sell—even if it didn't take off until summer—we could justify everyone working and perfecting it. And then our neighbors gave us a fudge recipe and we were very glad to move on to the fudge. And it worked. The fudge is working."

Shortly after taffy and fudge came calendars. "What started the calendar? I don't remember and I have a whole file on it so I wouldn't forget why it started. I think what started the calendar was I got a new computer, and there was a calendar program on it. I happened to have Bill Messina and Chris O'Brien working here who both love to take photographs and do a really good job. So we thought we could build a calendar and make a million dollars on it."

The next project was a line of packaged dried foods called Gunflint Viddles with the intentional misspelling of vittles. Sarah developed the recipes. Of the soup recipes she says, "I don't wander too far in spices. I know about three spices, maybe four. And they are all in every one of those. Garlic, sage, salt and pepper. And dried creamer, which makes everything good."

The latest project is a line of Dork clothing. When asked where the name came from, Sarah said, "It was just something we called each other here. Like a lot of people use it, you know 'Don't be a dork!' So we made shirts for the staff as a joke and we all wore them on Saturdays. And people loved them, loved them, loved them. So we made shirts to sell and people bought them. Then we made hats to sell and people bought them as fast as we could make them so now we have a whole new line of clothing."

Throughout all of her projects, Sarah has kept the main function of a restaurant in firm view—serving good food. It's the kind of food that locals enjoy coming in for week after week. Some recipes came from her mother. Others are from when the Liebertz family ran Trail Center.

Did you know . . .

Trail Center has had eight owners, but the main part of the lodge building is still the one built by Sam and Mayme Seppala in 1938.

Sarah Hamilton's Dork line of clothing is so popular that it was featured in an article in *Rolling Stone* magazine.

PIE CRUST MIX

Since pies were Thelma's specialty, we are lucky to have her recipe for crust plus an extra tip for baking perfect pies.

2⅔ cups flour
1 tsp. salt
1 cup shortening or ¾ cup plus 2 T lard

Mix thoroughly in a large bowl with a pastry blender. Put in a freezer bag and seal. This may be stored in the refrigerator for several weeks as long as you don't add water. When making pies for the restaurant, Thelma would multiply this recipe many times and fill a gallon size bag with the dry mixture.

When ready to make a pie, take out 4 handfuls (for a 2-crust pie) and put in a small mixing bowl. You will soon learn how much you need for the size pie you are making. Add 3 tablespoons of very cold water and mix just enough to make a soft ball. Add more water if necessary but don't get it too wet. A bit more flour mixture or a smidgen of water is easy to add as necessary. The remaining dry mixture can be stored in the refrigerator. Knead the dough for a minute on a lightly floured counter. Divide in half and roll out your crusts.

This is Thelma's additional tip for baking perfect pies. If you have old sheets or pillow case, tear a 2"-wide strip to go around the pie to help hold in the juices and keep it from browning too much. Wet it before putting around the pie. Remove the cloth immediately after taking the pie from the oven. Be careful as it is very hot. Thelma calls this a Band-Aid for the pie.

THELMA'S "PECAN" PIE

You will be surprised to read that this pie was made with walnuts rather than pecans. Very few people can taste or see the difference.

Crust for an 8" single crust pie
3 eggs, slightly beaten
¼ tsp. salt
⅔ cup sugar

Mix eggs, salt and sugar with a wire whip. Add margarine and syrup. Mix thoroughly with a wire whip. Stir in walnuts. Pour into prepared pie pan. Wrap a 2" strip of wet sheeting around the edge to keep it from browning too much. Bake at 375° for 35–40 minutes or just until it is set and not jiggly. Remove sheeting immediately upon removal from the oven.

FRIED ONION RINGS

Andy and Durae Lilienthal have both been cooks at Trail Center over the years. They got this recipe from a cousin in Des Moines, Iowa.

whole onions	pepper
flour	cold water
salt	

Slice your onions into rings. Separate and put rings into cold water. Remove the onion rings and let the excess liquid drain off in a colander. Dip the rings in flour combined with salt and pepper. Dip them into the cold water again. Return them to the flour mixture one more time. Fry in 360° fryer until golden brown.

FRUIT CRISP

Every cook loves this type of recipe that you can use with any fruit that is in season. Sarah took this recipe and made a dried version of it for the Gunflint Viddles line.

8 cups fresh or frozen fruit such as peaches, rhubarb, apples, blueberries or cherries (if using cherries, the quantity is 4 heaping cups)
¾ cup granulated sugar
1 T flour
¼ tsp. salt
1 tsp. cinnamon
½ tsp. nutmeg
¼ cup soft margarine

TOPPING:
¾ cup brown sugar
¾ cup granulated sugar
1 cup flour
1 cup oatmeal
¼ tsp. baking powder
dash of salt
1 egg
½ cup soft margarine

Melt the margarine in a 9x13" pan. Add the fruit combined with sugar, flour, spices and margarine. Use the cinnamon and nutmeg only with the apples. Combine the topping ingredients and sprinkle over the fruit and pat down. Bake at 350° for 45–60 minutes.

LENTIL SOUP

Ginny Backstrom says, "Soups have always been popular on the Poplar Lake Lodge menu. This one is an all-time favorite."

3 cup dried lentils
7 cups chicken or vegetable stock
2 tsp. salt
2 tsp. minced garlic
1 cup chopped carrots
1 cup chopped onions
black pepper to taste
1½ cup chopped tomatoes

POPLAR LAKE'S FAMOUS CHOCOLATE CAKE

When you are on vacation, there is nothing better than a little dessert to finish off a meal. This one will definitely fill in all the cracks.

3 cup flour
2 cup sugar
2 tsp. baking soda
⅓ cup cocoa
1 tsp. salt

¾ cup oil
2 T vinegar
1 tsp. vanilla
2 cups cold water

Mix the ingredients together by hand. Pour into a 9x13" cake pan. Bake at 350° for 30–35 minutes. Cool before frosting.

COLE SLAW DRESSING

This was a staple for Trail Center Cole Slaw. Its easy method of preparation uses only one measuring cup and one fork.

In a two-cup glass measuring cup put 2 ounces of vinegar. Add vegetable oil to the 6-ounce line. Add sugar to the 12-ounce line. Add water to the 16-ounce line. Stir well until the sugar is dissolved. There should be a little vinegary taste to the dressing.

Santa Fe Grits

Grits are not normally found on menus in northern Minnesota but this variation from traditional grits is a staple on the Trail Center breakfast menu.

10 lbs. breakfast sausage, browned but not drained
4 cups instant grits cooked according to the package directions
1 #10 can (6 lb. 3 oz.) diced green chili peppers, adjusted to your taste
12 eggs
2 T salt
2 T black pepper
2 T Tabasco sauce
4 cups grated cheddar cheese.

Combine all ingredients and place is a very well greased pan. Bake at 350° for 1¾ hours or until it is crisp on the outside and spongy on the inside. Cool overnight in the pan. The next day, to remove the grits from the pan, put in a 350° oven for 10 minutes. Invert the pan onto a large sheet pan. The entire mixture should come out as a loaf. Slice into individual servings and fry before using.

Sausage Gravy

This is another unusual breakfast item in northern Minnesota, but it's a favorite of the Trail Center regulars.

5 lbs. bulk breakfast sausage
2 tsp. salt
1 T black pepper
1 T dried sage
1 cup vegetable oil
1 cup flour
4 cups milk
4 cups water

Brown the sausage in a large pan. Add the seasonings. Add the vegetable oil until the meat is just covered. You may need more or less oil than is called for. Slowly mix in the flour and cook until thickened. It is very easy to add too much flour. Combine the milk and water. Slowly add this to the meat mixture and cook until the thickness is correct. Do this slowly as the exact amount may vary from day to day.

— Memories of —
Soderberg Cabins

The Soderbergs were once an active family on the Trail. Carl and Elinor founded Soderberg Cabins. They sold it to Floyd Soderberg who later sold the business to the Liebertz family at Trail Center. The Liebertzes had previously bought Trail Center from Floyd's sister, Eva, and her husband, George Cleaver.

Just a couple of bends up the road from Trail Center and on the right is where Soderberg Cabins used to be located. Carl and his brother Floyd Soderberg had been coming up to the Gunflint Trail since they were teenagers. After Carl married, he and his wife, Elinor, continued coming up. Their daughter, Carlene Soderberg Krumpack, remembers camping at West Bearskin and Flour Lake. Like many children who grew up on the Trail, Carlene has interesting stories of how it used to be.

"The first year my mom washed the towels and linens in a washtub and a scrub board. The next year we got modern and we had a Maytag gasoline powered wringer washing machine."

"In 1945 my dad, Carl Soderberg, began building cabins. My mom and I joined him in 1947 after I finished grammar school. We had a small operation, only three rental cabins. There was no electricity, phone or indoor plumbing. The only time you could listen to the radio was at night because the reception was so bad. We had a small radio that sat on top of a large battery. The battery was probably three times the size of the radio. We would get the news from Gabrial Heater.

"My mother made curtains, covers for feather ticks and comforters on an old treadle sewing machine. My mom also varnished all the cabins. In the summer we would pick berries, and she would put them up in mason jars so that we could have them in the winter. In those days my mom also used a pressure cooker for canning. I still have the pressure cooker in my attic. I do know that she canned everything from berries to fish and venison.

"Like everyone else up there, she made bread in a wood-burning stove. I remember she would put the dough in a large washbasin, cover with a dish towel, and hang it from hooks in the ceiling so it would rise. It sure hit the spot on those cold winter days with raspberry jam or just plain sugar bread.

"The first year my mom washed the towels and linens in a washtub and a scrub board. The next year we got modern and we had a Maytag gasoline powered wringer washing machine.

"I remember backpacking with my dad carrying minnow traps, pails, white eggshells and white bread and going deep into the woods to a floating bog area to clean and reset the traps and then hauling out the minnows, making sure to stop and pump the minnow pail on the way back to the road. Fishermen always preferred minnows over shiners. One day after being down by the lake, we returned to our cabin to find that the bear had just left. He had gone in one door, swiped and turned things around and then departed through the other door. We were glad we missed him.

"We always had the same guests back. In fact they insisted on coming to our place whether we had a vacant cabin or not. One summer we had to share our own cabin with them."

"During partridge season I would put the rifle over the handlebars of my bicycle and away I would go. I was successful. In those days even the women and girls knew how to handle a gun and always carried a hunting knife in a sheath on their belts. I would also show our guests how to fillet their fish.

"Our first Christmas tree had candles in candleholders that my mom bought. It was beautiful. The next Christmas my dad hooked a string of lights up to a car battery.

"On Christmas break we put up ice. My dad would saw the field of ice by hand and we would all pull and push the blocks of ice into the icehouse. One of my jobs was to put sawdust around each block of ice. Sawdust was insulation and prevented the ice from melting during the summer.

"When we moved to Poplar Lake we had an old LaFayette automobile. The next year we bought an Army surplus jeep. My dad taught me how to drive with that jeep. He showed me how to shift and go forward and backward and then went in the cabin for a cup of coffee and a cigarette. Of course, my mom asked where I was and he replied that I was driving. He said I couldn't get hurt, there were high snow banks on each side of the road and if I got stuck, I had four-wheel drive to get out.

Carlene and Carl Soderberg moving ice blocks

"My mother spent one winter alone, as my dad went to the Twin Cities to work. My mom did not have a car, electricity, phone or running water. She was snowed in for at least two weeks at a time. The plow was not able to get through and neither was the mail. She shoveled to the lake, chopped a hole in the ice and carried up buckets of water. The bucket gets heavier and heavier as it picks up snow on the way. She shoveled to the biffy and she chopped wood, baked bread and knitted. I don't know how she did it. I was in high school and could not hitch a ride up every weekend.

Elinor and Carl Soderberg with their full ice house

"We always had the same guests back. In fact they insisted on coming to our place whether we had a vacant cabin or not. One summer we had to share our own cabin with them. There was a door between the two rooms and we all just made the best of it. Some guests did not like well water or lake water so we would go to a spring over by Hungry Jack and haul the spring water back. Our guests became our friends and I would go portaging, hiking and swimming with them.

"At night when my parents and the adults would get together in one cabin, the young guests (pre-teen and teenagers) would go to another cabin to make fudge, pop popcorn, listen to records on a wind up phonograph and play 'Sorry.'

"I believe it must have been the late 1950s when my uncle Floyd Soderberg bought the cabins from us. In 1960 Floyd sold the cabins to the Liebertzes.

"It was a great place to live. The resorts would hire teens in the summer for help. I remember going with some of our young guests over to Hungry Jack to help dry dishes so we could all get together. Swimming, canoeing and portaging were my passions. I just loved the country and still do."

Did you know . . .

Solid blue ice that has been stacked and insulated with moss or sawdust in a well built ice house will last throughout the following summer.

Nor'Wester Lodge

Carl and Alis Brandt ended up in the resort business almost by accident. Carl came to run a logging business and built a spare cabin for visiting relatives to use. One day a fisherman offered to rent it for a week. The business grew from there.

The second resort we come to along Poplar Lake is Nor'Wester Lodge. It was started as Balsam Grove Lodge in the early 1930s by Carl and Alis Brandt. Carl and Alis were first generation Swedish-Americans. Alis made terrific pies and was soon well known for it. Her daughter-in-law, Luana, quickly mastered the art and even ran a small pie business for a time. Their son, Carl Jr., and Luana operate Nor'Wester now. It is laundry day and that's where Luana is.

"Laundry is one of those things that just has to get done. Then I hear it, the little chuckle and the lilting Swedish accent of my mother-in-law, Alis, saying, 'Isn't this fun? It is so easy to wash clothes now. A child could do it. Even with the weather not nice.' I have to smile as I recall the old days."

Carl and Alis Brandt came to the shores of Poplar Lake in 1930, intending to continue Carl's logging business. Unfortunately, the land had less saw lumber than anticipated, and with the Depression, lumber was not selling. The business prospects for this new family dimmed considerably. Times were not good and moving was not an option. Like many of their neighbors, they settled into a small, one room home on the property and decided to live off the land.

However small their home was, it soon filled with relatives and friends. It was a very small home and one morning on his way to the outhouse, stepping over family members sleeping on the floor, Carl decided he had had enough. He started construction on a building down the hill and next to the lake. He finished it with the lumber he was unable to sell from his previous logging days. He then had somewhere to put the visiting friends and relatives who came up.

One day, a fisherman offered to pay him the princely sum of $5 to rent the cabin for a week. Done. The family was in the resort business. Each year from then on Carl would build a cabin and furnish it from farm sale auctions as the less fortunate sold belongings during the Depression. Hoosier cupboards, round oak tables and chairs, iron bedsteads, springs and mattresses all made their way north to the new business of Balsam Grove Lodge.

Those beds, though, needed linens on them and those linens needed washing. With no electricity, the first laundry was done down at the lake with a scrub board and galvanized tubs. To get the sheets really rinsed, Carl would start up the old outboard motor and Alis would hang over the side of the boat as they ran up and down the lake, "rinsing" the sheets, towels and personal laundry. Carl soon determined he wanted nothing to do with this on a permanent basis and changes were made.

The following year, he built a garage next to their home and included a gas powered wringer washer as part of the equipment, as well as several galvanized tubs. Water, however, now needed to be bucketed 50 yards up the hill from the lake. Cold lake water needed to be heated on the stove and then poured into the washer and tubs. Wet laundry was then hung on the lines to dry. The lines were down hill near the lake, another 50-yard trek. Dry laundry came back up that same hill. Washday had improved but not much.

Times were not good and moving was not an option. Like many of their neighbors, they settled into a small, one room home on the property and decided to live off the land. One day, a fisherman offered to pay him the princely sum of $5 to rent the cabin for a week. Done. The family was in the resort business.

The next improvement came when Carl built a wash house down by the lake. This was only a few feet from the shore. Water could be bucketed into a metal trough with a wood fire underneath, then with a short turn it was poured into the waiting gas powered wringer washer and the necessary wash tubs with one containing bluing for a sparkling wash. Of course they were still hung outside on long lines but now were ironed on a new gas mangle. A contemporary picture shows Alis proudly standing in front of 96 sheets hanging on the lines.

This was the laundry status when Luana appeared in the picture in the mid-1960s. "After six weeks of fighting the washer, the mangle, and the weather I gave up on the entire arrangement. I stopped doing laundry. Sunny day followed sunny day as I never entered the building. At breakfast, at lunch, at coffee breaks, various family members mentioned laundry. Good day for doing it, good wind for drying it, etc. Finally on a drizzly, miserable, cool, gray day I cheerfully announced I was going to do laundry. The entire family thought I was certifiably crazy. Not yet, however.

"One of the employees stuffed bags of laundry into the old station wagon, I took a shower and grabbed two rolls of quarters. Smiling, I informed everyone that lunch was up to them and took off for town and the Laundromat. Several hours later we returned with piles of clean towels, sheets, pillowcases and personal laundry. Clean, dry, folded and ready for the shelves. We had also hit every gift shop in town. A year later we had our own Laundromat.

"Again I hear Alis saying, 'See, I told you laundry now is so easy it takes no time at all. You don't even need my recipe for washday chili. You can use it though if you wish. Did I ever tell you of the time I made chili for a trail meeting?'"

In the early days of the trail, owners decided to get together and work on getting more people up here. There was always a fall meeting to discuss what advertising they would do. The meetings were all held at different resorts and the lucky resort got to feed everybody. It was Balsam Grove's turn, and Alis had made hot cross buns and several loaves of bread, but needed something hot to serve

Alis with her father-in-law John August

and decided to make chili. However, when she went to the freezer all she could find was ground beaver meat. The hamburger was gone, so Alis served beaver meat. She laughed a lot though, because of all the compliments on the best chili they ever had. Luana remembers that chili. "You never knew what Alis used in it and it never tasted the same twice. Alis told me, 'Beaver haunch is good meat. It's kind of sweet and kind of like pork.' I'll have to take her word for it. On those nights that beaver was served I opted for a peanut butter sandwich."

Beaver trapping became a way of life. Beaver pelts brought in hard cash for taxes and machinery. After Alis died, the youngest son, also named Carl, found his first beaver license while sifting through family memorabilia. He had been three years old at the time it was issued. Up the trail, Bruce Kerfoot, six months older, was also trapping. The newspaper clipping attached to the old license commented that Carl was the youngest member of the trapping fraternity.

At the time the government was also paying a good bounty on wolves. However, trapping a wolf was no easy chore. It took Carl Sr. three years before he got smart enough to trap a dumb wolf. Smaller game was also here though, and Alis (along with Clara Dewar of Loon Lake) were introducing Alis's sons into trapping. Carl Jr. trapped his first mink a quarter mile from the house at age five. He proudly hauled it home, trap and all, for Mom to help him take it out of the trap. The crowning achievement became family lore because that day Carl Sr. came home empty-handed to a proud five-year-old holding a spitting, squirming, live mink. Several years later Alis would help her son make a pet out of a mink, and even let it drink from a cream pitcher on the table.

A self-described tomboy, Alis loved the outdoors and took every opportunity to enjoy the woods. Luana continues, "Again Alis's voice comes back to me, 'Oh, but I loved to go fishing. All winter long we would snowshoe up to Partridge to get small trout. I would slice up a loaf of my bread, butter every other slice, throw in some bacon and coffee and we would walk up there to fish. After the holes were made, Carl Sr. would start a fire. We would take turns watching the bacon, then slide it in between some bread for the boys. They were always a bit impatient. The first trout would be cleaned and plopped in the hot bacon fat, slid into a slice of bread and promptly eaten by the victorious fisherman.' Having experienced this family tradition, I agree. Restaurant trout cannot compare."

Many of the family traditions centered around gathering food, and then eating food. Some years blueberries were plentiful and the entire family would pick like mad. "Alis told me all the family stories saying, 'Paul would pick pretty good, but the other two ate more than they picked I think. Carl Jr. would put moss on the bottom and fill up the top, but they all liked to eat blueberry pie, so if they picked enough I would make a pie.'"

This love of blueberry picking lasted a lifetime. There are photos of Alis as a young girl with buckets of berries in front of her. She was still picking berries well into her nineties, as she taught her granddaughters to gather.

Alis, one of her sons and two helpers after a blueberry-picking trip

It is because of pies that Luana entered the picture. "I was working at a neighboring resort and Carl Jr. came over to meet the summer help. At the time I made lousy pie crust and wanted to improve on it. I mentioned this to a family friend, Lydia Miller. She assured me this new recipe was fail safe. My employer did not want me using her ingredients, but Alis Brandt had no problems turning me loose in her kitchen. Each night after work, I came over to Balsam Grove and made a pie. Each evening Carl Sr. ate several pieces of pie and critiqued my result. Whatever pie was left was eaten for breakfast. That meant unlimited experience with pie crust and unlimited pies to eat. It was a match without losers. By the end of the summer, I made fairly good pies, and Carl Sr. was ready to welcome a new person into the family.

"Carl and I married on a Saturday in June. The following Tuesday we arrived on the trail. Next morning there were sixteen people for breakfast. I was in the resort business. I had grown up in farm country and certainly had no intentions of marrying a farmer. Farming was just too chancy, between markets and weather, and very hard work. I was going to college so that I could marry someone with a good income and steady employment. Oh for the dreams of youth! Instead I married a resorter, dependent on weather and markets with a lot of personal hard work. Somehow I didn't make the connection. Dumb.

"In fact the day we married, Alis and Carl sat and talked for two hours over breakfast, quizzing me on why I wanted to get married, and all the downsides to being a resort owner. 'You know, there are times you are going to feel like the business is a logging chain around your neck. You can't run off and do things you want to do. You will be tied to the resort. Are you ready for that?' Alis asked. In that two hours, she pulled no punches as she tried to ascertain whether I would stick with this marriage and this business. Later she would tell me, 'I knew you were strong enough to stick, but my Carl wasn't quite sure yet and he needed to hear it from you.'

"Each night after work, I came over to Balsam Grove and made a pie. Each evening Carl Sr. ate several pieces of pie and critiqued my result. That meant unlimited experience with pie crust and unlimited pies to eat. It was a match without losers."

"That was the other thing we shared: names. Her youngest son was not really a "Junior" but to keep things simple, the family and friends had called him that. I couldn't. So between us, Alis and I devised a way to let people know whom we were talking about. Carl Sr. was Dad or my Carl for Alis. Carl Jr. was Carl or my Carl for me, and my father-in-law was Dad. After some time family and friends picked up on our verbal shorthand and the distinction was made for most. There are still friends and old guests who continue to call my Carl 'Junior.'"

There were numerous other things Alis and Luana shared. A kitchen for one. Alis walked out of the lodge kitchen and left everything there. Luana never had a new bride confusion about spices, condiments, or staples in the cupboard. All she had to do was replace those things she had used. Some things were easier to replace than others. "That first summer as I struggled to make sense out of my new surroundings, duties and expectations, I made numerous gaffs. One of the more memorable concerned dogs and pies. Dad had gone blueberry picking and came home with buckets of berries and I had made numerous pies. Unfortunately, I had put two of them on a low counter to cool. At the time Carl had a dog that was part Norwegian elkhound and part Labrador. This dog was large and tall enough to carefully lift a ten-inch pie tin from the counter, place it on the floor and eat half of a warm, blueberry pie. I was furious. Carl's pie was the other half of the one his dog ate! That dog and I did not see eye to eye on a lot of things.

The old cookstove and collections of cooking utensils

"One of Carl's favorite tricks that first summer was to tell the dog, Hardtack, to go wake me up, which the dog loved to do. In the bedroom he would pull off one blanket, pull off another blanket, then pull off the sheet. By this time a shivering, sleepy me is feeling around for a blanket. Now I would wake up to a grinning, smug, black face as Hardtack sat on the bedclothes. When I would get out of bed to swat him one, he gleefully backed away. If I were silly enough to pick up blankets and go back to bed, he would start the game all over again. Carl, of course, thought it great entertainment.

Nor'Wester Lodge

"It was not entertainment when Hardtack would try and 'save' us while we tried to water-ski. That blasted dog would jump on the back of the skis as we took off, guaranteeing a face plant in the water. When confined to the washhouse, he would bark, howl and occasionally push out one of the windows to save us from the water. Unfortunately, the antics of this pet were not appreciated until he turned up missing that first autumn, then his little idiosyncrasies became family stories.

"In the summer of '67, the Canadians celebrated their centennial and with it the role of the voyageurs and the North West Fur Company. They ran a group of Montreal canoes from Lake Athabasca to Montreal passing through the border country. A number of Canadian notables were on the Gunflint Trail. Among them was a couple from Fort William. George and Nancy MacGillvray suggested a name change. The following year, we became the Nor'Wester Lodge, named in part for those early voyageurs searching for furs and trade. The name change became necessary as too many Carls were answering the phone, and record keeping became confusing and difficult. There was now a clear line of succession and ownership that made sense to the public."

Over the next decade Luana and Carl changed more than the name. Cabins were remodeled while others were jacked up and moved off the property to be sold as summer homes. New units went in and the face of the resort changed. "I loved to swim and water ski, but the area in front was loaded with leeches. We solved the problem by developing a small beach and dock area. It was popular with the kids, unfortunately it was also the site of the death of our son. Time heals and with it came two additional daughters. Three girls in the same house added up to laughter and smiles."

In 1980, they made the last large addition as they tripled the size of the lodge to include new living quarters and a restaurant. "Things had changed once again and I was off to a new adventure as meals became more involved and I could no longer do it alone. Alis, of course, continued to over-see all the changes. Approving of most and gentle in her criticism, she became the sounding board on raising children, hiring employees and finding time for myself, as I balanced husband, children, resort and teaching full time.

"Oh, yes, I traveled the Gunflint Trail to town 182 days of the year to teach in Grand Marais. I became expert at blowing into the kitchen at 4:30 and having a full meal ready for guests at 6:30. Planning and a helpful husband were necessary. Although we were open year-round, the winter months were not as hectic, and teaching fitted into the time space available. Besides, when school started in the fall, I appreciated anyone else picking up the phone. I loved teaching and the variety in my life fit my ever-questing mind for new things to see and do."

Part of that quest was to develop new recipes for the restaurant. They would also develop a thriving pie business as Luana finally put to the test the search for a better pie. Over the years they developed over seventeen recipes for apple pie. The original was good, but Apple Praline, Dutch Apple, Bog Orchard and Swedish Apple soon followed.

Luana Brandt

"In 1997 we finally closed the restaurant and tried to slow down the frenetic activity. For the next three summers, our youngest daughter, Kathryn, continued to make pies. She had a sweet deal from her dad. He paid for the ingredients, she got to take the profits, as long as he could eat all the pie that he wanted. So life comes back to family, friends, laundry and pie."

Did you know . . .

Jerome, Paul and Carl Brandt were three of the pupils at Grace Boissenin's one-room schoolhouse on Clearwater Lake.

Blueberries contain no natural pectin, which is what thickens jams. Raspberry or strawberry jam can be thickened by boiling the berries long enough but blueberries need to have pectin added to make jam.

One of the subjects Luana Brandt taught in school was geography. As homework assignments, she would send her students home with a page of geographical locations to find on a world map. Many a family would find their night spent sitting around the dining room table with the list and atlas.

Like many Trail residents, Luana is a world traveler. She has spent many midwinter breaks taking local students on European trips. Poland and Russia are two of her favorite places to visit. Luana was one of the first people on the Trail to bring students from these countries over to work for the summer.

WALLEYE in PARCHMENT

Fish became a staple on the menu and nothing says northwoods better than walleye. Here is a recipe Luana developed after numerous experimentations. It has previously been featured in the Pioneer Press and another cookbook.

half a sheet of baker's parchment paper
½ cup julienne sliced carrots
½ cup julienne sliced celery
2 T water
2 walleye fillets, 2–4 ounces each

½ tsp. dill weed
½ tsp. lemon pepper
2 T butter
4 slices lemon

To wrap fish: Place parchment on shallow microwave dish or plate. Place carrots and celery with water in middle of sheet. Place fillets on top. Shake or sprinkle dill weed and lemon pepper on each fillet. Dot fillets with butter and cover with lemon slices. Bring 2 long edges of the paper together and make a double French fold, folding firmly on top of fish. Make a double fold on each end, tucking folds under fish. (Note: make sure all folds are secure enough to keep butter and steam inside. It should look like a well-wrapped parcel.)

To cook: microwave on high for 6 minutes in a 750 watt oven. Adjust timing to suit your microwave and the size of the fillets. Fish is done when it flakes with a fork. Unfold the parchment paper, folding it back, and serve the fish in the paper. Be careful of the steam coming out. Garnish with parsley and lemon wedges.

WILD RICE

When Luana and Carl operated a restaurant at the Nor'Wester, Luana came up with a list of menu options that reflected the lakes and streams of the BWCAW. One of them was a wild rice dish that proved a popular favorite.

5 cups chicken broth
2 cups wild rice
2 tsp. thyme
Gently simmer until rice has popped
    open and is tender. Drain and chill.

ADD:
2 cups sauteed julienne cut carrots
2 cups sauteed julienne cut celery

2 cups thinly chopped tops of green onions,
    sauteed
2 cups sliced and sauteed mushrooms
½ cup roasted slivered almonds

Toss all together and serve warm, with sauce of choice. This also freezes well and can be used at a later date if needed.

TRAIL MEETING HOT CROSS BUNS

This was a favorite of Alis's for potlucks or early meetings of the Gunflint Trail Association.

3 cups milk, scalded and cooled
¾ cup butter
6 tsp. yeast
3 tsp. cinnamon
¾ tsp. nutmeg
¾ tsp. salt
¾ cup sugar
13½ cups flour
6 eggs
3 cups raisins

Scald milk and cool to room temperature. Add melted butter and yeast into milk. Set aside to rise. Mix spices, sugar and flour together. Add eggs to cool yeast mixture, then add yeast mixture to dry ingredients a bit at a time. Fold in raisins last. Let rise until double in volume and punch down. Form into golf ball size pieces of dough. Place about ½" apart on baking sheet. Cover with cloth and let rise again. Bake in a 425° oven for 15 minutes.

PASTRY for PIE

Alis and Luana were always two of the best pie makers on the Trail. Add in the recipes and tips from the Boostroms and Thelma Liebertz and every reader of this book can easily become an expert pie maker.

4 cups flour
1½ cups shortening
1½ cups ice cold water

Blend flour and shortening. Slowly add the ice water. Sometimes you use less water, sometimes a little more. Dough should be mixed, but not sticky. Divide into 4 equal balls. Flatten and use a pastry stocking over the rolling pin, and a pastry cloth. Roll out into roughly a circle and use for whatever recipe you wish.

GRANDMA'S BLUEBERRY PIE

One of the most memorable events for Alis Brandt was the annual blueberry season. She loved to pick the shiny small berries and was once even filmed picking by a local TV crew. She continued to pick berries until well into her nineties. One of her favorite recipes was for blueberry pie. To cut down on the mess in her kitchen, and the inevitable "his piece is bigger then mine" argument, she would bake each of her three sons their own individual pie. Then she would send them off to the island to eat it and keep the mess and discussion out of her kitchen.

    5 cups of blueberries, fresh or frozen
    add 3 T flour if you use fresh berries, ¼ cup if frozen berries are used
    1 cup sugar
    ½ tsp. of lemon peel

Mix together. Pour into a pie tin covered with the lower pie crust. Attach upper crust. Seal and bake at 375° for 1 hour.

LUANA'S APPLE PIE

When Luana came into the picture, she learned that this family ate pie. She worked hard on a basic apple pie, even winning a blue ribbon at the local fair one year.

    crust for a 2-crust pie   1 tsp. cinnamon
    4 large Granny Smith apples, peeled and   ¼ tsp. nutmeg
        sliced (enough for 5 cups of apples)   3 T flour
    1 cup sugar

Mix together thoroughly. Fill pie shell and attach top crust. Bake at 400° for 1 hour, or until steam comes from the slit in the top crust.

Variations: Soak ½ cup of craisins in white wine for two hours, add to the apple mix OR soak ½ cup of raisins in Kahlua for two hours, add to the mixture.

Another variation is to top either of the two with a crumb topping instead of a second crust.

Crumb topping: 1 cup flour, ½ cup brown sugar. Mix well and cut in ½ cup margarine. Place on top of the apple mixture. Bake at 400° for 50 minutes, or until the mixture bubbles through the crumb topping. Cover the pie for the last ten minutes to prevent overcooking.

Windigo Lodge

Windigo's moose statue is the first moose that many Trail visitors see. At any rate, it is the most reliable moose to see. Because it is life-size, standing next to it gives you an idea of just how big moose really are. If you see moose from a car while they are standing in the water, they don't seem quite so big.

Next on Poplar Lake is Windigo Lodge. It was started by Genevieve and Harry Brown when they moved their entire operation down from Seagull Lake. In 1956 the Izaak Walton League bought the Seagull Lake peninsula that Windigo Point was located on. The Browns cut the main cabin in half, skidded the two pieces across the ice, and rebuilt it on Poplar Lake. The other three log cabins were dismantled, log by log, and put back together on Poplar Lake. To this day, those cabins still stand at Windigo Lodge.

Windigo's moose statue

Genevieve and Harry Brown operated Windigo Lodge until 1960. They sold the lodge to Ann and Helmer Larsen from Chicago. The Larsens maintained the small, seasonal resort until the fall of 1968 when it was sold to Jean and Harold (Ike) Ikola. Harold was a teacher in Grand Marais, so having a small summer resort was just what they wanted. They were preparing for their first endeavor of operating Windigo in the spring of 1969, for the Memorial weekend, when Harold had an untimely death on May 29.

Jean Ikola and her children, JoAnn and Dan, ran the resort for two summers as a small, family-style place with three completely furnished log cabins. The guests looked forward to late afternoons when the garbage cans were piled in the back of the truck, headed for the dump. The rattling of the garbage cans was like a dinner bell as the bears often climbed right on the truck for their evening feast.

Jean Ikola (now Williamson) tells of a few of her memories of running a resort.

"The one member of our family at Windigo who sometimes gets forgotten is Cricket, our dog. She always seemed to have interesting experiences. Cricket had a personality all of her own and had me well trained. Each morning she went into the kitchen and with her shrill bark demanded some food. I made her toast, buttered it and cut it into bite-sized pieces. This ritual went on for years. As a result she looked more like a pig than a black Labrador.

"Cricket spent hours running up and down the shore barking at her splashes. After tiring of that she would run up to the lodge, barking her persistent shrill bark, until I dropped everything I was doing to let her in so she could drink from her water bowl that had turned warm and possibly ridden with a fly or two.

"One day she went to Cabin 1 to inspect the fishing poles that were on their porch. Unfortunately, she caught her mouth on a hook and came squealing back to the lodge dragging the rod and reel behind her. The three-barbed hook was deeply fastened in her mouth with no way of removing it. I finally called Jocko's Clearwater Lodge asking for help and to my surprise they sent over a doctor who was one of their guests. Cricket patiently accepted his help but to no avail. He suggested waiting a few days to see if the hook would work its way out. Nothing was happening so plans were made for Cricket to be flown to Duluth to have it surgically removed. JoAnn and Dan looked at Cricket's great adventure with envy, as they had never been in an airplane. The morning of her trip came. While I was preparing breakfast, I looked down at Cricket and couldn't see the hook sticking out of her mouth. I yelled to the kids, and lo and behold, it was lying beside her bowl.

"During the second summer of running Windigo Lodge with the help of my two children JoAnn and Dan, I also worked at the Grand Marais State Bank. I commuted the 34 miles to and from work each day and, of course, had laundry and other chores to attend to when I got back. The lodge was for sale and I showed it to prospective buyers from time to time. My attorney strongly felt that the lodge should be in operation to make a sale more feasible.

"One Sunday afternoon Willie Williamson and Jerry Alms arrived on the scene. Of course, I thought I had a sale pending so I showed them the cabins and gave them the sales pitch. They seemed to hang around so I invited them in for coffee and conversation. The next Sunday, Willie arrived alone. I had a horrible cold but had work to do, so I was in the kitchen mangling sheets. Dan became suspicious and took JoAnn aside and said 'is Willie hustling MOM?' JoAnn just shrugged her shoulders. I dropped what I was doing and invited Willie into the living room for coffee and cookies.

"That was the beginning of our courtship. In the fall we went partridge hunting, snowmobiling in the winter, and canoeing or brook trout fishing in the summer. I don't think we would have ever gotten married if it weren't for Betty Backlund. We were all at the Harbor Light celebrating a 25th wedding anniversary when out of the blue and very unlike Betty, she asked 'When are you two getting married?' Willie was a man of few words, so he looked at me and said, 'How about in two weeks?'"

Did you know . . .

The original buildings at Windigo Lodge came from Windigo Point, a resort on Seagull Lake. Harry and Genevieve Brown sold the Seagull property to the Izaak Walton League. They and their family spent the summer of 1957 dismantling and moving buildings.

VENISON PARMESAN

Venison has long been a staple in the diets of Gunflint Trail residents, so they have developed lots of great recipes like this one.

1 lb. venison steak, ¼" thick
salt and pepper
1 egg
2 tsp. water
⅓ cup Parmesan cheese
⅓ cup fine dry bread crumbs
¼ cup olive oil
1 onion, finely chopped
2 T butter or margarine
1 6-oz. can tomato paste
2 cups hot water
1 tsp. salt
½ tsp. dried marjoram leaves
¼ lb. mozzarella or Swiss cheese, sliced

Cut steak into 6 to 8 pieces. Sprinkle with salt and pepper. Beat egg with 2 tsp. water. Combine Parmesan cheese and bread crumbs, mixing well. Dip meat in egg and roll in crumb mixture. Heat oil in large skillet and fry three pieces at a time until golden brown on each side. Save drippings in skillet. Lay venison in 13x9" baking dish. Saute onion in butter and reserved drippings until soft. Add tomato paste, hot water, salt and marjoram. Boil a few minutes, stirring well. Pour three quarters of the sauce over the steaks. Top with thin slices of cheese and pour remaining sauce over cheese. Bake at 350° for 30 minutes. Even it you aren't a venison lover, you're sure to like this!

Ground Beef Snack Quiches

With this recipe Jean said, "Here is a bit of puttery but the result will be rave reviews!"

½ lb. ground beef
¼–½ tsp. garlic powder
¼ tsp. pepper
2 cups biscuit baking mix
½ cup corn meal
½ cup cold butter or margarine
4–6 T boiling water
2 eggs

1 cup half and half cream
1 T chopped green onion
2 T chopped green pepper
2 T chopped red pepper
¼–½ tsp. salt
¼–½ tsp. cayenne pepper
1 cup finely shredded cheddar cheese

In a saucepan over medium heat, cook beef, garlic powder and pepper until meat is no longer pink; drain and set aside.

In a bowl, combine the biscuit mix and corn meal; cut in the butter. Add enough water to form a soft dough. Press into the bottom and up the sides of greased miniature muffin cups. Place teaspoonfuls of beef mixture into each shell. In a bowl, combine the egg, cream, onion, green pepper, red pepper, salt and cayenne. Pour over the beef mixture. Sprinkle with cheese. Bake at 375° for 20 minutes or until a knife inserted near the center comes out clean.

Chocolate Bavarian Pie

"The next recipe is an old family favorite," said Jean.

1¼ cups chocolate wafers
   (about 20–25 wafers)
⅓ cup melted butter
3 slightly beaten egg yolks
½ cup sugar
¼ tsp. salt

1 cup scalded milk
1 pkg. plain gelatin
¼ cup water
1 tsp. vanilla
1 cup cream, whipped
3 egg whites, whipped

Crush wafers, add butter, and line a 10" pie plate with all but a few crumbs. Set aside the reserved crumbs.

Combine the yolks, sugar and salt. Add the scalded milk. Cook like custard. Add the gelatin that has been dissolved in the water. Add vanilla and cool. Fold in beaten egg whites and whipped cream. Spoon into chocolate pie shell. Sprinkle with reserved crumbs.

Big Bear Lodge

In 1937 the original lodge burned at Old Northwoods Lodge (as it was then known). It was rebuilt, but in 1965 there was another fire. A youth group that was using white gas to fill their lanterns near the gas hot water heater spilled some and it contacted the heater's pilot light. The lodge burned to the ground except for the fireplace, which remains standing to this day. The resort stood empty and inactive until 1995 when Gale Quistad purchased the property.

Dr. Remple came to this area as a Russian immigrant and was the doctor at the Gunflint CCC camp. As so many others did, he purchased land here and started this resort around 1934 with a few trappers' shacks, eventually adding cabins and a lodge. The original lodge burned in 1937. Fire leveled the second lodge in 1965, and the stone fireplace stands as the lone survivor. At the approach to the lodge, this remnant of another era is visible.

The second owners were Ann and Ed Ruidl. They began to run the lodge in 1949. Ed worked for the Duluth, Mesabi, and Iron Range Railroad out of Proctor, Minnesota. They raised three daughters here and ran a tea room. Perhaps their most famous guest was Charles Schultz of Snoopy fame. They still have his letter thanking them for a wonderful vacation. At one time the resort had 22 cabins.

"Mom would bake bread every Thursday morning, then we girls would deliver a warm loaf to each cabin. The smell of that bread around the lodge was out of this world."

One of their three daughters, Mary, relates that their mother ran the lodge with the help of Ed's Uncle Carl, a couple of hired workers and the three girls. "Dad would come up to the lodge every other weekend. We were always happy to see him. He would bring fresh fruit and treats for all of us. Mom would bake bread every Thursday morning, then we girls would deliver a warm loaf to each cabin. The smell of that bread around the lodge was out of this world."

Mary, Kathy and Pat used to entertain the guests with their singing. Their most requested song was "I Didn't Know the Gun Was Loaded." Mary continues, "Pat is the youngest and she would belt out the chorus with her strong little voice. Everyone would be so surprised. Kathy was 10 years old, I was 7 and Pat was 5." The girls would go back home to school in the fall staying with their dad and grandmother. Their mother stayed until the last of the guests left. Then Ann would close up the resort and do all the things necessary to secure the resort for winter.

After the fire of the second lodge in 1965, the resort was not an active business for 30 years. Trail residents wondered if there would ever be a resort here again. Today, pulling up to the lodge and seeing the massive native white cedar log lodge is an impressive and welcome sight. The logs arrived in the winter of 1995, and Yelena Quistad arrived about six months later.

She came from Moscow, having met her husband, Gale Quistad, while he was vacationing in Russia. Since she was ten years old, Yelena had been studying impressionist painting, refining her skills and talents as an artist and winning awards in competitions in her homeland. She was a member of the Russian Trade Union of Artists, a prestigious group of fine artists.

Moscow and the Gunflint Trail had little in common, but Yelena was immediately drawn to the natural beauty of her new home. The setting to which she had moved was a beautiful spot, look-

Ed and Ann Ruidl with guests

ing west to Poplar Lake. Old Northwoods was one of the five original resorts on the Gunflint Trail (since the early 1930s), and it was ready for the new owners and their vision to bring it back to its former grandeur. Her talents would be called upon time and again as she and Gale brought the dream of a new log lodge to reality.

Gale rounded and shaped the timbers by hand and set them into position using a French-Canadian technique known as piece on piece log building, similar to the construction used in Fort William to the north. As Gale and his crew gave form to the lodge, Yelena infused it with character (and a lot of hard work right alongside the crew). Her artistic input is evident everywhere, from hand-painted wall treatments and dramatic fixtures to colors, fabrics and a gallery with her original paintings.

Her first winter in Minnesota was one of the coldest in years. Moscow had winter, but she was unprepared for the bitter cold she was to encounter in Minnesota.

"The temperature outside was -58°. In Moscow, -35° was extreme. We moved firewood into the cabin all day long, and we had to keep a fire burning in the fireplace plus use the gas heater just to keep from freezing." (This was during a time before the cabins were renovated, and the insulation was less than adequate.)

"Nobody in Moscow had a fireplace, so I had to learn how to use it—what kind of wood is best, how to get the fire started, how to let the smoke out."

And then in the summer, there was the challenge of growing things in the garden. "You can't depend on it," Yelena says. Since the weather didn't cooperate (it was either too cool, or windy, or rainy, or not), she thought it would be a good idea to put up a little greenhouse—but the weather had plans for her greenhouse, too. "The greenhouse was a metal frame covered with plastic. It was a windy day and

The second Old Northwoods Lodge building

I kept trying to tie it together and make it strong. Then, the wind just took it away. It flew away and it was gone. Maybe next year I will try again."

When Yelena speaks, it is often with excitement and at times, a unique turn of a phrase—a delightful aspect of having English as one's second language. Interesting word choices and expressions give color to her stories, like this one about the wildlife:

"Bears are close around you here, and so are deer and moose. One day there was bear on the porch eating birdseed. I was very surprised to see bear and he was surprised to see me. We ran in opposite directions. He was really close. It makes you feel very exciting for at least two weeks."

In 2011, Andy and Ida DeLisi bought Old Northwoods Lodge and changed the name to Big Bear Lodge.

Did you know . . .

The log construction of the main lodge at Big Bear is uncommon in this area. Gale placed a vertical log every eight feet. Between these logs he layered horizontal logs to fill in. The vertical and horizontal logs make a beautiful pattern for the eye to follow.

YELENA'S RUSSIAN POTATO SALAD

This potato salad has dozens of variations, and it is a very popular dish in Russia. A small scoop is sometimes served as a starter to a special dinner, or a larger portion could be served as a salad or a side dish.

Yelena says to use "whatever potatoes you can get. Up here, you don't always have a choice, but smaller potatoes are better. Red, medium-sized potatoes are perfect." Use a uniform dice for the potatoes and carrots; Yelena usually cuts the vegetables into cubes that are between ¼ and ⅓".

It's best to prepare this recipe a day before you will be serving it; it's important to let the flavors blend overnight.

8 med. red potatoes, skin on
2 carrots, diced
6 scallions (green onions), chopped
8 dill pickles, chopped
1 16-oz. can small early peas, drained

salt and pepper
fresh or dried parsley to taste (optional)
fresh or dried dill to taste (optional)
mayonnaise (homemade is preferable)
ranch dressing

Boil the potatoes until tender but not soft. Drain, cool and then remove the skins. Cut into uniform dice. Add carrots, scallions, pickles and peas. Mix gently and thoroughly and add salt and pepper to taste. At this point you can add the parsley and dill (or other herbs if you like).

Mix equal parts of the mayonnaise and ranch dressing. Mix dressing into the vegetables and herbs until the salad is evenly coated. Correct seasonings. Cover and refrigerate overnight. Serve cool. Keeps for up to 72 hours, refrigerated.

POOR MAN'S CAKE

Mary shared this recipe that her mother, Ann, made for everyone's birthday.

2 cup sugar
¾ cup raisins
¾ cup shortening or margarine
2 cups water
1 tsp. cinnamon

½ tsp. cloves
3 cups flour
1 tsp. salt
2 tsp. baking soda
½ cup chopped walnuts

Bring the first six ingredients to a boil and let cool. After the mixture has cooled, add flour, salt, soda and walnuts. Pour the mixture into a well-greased and floured 9x13" pan. Bake at 350° for 40–45 minutes.

Rockwood Lodge

Paul and Jenny Stoltz along with Jenny's brother Wally started Rockwood Lodge. Running the business was a family affair and you were never too young to help. Paul and Jenny's son, George, was born in 1933. He has memories of helping out, "My job when I started growing up was to keep the wood box full."

This next side road is actually part of the original Gunflint Trail and it takes us to the last resort on Poplar Lake. Rockwood Lodge was started by Jennie and Paul Stoltz and Waldemar (Wally) Anderson. In July of 1926 the three of them bought the land on Poplar Lake. Jennie and Paul's son, George, believes that the name "Rockwood" came from the difference in terrain from sandy Wisconsin to rocky Cook County.

Interior of Rockwood Lodge

Over the next six years the men built eight log cabins. In 1932 they started building the log lodge. All of the work was done by hand. The cabins used vertical log construction. The large logs in the main lodge came from a stand of red pine on the south shore of Poplar Lake. After felling the trees, the men would use a horse to drag the logs across the ice in the winter. Then the logs were stripped of bark and sat for a year to dry before being used in the lodge. In the 1930s Wally Anderson sold his share of the resort to Paul and Jennie.

George remembers that his mother was also very busy. "My mother did all the bookkeeping, took care of reservations and paid the bills. In addition to this she did a lot of canning of fruit, venison and vegetables to be put in the root cellar for the winter. One year we had over 100 Mason jars of raspberry sauce."

Originally Jennie was to have a cook but as George says, "Same as it is today, you have a hard time finding a cook. And you would find cooks you hired in May who would somehow in July end up going on a drunk or whatever, and my mother ended up doing the cooking. All the cooking was done on the wood stove, except sometimes she would use a 3-plate gas burner. If it was really warm, Cook County warm, 90° or something on three, four days a year, she wouldn't use the wood stove. Normally every day she would bake bread. The kitchen was very warm sometimes. My job when I started growing up was to keep the wood box full. I can still remember that. The lodge was a little ways from the woodshed and every day I had to get my wagon out and take the trip and fill the wood box."

Even after 60 years, Helen Shelley, a former guest at Rockwood, remembers Jennie as "a work-horse. She saw to the feeding and keeping the guests comfortable. She was a very good cook. The meals were delicious and substantial, perfect before and after a long day fishing."

George also remembers how his mother catered to their guests. "If someone especially liked certain food, such as apple pie or pineapple upside-down cake, Jennie would have it on hand for them. I think the personal touches that she added kept them coming back year after year.

"If someone especially liked certain food, such as apple pie or pineapple upside-down cake, Jennie would have it on hand for them. I think the personal touches that she added kept them coming back year after year."

"Paul and Jennie sold Rockwood to Ann and Dave Clark in 1946 for a little over $20,000. I think that they sold Rockwood after 20 years because they felt it was time for a change. My mother's health was not so good and my dad was ready to move on."

Ann and Dave Clark lived on the Trail for some years before purchasing Rockwood. Ann was a young, college-educated girl from Chicago. Her father and a group of men bought a cabin on West Bearskin Lake. Around 1930 she started coming up the Trail for a few weeks each summer. In 1934 her father built his own cabin on West Bearskin. By that time, Ann had met Dave Clark, a local guide. Dave had originally come up the Trail to work at the Weyerhauser logging camp on Rose Lake. He built a cabin on Arrow Lake out of rejected lumber from Weyerhauser. These two people from very different backgrounds met and fell in love. They were married in 1936.

Ann was a person who built her life around goals. Her goal after marriage was for them to own a resort, but in 1938 buying a resort must have seemed to be a very distant goal. They were living on West Bearskin. Dave guided at Swanson's Lodge for $5 a day, and Ann cleaned cabins for tips. She said it was the hardest work she ever did.

"We lived on the land—fish, venison, grouse and blueberries." Ann tells the story of a blueberry picking expedition during the summer of 1938.

"Marcia was 1½; my parents were living in the cabin next to ours on West Bearskin Lake. McNally, who worked for Weyerhauser Timber, had a motorized speeder for use on the railroad track that ran all through the woods for logging. He said that he would take us to Two Island Lake about 20 miles away and leave us there for three days to pick blueberries. Dave was good at packing for such a trip: macaroni, grease to fry fish, tea, a blanket to sleep on balsam boughs (under our canoe if it rained), a bushel basket, two water pails for the berries and a couple of small picking pails. Also a length of rope, a hatchet, matches, a frying pan and a kettle were included. The night before we left there was a bad wind storm and while going around a bend on the railroad track, we rammed into a big tree on the track. Our canoe took most of the punishment, but we still went fishing in it that night. Dave held the prow together with the rope. McNally left us in an endless sea of ripe blueberries and said he'd be back Saturday. I was uneasy on the lake. It was foggy. I was afraid we'd either get lost or sink, but we got fish for our supper. We went to bed and listened to the wolves howling all night. The next day when we started picking, I suggested to Dave that I sit under a tree with the bushel basket and that he take a pail and use his hunting knife to cut off branches of ripe berries and bring them to me. I could pick them very carefully so they didn't have to be looked over too much. When Saturday came, McNally was a few hours late picking us up. I was sure he had forgotten us and we'd have to walk. When we got home I had all those berries to can—the hard way—in a hot water bath in jars in a wash tub on our wood range. We had blueberries for a long time."

Dining room at Rockwood Lodge

Ann and Dave Clark bought Rockwood in 1946, finally reaching their dream of owning a resort. Ann remembers their beginnings at Rockwood. "We moved into Rockwood in September. Jennie Stoltz let me help her in the kitchen, the dining room, the laundry and the cabins. I could never have managed Rockwood without that month of apprenticeship. We took over in October and I had a month of operating it alone. When deer season came I had two women to help take care of the 45 hunters whom we had to feed, clean cabins, make beds for and entertain until midnight. Dave helped when he was there but he was very busy guiding. The next summer Dave's sister Rita came to work for us as cook. The six years at Rockwood were hard, many 18-hour days, many stressful days. But there was also lots of fun, dancing to the juke box and listening to fish stories."

Darwin and Loretta Noyes bought Rockwood Lodge from Dave and Ann Clark in 1950. Like many resorts owners, they were open for three seasons and wintered in warmer climates. The Noyes family lived in Phoenix during the winter. Their two daughters, Sandi and Janet, attended school in Grand Marais spring and fall.

The Noyes had seven rental cabins, a store and a dining room. The kitchen was always busy with guests, friends and family. Two of the guides, Clyde Boostrom and Carl Bornhoff, would occasionally boil up some beaver meat from their trap lines.

Some of the ducks that Don Lobdell helped bring to the Gunflint Trail

There was a root cellar dug into the hill across from the lodge that remained at the same temperature winter and summer, and was a cool place to hide on hot summer days!

The Noyes sold Rockwood Lodge in 1956 to Don Lobdell and Rick Whitney. The "Rockwood Boys" had some big ideas. They filled the lodge with antiques, focused on dining, acquired a liquor license and had a sauna cabin for a spa atmosphere. One specialty was a cup of borscht before dinner.

Today most of us take for granted the flocks of mallards that eagerly appear for corn handouts at docks along the Gunflint Trail. Justine Kerfoot in *Woman of the Boundary Waters* reminds us that these mallards weren't always here. "Years ago most ducks on the lakes were mergansers, known as fish ducks. Don Lobdell, who operated Rockwood Lodge on Poplar Lake, had connections with the McGraw Game Farm in Dundee, Illinois, and undertook transporting mallards to the Gunflint Trail. The Minnesota Game and Fish Dept. arranged to ship mallard ducklings to Don. Some of us along the Trail agreed to raise and release the ducklings, and we built houses with fenced enclosures. Don met them with his car. He transported them to Rockwood Lodge, which became the distribution center. We took 75 of these little balls of fluff and coddled, fed and pampered them. When they were a few weeks old, they were banded by Charlie Ott, one of the game wardens. It was a program repeated for three years. The banded ducks, who survived the firing line on their southward flight, returned each year to raise a new brood in the area." So next time you feed the mallards, say a few words of thanks to Don Lobdell.

In 1979 Dana and Tim Austin bought Rockwood Lodge from Rick and Don. It was the beginning of an entirely new life for the Tim and Dana, a life that would be full of surprises and unexpected encounters. Dana has vivid memories of resort life.

"Running a restaurant in a remote and wild area can be a challenge. When we purchased Rockwood Lodge on the Gunflint Trail in 1979, we had no idea what we were getting into. Rockwood is one of the few remaining original log lodges left in northern Minnesota. The road that runs in front of the lodge was part of the original Gunflint Trail. The lodge had an American plan and served food to the guests, but we decided to make the dining room into a restaurant that was open to the public. Some of the incidents that occurred after that were sometimes hilarious and also challenging.

"Most of the things I remember involved animals—not the people in the dining room—but the four-footed kind. Of course, there were often the bears that seemed to come around to entertain the guests. It was not entertaining when one would stand at the door and make it difficult for the guests to leave or would walk around the roof making a lot of noise.

"The banded ducks, who survived the firing line on their southward flight, returned each year to raise a new brood in the area."

"There was the time we had a full dining room and everyone was having a good time when, out of nowhere, a flying squirrel appeared on one of the tables. Everyone got a laugh out of it but getting it back outside was a little difficult.

"There was also the time I tried to lure a duck into the kitchen with a doughnut and ended up with more than a dozen ducks in the kitchen, none of which would leave, and they panicked and flew around the lodge instead of out the door.

"Skunks are never pleasant to have around a restaurant and we discovered that chasing them off only makes them spray and smell up the dining room.

"We had a couple that had been coming up the Gunflint Trail for years looking for moose and had yet to see one. They were sitting at a table for two (that we called the honeymoon table) in the dining room and asked our son Rick where a good place to see moose might be. Just as he was about to give them some suggestions, he looked out the window and suggested that they look out the window where a big bull moose was swimming right in front of the lodge. What a coincidence!

"Another critter that is cute to watch but can make an awful mess is the pine marten. We have had problems with several of them. One chewed through the hardwood floor in the Lodge in the middle of winter and we saw it sitting on a curtain rod when we walked by. Getting it back out was tricky. Then there was the family of pine marten that got in the laundry room one winter and tore up blankets and mattress pads to make nests for their babies. We tried to lure them out with food and left the door open but nothing worked. Finally we borrowed live traps from the DNR. The food would be gone every day but no martens.

"As a last resort Tim set a trap but by then the martens had disappeared. He tried to close the trap and caught both hands in it. Being in severe pain and unable to open it with both hands trapped, he was rather upset. I just happened to walk down to see how things were going and found him trying to pry it off. After laughing for some time we finally got him free and threw the trap away.

"The resort business was rewarding in so many ways. The people that you meet and feed and try to make vacations special for are the people that made running a resort and restaurant special for us.

"We had one family that had an autistic son who had never spoken a word. He played with our dog Neka and seemed to have a really good time. After their first summer vacation at the Lodge, they went home and their son started saying Neka all the time. They came back summer after summer and each time he spoke more words. One of his favorites was 'pie.'

"We also had a couple that took a three-week canoe trip. During their time in the woods it rained for days, then got extremely cold, snowed and was generally miserable. We worried about them and were sure that they would be back early and that they were having a terrible time. At the end of their three-week trip they came back and raved about what a wonderful time they had. In fact, when they packed up to leave, they cried because they didn't want to go."

Lin and Mike Sherfy

In 2003 the Austins sold Rockwood to Mike and Lin Sherfy. Lin recalls how they came up here. "We arrived on the Gunflint Trail by serendipity. We had listed our resort in north-central Minnesota for sale and were preparing for the 2003 season when our agent called with an offer too good to pass up. We looked at resorts all over Minnesota without finding one we liked. One day an agent asked us to meet him in Grand Marais as he had a new listing that he thought reminded him slightly of our old home. We drove up the Trail to Rockwood, fell in love with the place and the area, and that was that. Our roots are in rural Iowa. After years in the office rat race, we were ready for a change—and a return to the outdoors we love. The Gunflint Trail has become home—we love the area, the people, operating a lodge and outfitting."

Like all resorters, Lin has a good story about people adjusting to having real animals in the woods. She says, "Last summer we had a permanent guest. He lived under the old boathouse behind the outfitting building and managed to cause quite a bit of excitement every so often. One morning in July two of our guests came into the lodge right after breakfast. "There was a bear around our cabin last night!" exclaimed the man from Cabin 3. "We heard him dive into the lake and splashing in the water. He took the stringer of fish we had tied on the dock!"

"That must have been our otter," I replied.

"No, it was huge! It must have been a bear!"

"Our otter is around 50 inches long and loves swimming and free fish," I answered. "He's stolen fish stringers before."

"Well, that explains my mystery," said the man from Cabin 2. "When I went out this morning our dock smelled like fish and was covered in fish scales!"

The next evening, Cabin 2 tied a second stringer of bass to his dock and kept watch with a flashlight. Sure enough, our otter turned up right on schedule, helped himself to fish, and then put on an acrobatic swimming show in gratitude.

Did you know . . .

One of the big social events on the Trail used to be Saturday night dances at the various resorts. Whole families would go. The kids eventually would be put to sleep in a back room while their parents danced the night away. A juke box or local band provided the music. This type of entertainment has been lost on the Gunflint Trail today.

Under Rick Whitney and Don Lobdell, Rockwood Lodge was the first resort on the Trail to get a full liquor license. The new bar was very nicely done but it kept local tongues wagging for a summer.

When Rick and Don ran Rockwood Lodge, they divided their responsibilities. Don worked the front of the house. Rick cooked and ran the kitchen.

ROCKWOOD'S FAMOUS WALLEYE

Everyone on the Trail served fried walleye but the inclusion of potato meal in the breading adds a little something extra to the flavor.

1 cup flour
1 cup white corn meal
1 cup potato meal
walleye fillets
oil for frying

Combine flour, corn meal and potato meal.

Wash walleye fillets and do not dry. Dredge in flour mixture and fry in hot oil until golden brown on both sides.

RITA'S MINCEMEAT "POCKET BOOKS"

Dave Clark's sister, Rita, used this recipe while she cooked at Rockwood Lodge.

1 cup margarine	1 tsp. salt
1 cup brown sugar	2 tsp. soda
1 cup white sugar	1 tsp. cinnamon
3 large eggs	1 tsp. nutmeg
3½ cups flour	1 package concentrated mincemeat filling

Cream margarine and sugars together. Add eggs. Sift dry ingredients and add to mix. Form into rolls, about 2" in diameter. Wrap with plastic wrap and refrigerate overnight.

Prepare mincemeat filling according to package directions.

Slice the refrigerated rolls into ¼" slices and place on ungreased cookie sheet. Put ½–¾ tsp. of mincemeat filling in the center of each and top with another slice. Use the side of your thumb and fingers to press one side together and a fork to press the remaining edges together. This forms the shape of a pocket book, round on the bottom and flat across the top. Bake at 350° for 10–15 minutes.

FISH CHOWDER

With all the fresh fish available on the Gunflint Trail, it was just natural that local cooks developed chowder recipes.w

3 lb. pickerel (northern)
7 potatoes, cubed small
4 onions cubed small
½ lb. salt pork, diced very small

salt and pepper
1 quart rich milk (or part evaporated if desired)
1–2 T Worcestershire sauce

Cook skinned and boned fish in boiling water. Save the juice. Pick fish meat from bones and set aside. Salt and boil potatoes and onions together. Add fish juice and simmer. Fry pork and remove grease. Add salt and pepper to taste. Add to potato and onion mixture. Add milk. Add fish meat and heat thoroughly. Add Worcestershire before serving.

POTLUCK CHICKEN CASSEROLE

This is one of several recipes that have come down to us from Loretta Noyes.

½ cup chopped fresh mushrooms
3 T chopped onion
2 cloves minced garlic
4 T butter, divided
3 T flour
1¼ cup milk
¾ cup mayonnaise
4 cups cooked chicken, cubed

3 cups cooked rice
1 cup chopped celery
1 cup frozen peas, thawed
1 12-oz. jar diced pimientos, drained
2 tsp. lemon juice
1 tsp. salt
½ tsp. pepper
¾ cup coarsely crushed corn flakes

In a saucepan over medium heat, saute mushrooms, onion and garlic in 3 T butter until tender. Stir in flour until thoroughly combined. Gradually add milk; bring to a boil. Cook and stir for 2 minutes or until thick and bubbly. Remove from heat; stir in mayonnaise until smooth. Add chicken, rice, celery, peas, pimientos, lemon juice, salt and pepper. Mix well. Spoon mixture into an ungreased 9x13" baking pan. Melt remaining 1 T butter; toss with corn flakes. Sprinkle over casserole. Bake, uncovered, at 350° for 30–35 minutes or until bubbly.

Presbyterian Meatballs

This recipe is so popular in Lin's hometown that the grocery store sells packages of the meat mixture ready mixed! "I've been purchasing ground ham, sausage and beef and mixing it myself since we moved north." (One of the variants of this recipe is called "The World's Best Meatballs.")

1 pound ground ham
1 pound pork sausage (unseasoned)
½ pound ground beef
2 eggs
1 cup milk
2 cups ground graham cracker crumbs

SAUCE:
½ cup ketchup
½ tsp. ground mustard
1 cup brown sugar
¼ cup plus 2 T vinegar

Mix the meats together thoroughly and add eggs, milk and crumbs. Work the mixture into balls or small individual loaves and place in greased pan. Bake one hour at 300°. Mix sauce ingredients and pour over balls and bake uncovered an additional hour at 250°.

Baked Beans

Dana's recipe shows that with a little effort baked beans can be much more than just opening a can and heating it.

½ lb. hamburger
½ lb. bacon
1 onion, chopped
½ cup celery
½ cup chopped green pepper
1 tsp. salt
½ cup ketchup
¾ cup brown sugar

1 tsp. dry mustard
2 tsp. white vinegar
½ cup white sugar
1 can pork and beans
1 can kidney beans
1 can lima beans
1 can butter beans

In a heavy stock pot brown hamburger, bacon and chopped onion. Drain grease and add celery and green pepper. Cook and stir until semi-tender. Add salt, ketchup, brown sugar, dry mustard, white vinegar and white sugar. Drain cans of pork and beans, kidney beans, lima beans and butter beans. Add to mixture and bake at 350° for 1 hour and 30 minutes.

GRAN'S FARMHOUSE DINNER ROLLS

Lin says: "These were a special favorite at Sunday dinner on the farm when I was growing up. The cinnamon and pecan versions were an extra special treat!"

2 packages dry yeast	3 tsp. salt
1 cup lukewarm water	9–10 cups flour, divided
¾ cup sugar, divided	2 eggs, beaten
1 pint milk	⅔ cup melted shortening (warm, not hot)

Pour yeast and water into bowl. Add 1 teaspoon sugar, stir. Let stand about 5 minutes. Scald milk (heat just to boiling) and add salt and remaining sugar. Stir. Let mixture cool. Add about half of the flour to the cooled mixture and beat smooth. Add the beaten eggs and shortening. Work in enough additional flour to make a smooth dough as soft as you can handle—not as stiff as bread dough.

Place dough in a large greased bowl and cover tightly. Let dough set in a warm place until doubled. Knead the dough down and let rise again. Shape into individual dinner rolls. Let them rise until doubled in size.

Bake on a greased pan in a 400° oven for 15 minutes.

For cinnamon or pecan rolls, use the same recipe with a bit more sugar.

Cinnamon rolls: Roll out dough. Spread cinnamon, sugar and butter on top and roll up. Put in pans to rise until double. Bake at 400° about 15 minutes.

Pecan rolls: For pecan rolls use the same method, only put brown sugar and butter on the bottom of the greased pan and place rolls on top. Bake the same.

BLUEBERRY-RHUBARB JAM

Of course, Dana has several recipes from the restaurant to share. This is a unique jam combination.

4 cups sugar
7 cups fine cut rhubarb
1 6-oz. box raspberry jello
1 can blueberry pie filling

Mix sugar and rhubarb and let sit for 10 minutes, stirring occasionally. Boil for 8 minutes, stirring often. Add raspberry jello and stir well. Add blueberry pie filling and stir well. Put in jam jars and freeze.

Ann Clark's Blueberry Dumplings

Marty Clark, Ann and Dave's son, shared this recipe from his mother.

SAUCE:
2 cups blueberries
½ cup water
½ cup sugar
⅛ tsp. salt

DUMPLINGS:
½ T butter or margarine
¼ cup sugar
¾ cup flour
¾ tsp. baking powder
¼ cup milk
pinch of salt

Combine blueberries, water, ½ cup sugar and ⅛ tsp. salt and cook until berries are tender.

Cream butter and ¼ cup sugar. Stir in dry ingredients, alternately with milk, to make a dough. Drop by teaspoon full in boiling blueberry mix. Cover tightly and cook over medium heat for 10 minutes. Don't peek! Cool slightly before serving.

Kringla

Our first Christmas in Minnesota I offered to make the Kringla for our WELCA (Women of the Evangelical Lutheran Church) Christmas gift trays. I was startled to discover that my new Minnesota Norwegian friends had never heard of Kringla. I must have over a dozen recipes gathered from my grandmother's Norwegian friends and neighbors, but this one seems to be the best.

2 beaten eggs
1 cup sugar
1 cup sour cream
1 tsp. vanilla
1 stick melted margarine

3 cups flour
1 tsp. soda
1 tsp. baking powder
½ tsp. salt

Beat eggs. Add sugar, sour cream, vanilla and melted margarine. Sift together dry ingredients and stir into the wet ingredients. Chill overnight. Roll out on lightly floured board. Make a pencil size roll about 12" long and shape into a figure eight. Bake on a dry cookie sheet for 10 minutes at 350°. Makes about 50. Serve warm with butter. Can be frozen for later use.

Loon Lake Lodge

Clara and Jack Dewar started Loon Lake Lodge about 1927 or 1928. They built the road and started with what is now Cabin #7 and worked their way down, building cabins as they went. The lodge was the last to be finished. When the building was complete, Jack took off and Clara ran the resort for seven years. Clara continued to live on Loon Lake after she sold the place.

Willard Johnson recalls when Clara built her last cabin on the lake where the road now makes a very sharp turn to the right. "She decided to build this little log cabin beside the road. She'd go across the bay and pick up the dead spruce. They'd be in good shape, but dead, and haul them up the hill. And I said 'Why don't you haul them to the dock and we'll truck them up for you?' 'Oh, no, I love to work hard.' Work is what she existed for. She was telling me about some of the girls working for her. She had to fire them right away because they couldn't keep up with her. Who could?" Clara was probably in her seventies when she built that cabin.

Luana Brandt from Nor'Wester also has memories of Clara. "When I first met her she was a feisty little lady sitting on the floor braiding wool rugs and talking a mile a minute. She was one of the 'must-sees' Carl took me to meet when I first came to the Trail. As a young woman, she and her husband Jack had bushwhacked a switchback road into Loon Lake and built a log lodge with numerous cabins, thus starting Loon Lake Lodge. An experienced woodswoman, she had taken the time to show a young Carl Brandt how to trap mink. His first mink, at age five, was thanks to her careful teaching. Now in retirement she

Loon Lake Lodge

sat on the hard floor cheerfully talking about hunting and trapping and her raspberry patch as her hands flew through the braids. On the stove simmered her usual pot of soup, which never contained the same mix of ingredients twice. 'I just take whatever comes to hand and put it into the pot.' Her coffee pot was always on and ready for a quick cup of what had to be the strongest java on the trail. No matter the tragedies life had thrown at her, she continued to see the glass half full, and filling rapidly. In the short time I had to know her, her unfailing cheerful demeanor never wavered. Today her rugs continue to warm my floors, and memories of her warm my heart."

In 1935 Clara sold the resort to Marie and George Stapleton. George had been a salesman of office furniture. All the neighbors were shocked when he paid cash for the business. Stapletons added a cabin in 1941 and made improvements like running water. After they sold, George Stapleton went on to be the Postmaster for the Gunflint Trail from his new home on Pope Lake. He got paid by the piece so to increase his income, he would run ads in magazines selling things like Princess Pine decorations and Christmas wreaths. He would get paid not only for the decorations but his income from the mail would increase with the incoming and outgoing mail. This arrangement lasted for a couple of years.

In 1948 Willard Johnson, Kermit Johnson and his wife, Ethel, and Cliff Hammerberg bought the resort. Kermit and his wife were divorced about 5 years after they bought the resort. Cliff stayed about 8 years and then left to take care of his mother in Duluth. So by the middle of the 1950s it was just the brothers—Willard and Kermit—running the resort.

Willard Johnson with guests and their catch

Willard remembers how he came up here, "I used to come up here fishing. And I used to go down to Greenwood and Frank Fuller's place at Tuscarora. I stayed there and then I stayed at Clearwater and then I was down at Bearskin. I just decided that I would like to live up here."

In the beginning Ethel Johnson was the cook. After she and Kermit parted ways, the brothers hired a variety of cooks over the years. Willard said, "I guess I started cooking when I had to. There was nobody around. I don't want to remember the first year I cooked because who wants to remember that, not when I was forced to. And I was still supposed to guide. I had one hard time. If it was just a couple people here, I'd guide and take them with me. We served 25 or better sometimes but on the average it was 10 and 15."

The next owners of Loon Lake Lodge were Tom and Terry Caldwell. Tom was working for his stepfather Don Lindquist at his gas station in Grand Marais. Tom relates the story of how they got to Loon Lake, "I think it was 1968 and Kermit had called Don to say that the land in the bay was going out for lease. They were looking for some people they knew to take out leases. At that point the lease was twenty-five bucks. I had twenty-five bucks. We had a double garage full of lumber just sitting there. Other people came up to help build. Ollar Snevets helped get the logs. I was working for the power company, REA, during the summertime. We had replaced a bunch of poles out in the east end of the county. They said 'take as many as you want.' So Ollar came up and helped me level them off and Don and other people helped put the cabin up over the years.

"I think it was 1984 and Terry and I were sitting on the deck talking. At that point Willard was seventy-two and Kermit was seventy-six. She said, 'You know, I think that's something you've always wanted to do. It's only open in the summer. How much work can it be?'

"I talked to Willard because Kermit was retired. I just asked Willard, 'Are you interested in taking on a partner?' The biggest shock to me was he didn't say no or throw me out. So we just kind of walked around for a little bit. He didn't say one way or the other. Then Willard said, 'Well, why don't you work for a couple weeks and see if you can really get used to it?' And so I worked for a couple weeks and we didn't kill one another and we survived. I think Terry and I both worked the whole season. We never left. We've been here since then and I think it's worked out for both of us. It's given Willard an opportunity to stay and slowly phase out. I always tell people, 'Willard's like the furniture. He came with the place.'"

Willard Johnson

Because Tom was a school teacher, he was at the lodge during his summer vacation. Terry came up for a shorter vacation and weekends. Tom also became the cook, continuing in Willard's footsteps. They serve meals to guests and by reservations to the general public.

After almost twenty years, Tom and Terry moved up full time to Loon Lake in 2004. A new log cabin home was built for them and they are now open during the winter with three cabins. After announcing this new season with a newsletter, it was very gratifying to hear from many customers who have been wanting to see the area in the winter. It has been an exciting first winter for both of them.

When it came time to talk about recipes, Tom went into the kitchen and brought out the old recipe box. The two men discussed which favorites to pass on.

Did you know . . .

Willard Johnson was the cook at Loon Lake Lodge for over 40 years.

After she sold Loon Lake Lodge, Clara Dewar made and sold beautifully braided rugs to many people on the Gunflint Trail. They were very heavy and lasted for years. Luana Brandt at Nor'Wester Lodge is still using her braided rugs.

World's Greatest Meatloaf

Every cook has his own recipe for this comfort food. Here is Willard's.

1 egg
1 tsp. salt
¼ tsp. pepper
½ tsp. dried basil
½ tsp. dried thyme
¼ cup ketchup
parsley
2 tsp. Accent (optional)

2 tsp. prepared mustard
1½ cups soft bread crumbs
2 beef bouillon cubes
1 cup boiling water
½ cup finely chopped celery
½ cup finely chopped onions
1 cup shredded cheddar or Swiss cheese
2 lbs. ground beef

Beat the egg lightly in a medium bowl and add salt, pepper, basil, thyme, ketchup, parsley, Accent, mustard and bread crumbs. Dissolve bouillon cubes in boiling water and add to bowl. Mix well. Mix celery, onion and cheese into the bowl. Break up meat and add to other ingredients. Put in a pan and bake at 350° for 1 hour or more.

Loon Lake Bar-B-Q Ribs

Tom has gotten rave reviews for these ribs with the extra taste of pineapple.

1 rack of ribs
1 onion, quartered
8 oz. crushed pineapple with juice
⅔ cup water
½ cup BBQ sauce

Cut the rack of ribs into thirds. Put in a pot and add onion, crushed pineapple, water and BBQ sauce. Bring to a boil and reduce heat to a slow boil for 2 hours. Place the ribs on a cookie sheet. Hold in a refrigerator until half an hour before dinner. At than time put in a 350° oven for 30 minutes. Baste with the sauce as they cook.

Banana Cake

Bananas are the most popular fruit in America. Here's another wonderful way to use them.

½ cup shortening
2 eggs
¼ tsp. baking powder
½ tsp. salt
½ cup sour milk

1½ cup sugar
2 cups sifted flour
¾ tsp. baking soda
1 tsp. vanilla
1 cup mashed banana

Combine all ingredients and bake in a greased 9x13" pan at 350° for about 45 minutes. Frost hot cake with an icing made of powdered sugar, margarine and almond flavoring.

Rhubarb Cake

Rhubarb is the first thing to be harvested from gardens on the Gunflint Trail and Willard has this favorite way to use it.

1⅓ cups brown sugar
1 egg
2 cups sifted flour
2 cups cut up rhubarb
½ cup shortening
1 cup sour milk
1 tsp. baking soda
¾ cup coconut or chopped nuts
½ cup sugar
1 tsp. cinnamon

Combine brown sugar, egg, flour, rhubarb, shortening, sour milk and baking soda. Put in a greased 9x13" cake pan. In a separate bowl combine coconut, sugar and cinnamon. Sprinkle over the top of the cake dough. Bake at 375° for about 45 minutes.

Gunflint Lodge

Gunflint Lodge will always be known as the home of Justine Kerfoot, a woman who was liberated before anyone had heard of the term. Justine, to some extent, was just following in her mother's footsteps. Mae Spunner was a strong-willed woman who made the move from a life of wealth and privilege in Illinois to subsistence living in the Northwoods.

The first resort on the road is Gunflint Lodge. It is one of the older resorts on the Trail. Since 1929 the Kerfoot family has owned Gunflint Lodge, but it was started by Dora Blankenburg and her son, Russell. During the early 1920s Dora and Russell operated Lighthouse Lodge in Eagle River, Wisconsin. While operating this lodge, Russell noticed that there was a trend among their guests to move on north as the roads opened up new fishing areas and lakes. When one of Russell's best customers, a doctor from Milwaukee, told him that next year their party would be going up to a newly opened area called Gunflint, Russell

Old Gunflint Lodge

decided to come up to this area and look around. He made a couple of trips and eventually decided to buy land on Gunflint Lake. He and his mother opened Gunflint Lodge in 1925.

After operating the resort for a few years, Mrs. Blankenburg tired of running one place in Wisconsin and another one in Minnesota. She decided to sell Gunflint Lodge. Among her friends were George and Mae Spunner. The Spunners owned a summer place on Lake Zurich, Illinois, next to a home owned by Mrs. Blankenburg. George had given Mrs. Blankenburg advice when she bought Lighthouse Lodge. Mae was interested in trying her hand at running a business. After checking to see if her daughter, Justine, would help run the place during her summer vacations from college, Mae Spunner bought Gunflint Lodge in 1929.

That fall Mae contracted with local carpenters to add on to the lodge and to build a couple of cabins. She wanted to run a first-class resort and to expand the business. Mae and Justine also bought some property on an island in Saganaga. They had a small lodge building and tent cabins built on the island, and called it Saganaga Lodge. Guides took guests down the Granite River for a few days of fishing on Sag. At the end of their trip Justine picked them up by car at Seagull Lake.

Justine hired a Northwestern University classmate of hers named Val McIlhenny to run the camp. During the winter Val continued to work for her master's degree at Northwestern. She later married Benny Ambrose, the reclusive guide who lived year-round on Ottertrack Lake for most of his life.

Justine and a guest with Lake Trout

In October of 1929 the stock market fell and the Depression hit. The resort was worth a fraction of the purchase price. It had a large mortgage. In addition, there were outstanding bills for the new construction. Saganaga Lodge was a casualty, as they did not have the money to keep both Saganaga Lodge and Gunflint.

Mae and Justine went to work to dig themselves out of their financial hole. Justine visited the creditors and worked out extended payment plans. She was very careful to only promise amounts that she was certain to be able to pay. The family's affairs deteriorated further when a bank George had stock in failed and ruined him in the process. In a very short time they went from being a relatively wealthy family from Barrington, Illinois, to being the owners of a marginal resort in northern Minnesota. Justine's dreams of becoming a doctor fell by the wayside as she struggled to keep the small resort going. She and her mother divided the responsibilities. Mae would do the correspondence, run the dining room and manage the help. Justine would pay the bills and take care of maintenance. George would help guide and grow a large garden. It was a subsistence living but they made it work and gradually paid all the bills.

In 1933 young Bill Kerfoot was also feeling the affects of the depression. Gone were his dreams of joining the Foreign Service. He decided to move up to the Gunflint Trail and camp until he could find work. The sand beach at the west end of Gunflint became Bill's campsite. Maybe he could talk the people at Gunflint Lodge into taking him on for room and board. Bill was always a glib talker. Justine took him on.

Pretty soon the two of them were working together to keep the resort going. With Bill shouldering some of her load around in the resort, life became a little easier for Justine. By 1934 they decided to pool their resources and get married. The marriage would produce three children and last until the late 1950s. After they divorced, Justine remained to run Gunflint Lodge and Bill moved to Duluth. Justine would live the rest of her life at Gunflint and become a much beloved figure on the Gunflint Trail.

Justine is no longer around to greet us, but one of the Kerfoots will be around. In fact, it's Miranda at the front desk. She is married to Justine's grandson, Robert. Miranda is a Missouri girl who recently joined a long line of women who moved to the Trail from elsewhere and had to adjust to the remoteness.

One of the questions for Miranda is about a cookbook in Grand Marais that had a recipe for Justine's Muskrat Stew. Miranda didn't know anything about it, but Sue, Justine's daughter-in-law, answered, "Any recipe attributed to Justine is a mistake. Mom was admired for many things but certainly not her cooking. In Justine's writings, I found the origin of Muskrat Stew. Mom wrote that muskrat was a delicacy in France and then went on to tell how she got the recipe."

There is an island in Magnetic Lake that is known to locals as Gallagher's Island in memory of Ben and Lucille Gallagher who owned it from the early 1920s until the 1970s. Ben was a wealthy playboy from Omaha where his family owned Butternut Coffee and a wholesale grocery and liquor business. Lucille (or "Mama" as she preferred to be called) was a French widow whose first husband had been killed in World War I. They met at an international skeet-shooting contest where both were champions. They married and came to the States. Allergies made Omaha living difficult for Mama in the summers so they lived at their Magnetic Lake home from the first of June until the first of October.

Justine preparing a shore lunch for guests

Justine wrote that Mama had her cook bake a young muskrat. She then sent it across the lake while still warm for Justine to try. Justine found it "absolutely delicious." Not recognizing the herbs used, she asked Mama for the recipe, which was graciously given.

Sue continues her story, "Justine might not have been much of a cook but she recognized that good food was important to her guests. I am sure that a lot of this goes back to her mother, Mae Spunner. In the early years Grandma Spunner would supervise the kitchen and dining room while Justine was out doing other things.

"I recently came across a diary that Justine kept during the winter of winter of 1936–37 illustrating some of those 'other things.' It seems possible that the diary was kept with the idea that she could have an answer to all the people who wanted to know what everyone did during the winter."

The diary was kept in a little green calendar book given out by A. M. Anderson of the Grand Marais State Bank. Jimmy Dunn and Rosie Rosecrantz, both from Seagull Lake, kept similar diaries in the same green book from A. M. Anderson. None of the entries in any of these diaries are very long but their brevity really makes you wish for more of the stories.

During the fall hunting period of 1936, Justine made a few entries that give a glimpse into the hard work and long hours of those early years. On November 14, 1936, a large group of hunters checked into Gunflint Lodge. Art Smith from Loon Lake and Justine and Bill were going to guide the party on their hunting trip.

The first day started out pretty easily. The guides and hunters spent the day looking over some territory near the Clearwater Road. Justine also recorded getting 200 pounds of corn meal for the dogs for $5 that day. During those years she fed the sled dogs corn meal mush every day.

On Sunday, November 16, they were up at 3:45 a.m. to get into the woods by daylight. The party hunted all day around Clearwater but didn't get anything.

Monday morning they were up at 3:45 again and went to the Birch Lake area. Justine, Bill and one of the guests got deer in the morning. In the afternoon Bill continued to hunt while Justine walked back out from South Lake to get the toboggan at the road, a distance of three miles. By 2 o'clock she had hauled the toboggan back into South Lake. They loaded two deer on the toboggan and pulled it out. The group got home about 7 o'clock.

Interior of the old Gunflint Lodge

Tuesday morning they were up at 3:45 for the third morning. They decided to run the dog team down on the Birch Lake Trail. Bill hauled out two deer plus four deer from South Lake. Justine took the last man hunting. He got a doe and the two of them hauled it about a mile. Then Justine walked further out to meet Bill with the dog team. They took the dogs back to the hunter and his doe and hauled them out.

On Wednesday they got up at 3:45. First they took the dogs into South Lake to get Bill's deer. They had to drag the deer to the dog trail and then run to Rockwood Lodge with the dogs. They also went to another lake to haul out a 250–300-pound buck that Art got. A doe was pulled out at the same time.

Thursday the hunters left and Justine noted, "We took it easy. I was pretty pooped." To Justine this type of work was physically harder but much more interesting than being in the kitchen.

The kitchen at Gunflint Lodge was filled with a succession of local women who would come up to cook for a summer. Women such as Mabel Lindskog and Aggie Jackson spent summers at Gunflint Lodge putting out huge quantities of tasty, made-from-scratch food. They learned their skills cooking for large families or in logging camps.

Aggie Jackson kept her logging camp work habits all her life. Every morning she was the first person in the lodge. By the time the next person came in, her bread was rising, pies were in the oven, homemade doughnuts were waiting, soup was started and breakfast was ready—all before 7 a.m. To Aggie, anyone who came to work as late as 7 in the morning was just a lazy bum. Aggie's day

Buffet at Gunflint (Bruce is on the right)

ended in the evening hours after the last dinner was served, her prep area was cleaned and her floor was swept. She liked to retire to her cabin with a small sandwich of meat on a dinner roll. While eating her dinner, Aggie listened to her radio for a bit before retiring for a well-deserved rest.

When Bruce was in college, he brought home Ollie Sells, the cook from his fraternity to lead the kitchen efforts. She was interested in and eventually convinced the Kerfoots to start Gunflint's Sunday smorgasbords. From 5:00 to 7:00 guests and neighbors ate roast turkey, ham, potato salad, Swedish meatballs, sauerbraten, fresh fruit salad, jello salads, potato salad, three-bean salad, mashed potatoes, wild rice and homemade breads, all topped off with Baked Alaska, German Chocolate Cake or Blueberry Pie. After serving all the guests, the staff would finish off the leftovers.

"I don't know that I could have done that kind of physical work Justine did," Sue continued. "For me the challenge was first learning how to cook for two people and then translating that into cooking for guests. My first test came the second winter we were married. At that time the Canadian side of Gunflint was open for moose hunting well into January. We had a party of hunters up and they asked Bruce where they could get a meal. Bruce replied that Sue could cook them dinner. For the next twenty years our home was the winter lodge and I would serve meals to guests regularly.

"On holiday weekends with ski clubs in, we could serve up to 45 people in the house. Everything was buffet and we tried to use a pack lunch as much as possible. As with many young resort families, the entire family participated in serving the guests. Our sons, Robert and Lee, learned to deliver beverages, bus tables, and re-set for the next meal.

"At other times we would have just a couple of people. Many of the conversations were quite fascinating. One time Justine's friend, Grace Lee Nute, was our winter guest for several days. Grace was a prominent author of Minnesota history and Mother knew everything about this area. It was hard to keep up my end of the dinner conversation. I wish I had known enough to ask Grace more questions. One night she told us of her experiences sitting on the grand jury in St. Paul. Of course, Grace first reminded us that grand jury members are chosen and not drawn blindly from a pool of voters."

"By 1990 the number of winter guests overwhelmed our home/winter lodge. We bit the bullet and winterized the main lodge building. We totally changed our dining room service to the five-entree changing menu we still use. With the addition of Chef Ron Berg, our entrees advanced beyond the home style cooking of the past.

"We kept, however, a few favorites. One of these was to have a barbecue cookout one night of the week. Smorgasbords were discontinued and Sunday night became barbecue night. On the advice of some friends from Missouri, Bruce bought a huge covered grill that is about the size of a sheet of plywood (4x8'). We also journeyed down to Missouri to pick up some real hardwood charcoal. Each Sunday night during the summer whole chickens and racks of pork ribs are slow cooked on this grill. As an alternative to our normally upscale menu, this meal has remained the most popular night of the week."

Bruce and Sue Kerfoot

The current Kerfoot woman running Gunflint Lodge is Miranda, Robert Kerfoot's wife. Like the two women before her, she came to this area from another part of the country.

"Sixteen years ago as a girl growing up in the suburbs of Missouri, I spent an evening following my parents at the Kansas City Sport Show wondering if they had finally fallen off the deep end, all at the thought of spending our summer vacation in northern Minnesota. Driving home I had decided that my father had been hypnotized by the tall tales of a tall, thin fishing guide by the name of Kevin Walsh who had been weaving tales of 31" walleye, smallmouth bass and lake trout. With our first trip to the Gunflint I, too, fell in love with the beauty and peacefulness of the area, not to mention a small crush on a young fellow by the name of Robert. As summer trip after summer trip passed, I had my first real northwoods date with a trip down the Trail for malts at Poplar Lake Lodge, and a romantic stop at the local dump for an up-close visit with some of the local bear population. My dreams of dates at the movies with dinner were replaced with dates at the dump, gravel pits and boat trips on the lake. Thinking that this was all a summer crush that would pass like the seasons, a year passed and I got my first summer season of employment at the outfitters, my first trip from home and my first trip from the big city.

"I spent the summer of 1996 working here at the outfitters with every spare moment spent getting to know a living legend by the name of Justine. I spent evenings reading her books or sitting in on talks she would give in the evenings at the lodge. I knew my true test was to come when I was invited to stay for the winter season. In turn, it was Bruce and Sue's first real look at me. I was to spend the winter living with them in their home.

"Winter greeted this Missouri girl with 60-below temperatures and snow banks that were head high. I found early that the snow banks when high and frozen enough proved to be good bumpers for a mini van and prevented many trips to the ditch. In November of that year I had the pleasure of traveling to the Florida Keys with Justine. I spent six wonderful hours in the car going to Minneapolis hearing of the trials, travels and adventures of possibly the most amazing woman I have ever met. I learned of little known lakes that she had personally stocked with fish, how the lake feels the first time you fall through the ice and how to swim with the current that is life on the Gunflint rather than trying to always swim upstream. Now being part of such a family tradition is exciting and overwhelming all at the same time, so I always try to think of Justine and just keep swimming with the current and remembering that I am living surrounded by some of the most independent women around, who all have a wealth of knowledge and help for a city girl from Missouri."

Robert and Miranda decided to move on to other work, so Bruce and Sue are now running the lodge.

Did you know . . .

Native Lake Trout, as shown on page 144, were often called land-locked salmon because their flesh is colored pink just like a salmon's. Planted lake trout in the same lake will have white flesh.

In October, 1955, Justine Kerfoot, her three children, and Eleanor Matsis took a canoe trip. Due to the demands of running a business and raising a family, it was the first canoe trip Justine had taken in 16 years!

In 1943 Francis and Florence Jaques spent part of a winter living with the Kerfoots at Gunflint Lodge. In 1944, Justine and Bill received a package from the Jaques. It contained *Snowshoe Country*, which Florence had written and Francis had illustrated about their stay. The Kerfoots had never suspected that a book was in the works.

Sue recalls that Justine's right hand was so strong that even in her nineties, Justine would open sealed jars that Sue could not.

Gunflint Walleye Cakes

Walleye is a specialty of the Gunflint Trail and everyone is glad to get a new recipe like Miranda's.

1 small red onion
2 celery stalks
2 T butter
5 walleye fillets (about 10 oz. of fish)
1½ cup panko flakes or fine bread crumbs
1 cup mayonnaise
½ tsp. cayenne pepper
kosher salt to taste
cracked black pepper to taste

Finely chop the onion and celery, and saute in butter until translucent. Coarsely puree in a food processor. Cook the walleye by steaming or pan frying until flaky and white. Mix walleye, onion and celery mixture, bread crumbs, mayonnaise, cayenne, salt and pepper. Form into cakes and pan sear. Finish in the oven at 350° to heat through.

Gunflint Sauerbraten

HERITAGE

Sue says, "This recipe originally came to Gunflint from Bob Cardinal, who was our Sexton Foods salesman during those years. It is the only sauerbraten recipe I have ever seen that calls for grape jelly."

20 lbs. uncooked roast beef
4 cups burgundy
4 cups water
2 cups grape jelly
4 cups cider vinegar
2 cups brown sugar

2 T salt
1 T pepper
2 T whole allspice
4 cups sliced large onions
cornstarch

Place the roast beef in an extra large roasting pan. In a separate bowl, combine all other ingredients. Pour marinade over roast beef. Refrigerate for three days. Roast at 375° until meat is tender but not falling apart. Remove meat from the juices and carve into bite-sized pieces removing excess fat. Adjust the sweetness of roasting juices to taste. Lightly thicken juices with cornstarch as needed. Return cubed meat to thickened juices and serve.

BARBECUED PORK RIBS

After much research, this recipe has been our most successful rib recipe. It works on the premise that bottled barbecue sauce is just spices and tomato sauce. The tomato sauce easily burns so let's sprinkle just the spices on raw ribs before cooking. An easy trick at the end releases the meat from the bones. Curtis Martinson, one of the lodge chefs, has adapted the commercial recipe for home use.

1 T black pepper
2 tsp. cayenne pepper
2 T chili powder
2 T cumin
2 T brown sugar
1 T granulated sugar
1 T ground oregano
4 T paprika
2 T salt
1 T ground white pepper
3 T celery salt
3 T garlic powder

Thoroughly combine all the ingredients. Liberally sprinkle the raw racks of ribs with the spice mixture. Use your hand to press the spices into the meat. Wrap the meat tightly and refrigerate overnight.

About four hours before you wish to serve the ribs, in a charcoal grill with a tight lid, place about 40 hardwood charcoal pieces off to one side. Ignite them. After the charcoal is going nicely and has a fine layer of gray ash, lay in 2 cups of smoking chips wrapped in foil with holes punched in the top. Place your grill on top. Lay the seasoned ribs on top of the grill opposite the burning charcoal. Close the vents on your grill until they are about half open. During the entire cooking process the temperature inside the grill will range from 350° at the start until about 100° at the finish.

Every half hour or so, turn the ribs. Cook the ribs for two to three hours. When the meat starts to pull away from the bones, the ribs are done on the grill. In a baking pan large enough to hold all the ribs, place a trivet. Pour into the pan about 1–1½ cups water. Place the ribs on the trivet. Tightly seal the entire pan. Place in a 250° oven for one hour. This last step will release the meat from the bones and guarantee tender, tasty ribs. At the end of this baking, serve the ribs hot with hot barbecue sauce on the side.

Vic's Vegetable Salad

Sue says, "Because my family got bored during the winter months if I served the same kinds of food over and over, I was constantly looking for new recipes—not just for entrees but also for basics like salad. Also during those years we tried to add some variety to the dinner salads served in the lodge over the summer months. This recipe came from the sister of one of our cooks. The basic recipe serves 10 people."

10 slices of bacon	1 bunch broccoli
1½ cups mayonnaise	1 small head cauliflower
½ cup sugar	3 apples
2 T apple cider vinegar	½ cup chopped pecans
¼ cup diced onions	

Cut the bacon into small pieces. Cook until brown and crisp. Drain and set aside. In a small bowl combine mayonnaise, sugar, vinegar and onions. Blend well and set aside. Cut broccoli and cauliflower into small bite-size pieces. Core and dice the apples. Add to the vegetables. Add the pecans and bacon pieces. Add the dressing and toss until everything is well blended. Refrigerate until served.

Eggs S. O. B.

Some winter mornings I just knew there was no way I could get the boys off to school and everything done for the guests' breakfast. My solution was to prepare these eggs the night before and just pop them into the oven in the morning.

1½ lb. sausage or bacon
9 eggs
3 cups milk
1½ tsp. salt
1½ tsp. dry mustard
3 slices of white bread, cubed
1½ cups grated cheddar cheese

Cube and fry the meat. Drain well and set aside. Beat the eggs until well mixed. Add all other ingredients. Pour into a greased 9x13" baking pan; cover and refrigerate overnight. In the morning remove the cover and place in the 350° oven for approximately 1 hour, or until set. Let stand 5–10 minutes and serve.

CRANBERRY-PECAN TARTS

Even at resorts with a kitchen staff, the owner occasionally ends up helping with cooking and baking. This is one of Miranda's favorite recipes on those days when she fills in for the baker. She also reminded me that cranberries grow wild on the edges of some of our small swamps and ponds. The key to where they grow seems to be finding a place where black spruce trees grow.

CRUST:
3 oz. cream cheese, softened
½ cup butter, softened
1 cup all-purpose flour

FILLING:
½ cup orange juice
¾ cup dried cranberries, coarsely chopped
¾ cup light brown sugar, packed
1 large egg
1 T butter, melted
1 T cornstarch
1 tsp. vanilla extract
⅛ tsp. salt
1 orange, zested
½ cup pecans, chopped

Blend crust ingredients together. If making small tartlets, divide into 24 small balls. If making a large tart, divide into 12 balls. Cover with plastic wrap and chill. Press each ball onto bottom and up sides of tart tins and chill until ready to fill.

Meanwhile, bring orange juice to boil in a small saucepan. Take off heat and add chopped cranberries. Cover and let soak for 15 minutes. Then drain the cranberries well and blot with paper towel; set aside.

Preheat oven to 325°.

Mix all remaining ingredients, except the pecans, until smooth. Then add pecans and reserved cranberries. Divide the filling evenly among the tart tins and bake for approximately 35 minutes for the small tarts and 45 minutes for the larger tart or until the crust is golden brown. Serve with a dollop of orange-flavored whipped cream.

Gunflint Northwoods Outfitters

Just across the road from Gunflint Lodge is Gunflint Northwoods Outfitters. Justine Kerfoot started the outfitters, but for nearly twenty-five years a woman named Janet Hanson was her business partner and the operating manager of the outfitters. Janet's move to the Gunflint Trail started in 1945. During World War II she had served with the Red Cross in France as an ambulance driver. Upon returning to her home in Duluth in the fall of 1945, Janet took time to reflect on her life. She had a master's degree, some teaching experience and an uncertain future. To give herself some breathing room, Janet called Justine to ask about spending some time at Gunflint Lodge.

Justine barely remembered Janet from a brief meeting when Janet, as a girl scout, had taken a canoe trip from Gunflint in 1932. In the intervening years Justine had married Bill Kerfoot and had three children. The lodge didn't have any guests when Janet called but Justine agreed to let Janet stay with them in exchange for Janet's help with chores.

The time at Gunflint was an eye-opening experience for Janet. She was a single woman joining a bustling family of five in a wilderness setting with a team of sled dogs to care for as a bonus.

After Janet had been at Gunflint for several days, Justine received a phone call from her father in Florida. Justine's mother had suffered a stroke and she needed to go to Florida immediately. Janet agreed to stay and keep the household chores under control. It was a struggle but she would manage. Janet herself relates the ultimate test she faced while Justine was gone.

Janet Hanson with a canoe party

"It was on my tenth day of drudgery that Bill strolled into the kitchen casually in mid-morning, and deposited five uncleaned frozen chickens on the table. He announced, 'There are 14 hunters coming out tonight.' He grinned at me, raised his eyebrows challengingly and added, 'Can you cook up some kind of dinner for all of them?'

"I stopped in the middle of the room. My mouth fell open. 'Fourteen hunters for dinner? Are you crazy? I can't even cook a decent meal for you and the kids. Now you want me to cook for 14 hunters besides!'

"'They're not fussy,' he replied. 'You can concoct something for them. It doesn't have to be fancy, just filling.'

Janet Hanson with Justine Kerfoot

"'Bill,' I complained, 'we're almost out of bread, there is no dessert made, and besides, damn it, I never cleaned a chicken in my life.'

"'Oh, hell, I never cleaned one either,' he admitted, 'but they must be like a partridge, and you've cleaned them, haven't you?'

"'No,' I said crisply. 'I never cleaned a partridge either and furthermore, I'm not sure I want to learn.'

"'Well,' he said soothingly, 'just let them thaw for a while and later I'll help you clean them. It can't be too hard.'

"With that he was out the door in retreat before I could think up any more excuses. I stood there for a moment, debating whether to grab my suitcase and hike the 47 miles to town or stay and face the impossible task of preparing a dinner for 19 people. Even while I argued with myself, I knew I could not walk out.

"I decided to make hot muffins—the only bread-like substance I could make that I was certain would turn out to be edible. Then I could bake a big cake and serve fruit sauce with it. Bushels of potatoes would fill up the men. And as for the chickens, I had in the past used my mother's big four-gallon pressure cooker for stewing; there was a similar cooker standing in the corner.

"Soon I was in a storm of preparation. The children and the cat, sensing the tension in the air and my shortness of temper, kept out of the way and watched—from the corner of the room or from under the table or from a convenient doorway—the unusual rush of pots and pans and flour and potato peels as I met the crisis head on. Later, Bill tentatively poked his head in the door to see how things were going, and when reassured that it was safe to enter, came in and helped clean the chickens. Because the chickens were destined to become stew, neither of us was disturbed by our unskilled surgery upon them.

"That night all 19 of us stuffed ourselves on stewed chicken, mashed potatoes and peas. The hunters paid little attention to the lumps in the gravy, the hair-raising strength of the coffee, or the canyon in the cake where it had fallen. They were much too busy discussing the possible whereabouts of the deer population and making plans for the big hunt, which would start at

Old Gunflint Northwoods
Outfitters brochure

daybreak the following morning. Finally, Bill took them to the cabins that he had prepared for them and I herded the children off to bed, then went back to the kitchen to face the last ordeal of the day—a mountain range of dishes.

"I was almost finished with them when Bill returned. He patted me on the back and said, 'You did a swell job, Janet.'"

Women up and down the Trail repeated Janet's experience of a first meal for guests. Some learned to be wonderful cooks while others decided it wasn't for them. This second group either hired cooks or went into a branch of tourism with no cooking— canoe outfitting or housekeeping cabins. Occasionally there was a little crossover between cooking or not cooking. For example, Gunflint Northwoods Outfitters developed an oatmeal bar for canoeists. It is still baked on the property and provides a nice addition to dehydrated food. Below is the recipe for that oatmeal bar.

HUDSON BAY BREAD

This recipe is baked in a hotel size sheet pan, which is about the same size as three 11x16" sheet pans with a 1" edge (a jelly roll pan).

4 cups margarine	⅓ cup corn syrup
4 cups granulated sugar	⅔ cup honey
⅓ cup cornstarch	20 cups uncooked oatmeal

Cream the margarine and sugar. Thoroughly combine with all remaining ingredients. Press into an ungreased restaurant-size sheet pan. Bake at 350° for 25–30 minutes in a convection oven or a little longer in a standard oven. Take out when just starting to brown and still quite soft. The bars will firm up considerably as they cool. Let cool for 15 minutes before cutting into 48 pieces. Do not let the bars cool completely before cutting.

Did you know . . .

Most people on a canoe trip take dehydrated food for granted, but it did not come into common use until the late 1960s. Previous to that time, canned foods were used extensively. The two greatest selling points were that dehydrated foods were lightweight and produced no litter from cans.

Gunflint Pines

Gunflint Pines was another sideshoot of Gunflint Lodge. In the late 1960s Bruce Kerfoot added a small campground and three A-frame cabins. Ten years later Dick and Ronnie Smith from Milwaukee were working for the Kerfoots and looking for a place to buy. A deal was struck and a new business started.

In the 1960s Gunflint Lodge bought some property on the east side of the resort from Ray Merry, a longtime Gunflint Lake property owner. Bruce Kerfoot had just returned from college and the Army. He wanted to expand the resort offerings, so this land was used to build four housekeeping cabins and a small campground. By 1977 Dick and Ronnie Smith had been working for Bruce and Sue for several years. The Smiths wanted to own a resort so Bruce and Sue sold them the four A-frames and 18 campsites. In the spring of 1978 they formally started Gunflint Pines Resort and Campground.

Ronnie and Dick Smith with their son Aaron and Ronnie's father

Dick and Ronnie quickly started to make additions to the resort. A home and small office/lodge area was built. A marina with boat and canoe rentals was added. In the fall of 1982 an addition was put onto the main lodge to provide space for a gift nook, grocery area and snack bar. The resort soon became known on Gunflint Lake for its homemade pizzas and ice cream shakes and malts. By 1989 the Smiths were ready to move their family from Brookfield, Wisconsin, to Gunflint Lake on a permanent, year-round basis. As part of this move, they opened the resort for winter business. In 1991 they added two more cabins and then a laundromat and apartment in 1993.

Through all these changes, the Pines remained a family run and operated business. Tracy and Aaron, their children, were known to all the guests. As is typical of resort children, they learned to do all the jobs required at the resort: housekeeping, guiding, renting boats, hauling garbage and making milkshakes. Ronnie relates about an incident in those early years when the children were not old enough to help.

"As many people may know, doing repair work at a remote resort is a challenge. You have to be able to fix, repair and remodel most every area of your business. On the week before the 4th of

Ronnie and Dick Smith

July, Dick was trying to get a new floor put in the bathroom of one of the cabins. Of course, when the kids were little, my husband had to have at least one of them with him so I could have the other under control in the lodge. Aaron was with Dick helping (?) put in the bathroom floor. Aaron was told to sit on the toilet and just watch while the job was being completed. He got tired so he leaned his hands on the toilet paper roll not knowing that it would give way. Well, it did and his head went down and got stuck between the prongs of the toilet paper holder. This was a metal holder so when his forehead hit he got quite a cut right between his eyes. This was not a good day to have to run to the hospital miles away, but away we went with his sister for support. After a lot of crying, three stitches were put in and to this day my son has a scar between his eyes. Evidence that a toilet paper roll will not hold the weight of even a three-year-old."

In the fall of 2001, the Smiths sold Gunflint Pines to Bob and Shari Baker. Shari tells how this came about.

"I first came to the Gunflint Trail on a dreary day in early June, 1983, with no idea where I was really going or what I was getting myself into. At 18 years of age, I had applied for a summer job at the Gunflint Lodge and anxiously accepted whatever work they would offer me. After all, a guy I fancied had been hired as a fishing guide for the summer. I never told him I had accepted a position. When I finally arrived to begin my glamorous position as kitchen helper (pot and pan washer), I quickly learned that he had already left for home. No bother; being a bit of a tomboy, I sort of liked my rustic surroundings and decided to stick it out for the summer.

Shari Baker

"By the end of the season I was helping out in many areas of the resort, even cooking dinner on the chef's day off. I knew I had found a variety of life I loved. I returned to work each summer through 1987 and met my husband at the resort in the summer of 1985. I even changed my college major to Hotel and Restaurant Management. After graduation I followed the corporate path, accepting a management position with the Hyatt Hotel Corporation, but always thought of my wonderful summers 'back home.'

"By 1990 we had had enough of city life and the corporate world. We decided to return to the Northwoods. We accepted year-round positions at Gunflint Lodge, but always dreamed of owning our own resort, bed & breakfast or some business.

Entrance to Gunflint Pines

"In the fall of 2001 our dream came true and we purchased the Gunflint Pines Resort and Campground. The property was originally owned by the Kerfoot family as part of the Gunflint Lodge, but was purchased by the Smiths in 1977 to become its own resort and campground.

"But with a new business and two toddlers, life became very hectic. Resort life often finds me grabbing a candy bar and a soda to keep going. If we wanted a good meal, I would have to plan ahead. I love cooking, especially for a crowd, but I've never particularly been a hot dish person. I like to eat well. I prefer fresh foods and vegetables when possible, but living 43 miles from the nearest town does have limitations. I try to keep fresh vegetables on hand, but often use a mixture of frozen meats and some package foods. Thank goodness that I have lots of freezer space and a convenience grocery for guests here at the campground."

Did you know . . .

Resort owners are always figuring out new ways to attract guests. For several years, Dick and Ronnie Smith brought in an instructor to give scuba diving lessons. In addition to their guests, several residents on the lake got their PADI certifications for open water diving.

Although Bob and Shari Baker are a new family to own a resort on the Trail, Bob has roots to the Trail through his father. Father Bob Baker worked for Justine Kerfoot as a guide when he was growing up. When Bob was in high school, his father brought him to Bruce Kerfoot and announced that this was Gunflint's new guide. Father Bob was right.

Chicken Stir-Fry

The best thing about this recipe: it's flexible. You can use whatever vegetables you have on hand.

4 4-oz. boneless, skinless chicken breasts
¼ cup soy sauce
2 T lemon juice
1 head broccoli, cut into florets
2 carrots, peeled and sliced diagonally
½ cup whole almonds

1 cup fresh snow peas, sliced diagonally
1 can sliced water chestnuts
1 medium onion, cut into sliver wedges
2 stalks celery, sliced diagonally
4 cups prepared white rice
cooking oil

Cube chicken and marinate in the combined soy sauce and lemon juice.

Place the broccoli and carrots in a microwave-safe bowl. Add 2 tablespoons water and cover with plastic wrap. Microwave on high for 3 minutes. Set aside.

In large saute pan over medium heat, heat 1 tablespoon cooking oil. Cook the almonds, stirring constantly until toasted. Set into large bowl. Heat 1 tablespoon cooking oil and lightly fry onion and celery stalks to tender. Add to the almonds. Heat 1 tablespoon cooking oil and lightly fry broccoli and carrots. Add to almond mixture. Heat 1 tablespoon cooking oil and lightly fry water chestnuts and snow peas. Add to almond mixture. Drain marinade from chicken. Heat 1 tablespoon cooking oil and fry chicken until tender. Add the almond mixture to saute pan to quickly reheat and stir the mixture. When thoroughly warmed, serve with rice.

Dick's Slow-Cooked Stew

Some days there just isn't enough time to cook dinner for the family. This recipe is Dick Smith's solution.

2 lbs. beef chuck cut into 1–2" cubes
⅓ cup dry bread crumbs
1 tsp. salt
dash of pepper
1 large onion cut into eighths
3 carrots, peeled, split and cut into 4" strips
3 medium potatoes peeled and cut into
    1–2" cubes

4 celery stalks cut into 1" pieces
1 tsp. leaf basil
⅓ cup quick cooking tapioca
1 can mushroom slices, undrained
1 tsp. Kitchen Bouquet
2 10¾-oz. cans Condensed Tomato Soup
1 cup beef broth

Wipe beef cubes well. Combine bread crumbs with salt and pepper and toss with beef. Place coated beef cubes in a crock pot and add remaining ingredients; stir well. Cover and cook on low for 8–10 hours or on high for 3–5 hours. This recipe will serve six people or one hungry resort family of four.

Ronnie's German Potato Salad

Charlet Kratoska's German Potato Salad was well known on the Gunflint Trail, but Ronnie Smith is from Milwaukee and can cook a pretty mean potato salad herself. Naturally the ingredients are just a little different but equally delicious.

5 lbs. red potatoes, boiled in skins
1 lb. bacon, diced
6 medium eggs, hard-boiled, peeled and sliced
1 small onion, diced
¼ cup flour
1 cup sugar

1 tsp. salt
¼ tsp. pepper
dash of celery seed
1 cup water
½ cup vinegar
fresh parsley

Peel the potatoes and slice them. Cook the bacon until crisp. Remove the bacon from the pan and saute the onion in the bacon fat until cooked through. Blend in flour, sugar, salt, pepper and celery seed. Cook over low heat, stirring until smooth. Stir in water and vinegar. Heat to boiling, stirring constantly. Slowly pour the hot sauce over warm potatoes. Add cooked bacon and sliced eggs. Stir gently. Sprinkle with parsley and serve warm.

Gunflint Pines Spinach Salad

This next recipe is a great alternative to lettuce salads.

1 cup vegetable oil
⅔ cup sugar
½ cup ketchup
¼ cup vinegar
1 tsp. Worcestershire Sauce
1 small onion, diced

1 bunch spinach, broken and washed
4 medium eggs, hard-boiled and sliced
1 small can water chestnuts, drained and sliced
½ lb. bacon, diced and cooked
1 cup bean sprouts, drained

Combine the first six ingredients to make the dressing. Combine the next five ingredients in a large bowl. Add the dressing and toss or serve the dressing on the side.

Heston's Lodge

Long before it was fashionable, Peggy Heston fed the deer during the winter at her lodge. Many deer came in so regularly that Peggy named them Prince, Goldfine, Banjo Eyes and Gentle Boy. As the bucks dropped their antlers, Peggy was often able to match an antler to a specific deer. The antlers with identifying tags soon filled the lodge. The healthy deer herd on Gunflint Lake is a direct result of Peggy's early deer-feeding efforts.

This is another one of the grand old dames of Gunflint Trail resorts. It was started and operated in the beginning by Al and Luke Finn with their young son, Randy. Life in the woods at The Border Camp, as it was known then, was sometimes wild.

Kerosene was her preferred method for starting the fire in the cookstove. Boom! The morning would start with a bang.

In the late 1930s, Luke and Al Finn and son, Randy, had retired for the night. Awakened from a sound sleep by a terrible commotion in the kitchen, Al arose to investigate and told Luke to take the baby and hide in the closet. When he went out into the living room, which was between the bedroom and the kitchen, he was terrified by the sight of a very large bear, the kitchen table astride his back, trying to force his way into the living room through the French doors separating the two rooms. Al watched as the bear crashed through the doors leaving the table behind. As the bear burst into the living room, Al retreated back into the bedroom, shut the door and braced it with the dresser. Eventually the bear made his escape through the living room door amid screams and shouts from Al, Luke and baby Randy.

The next owners at the lodge were Peggy and Myrl Heston. The smell of baking caramel rolls often greeted visitors at Heston's Lodge when Peggy Heston was in the kitchen. From 1943 to 1971, Peggy and her husband Myrl ran the resort on Gunflint Lake. She continued on until 1979, after Myrl passed away. An adept baker of both caramel rolls and bread, she was usually up at six in the morning to begin the day. For many of these years, she did all of her baking and cooking on a wood-fired stove. To Peg, that was the only way to go. Kerosene was her preferred method for starting the fire in the cookstove. Boom! The morning would start with a bang.

Peggy's bread became fairly well known to neighbors and friends. In addition to keeping her grandchildren fed, she would sell bread to her neighbors. One couple, out on a canoe trip, had heard about this bread. Early one day, they began canoeing to the lodge, in order to buy a loaf of bread before it was all sold or eaten. Imagine their disappointment to learn that Peggy had not baked that day. "That poor woman, she almost cried!" related Peg.

In addition to all of the usual chores that any resort wife has, Peggy had a job that a neighbor wanted her to do. His name was Charlie Olson, and he had a pin cherry tree in his yard. Each year, Peggy would stop by to pick the cherries when they were in season. She would then put them up into jam

Peggy Heston

and jelly. One year, she was particularly busy, and she just couldn't get down to Charlie's to pick the cherries. He got so upset over this that he cut down the tree! He put it into his boat and rowed over to the lodge. If she wasn't going to come and pick the cherries, then he was determined to bring the cherries to her.

When asked if she ever got lonely up there in the woods, Peggy said "No, not ever." There was always someone around, be it family, guest, neighbor or one of her many animal friends. For several years, she fed corn to the deer that lived on the south shore of the lake. Observing them on a daily basis allowed her to identify individual animals and their distinguishing characteristics. As a result, they became like pets to her, and she would name them. Prince, Goldfine, Banjo Eyes and Gentle Boy were four bucks that came in regularly. When a deer would lose an antler, Peggy would leave the store unattended to go and search for the missing antler. Sometimes, by the shape of the antler, she would know which deer it came from.

One time a fellow stopped by just as Peg was finishing the evening feeding. He was amazed at the sight. As the deer slipped away, the fellow asked, "How do you get them to come in to eat?" Peggy said, "Why, they know their names, of course." The gentleman seemed quite surprised and skeptical about this. So Peggy said, "Watch." She refilled her bucket with corn, and as she shook the can, she called out Gentle Boy's name. Lo and behold, a buck came in from the woods. The visitor was amazed, and he could hardly believe "how that deer knew his name!" Peggy later said that she could hardly believe it herself that a deer had actually shown up at that moment, a conspirator in her little guise.

Another gentleman visitor had a much different animal encounter with Peggy. This happened in the early years when Peggy and Myrl were working in the summer. They repeatedly had visits from a bear, which was fast becoming a nuisance. One night they determined that the bear needed to be killed. Their daughters, Sharlene and Beverly, were with them at the lodge, and they feared for the girls' safety. So that night, they settled in to wait for the bear. They made a big bowl of popcorn and sat and waited. When the bear didn't show up, they all went off to bed, leaving behind the remaining popcorn. Not long after, a ruckus outside ensued and alerted them that the bear had finally returned. Everyone scrambled out of bed. In their haste, the bowl of popcorn went flying across the room, and the family dog was barking loudly. All of this noise easily frightened the bear away.

Peggy grabbed the gun, turned on the light and flung open the door. There stood a fisherman. Startled at this unexpected sight, Peggy said, "Mister, you don't know how close you came to being shot!"

They knew that he would return the next night, so this time they decided that they would really be prepared. No popcorn that night. The gun was propped in the corner near the door, close at hand and already loaded. With the preparations done, they all went to bed. Sure enough, about three in the morning, footsteps on the porch awoke everyone. The bear had returned! Peggy grabbed the gun, turned on the light and flung open the door. There stood a fisherman. Startled at this unexpected sight, Peggy said, "Mister, you don't know how close you came to being shot!" He took a step backward and said, "I just wanted to rent a boat!"

In addition to deer and bears, Peggy and Myrl had a pet raven that would accompany Myrl on his daily activities. They had an ermine that took up residence in the lodge one winter. Not a single mouse could be found in the lodge during that visit. Peggy admitted that the ermine even slept in their bed at night.

Another favorite pet was a red squirrel. This little fellow would climb up onto Peggy's shoulders and sit there under her hair. All day long he would stay there with her, as she did her chores. At that time, Peggy and Myrl were only running the resort in the summer. When fall came and it was time to go back to Chicago, Peggy asked her neighbor, Charlie Cook, to take good care of her squirrel over the winter. Charlie took the squirrel home to his cabin on the Canadian side of the lake. Next spring, when Peg returned, Charlie no longer had the squirrel. He had "taken care of it" all right. Says Peggy tartly, "I didn't talk to him for a long time after that."

No story of Peggy's animals would be complete without mention of her owl. Ole, as she named him, was a barred owl that she discovered in the yard one summer day. He was abandoned after he had fallen from the nest. Thanks to Peg, his new home was a box on the screen porch of the lodge. He would sit out there, greeting all of the guests and eating his meals of mice caught in traps. He thrived under her care. Eventually, the DNR said that Ole had to be released back into the wild. To prepare him for this, Peggy taught him how to catch mice for himself. She started with a toy mouse on a string, pulling it along until he pounced on it. Next, she replaced the toy with a dead mouse from a trap. Finally, after many lessons, she set him free from the porch. A while later, a strange noise was heard at the door. Upon opening it, Peggy found Ole there waiting for her. He dropped a mouse at her feet, as if to say, "Look, Mom, I did it." To this day, whenever a barred owl is heard calling, folks at Heston's still say that it is Ole.

Fortunately for her nine grandchildren, mice were never a part of the recipes that Peggy cooked for them. Instead, they, too, were often treated to those fresh caramel rolls that the guests got. Peg will still occasionally bake them for neighbors and friends who stop by to visit at her apartment in Grand Marais.

Peggy's daughter, Sharlene, was the next generation of the family to run the resort. Many of her memories center around the local bears.

"My first experience with a bear, other than an occasional sighting with my parents, came when I was just 10 years old as my cousin and I were playing in one of our small cabins. We heard a noise outside the cabin window, looked out, and there was a bear rubbing his backside on the cabin logs. We waited until he ambled off and then armed ourselves with a butcher knife and an ice pick. We ran for the lodge and excitedly told our story to the grownups. I'm sure we were in more danger from the weapons than we were from the bear!

"Our nearest neighbors, Walt and Addie Yocum, lived half a mile down the road where later Helen and Ade Hoover resided. Walt and Addie often joined us for an evening of singing while Walt played his guitar. In between songs Walt often discussed how to utilize all parts of the meat he shot. We lived a subsistence lifestyle here in the Northwoods, utilizing wild game, fish, partridge and berries. Food was scarce. It was a long way to town (50 miles) and in the winter the road was seldom plowed, making shopping impossible. Walt told us how great bear meat was, and how we could render the fat and make use of it in many ways.

"Not long after that a large, pesky black bear made a habit of following Addie and young son, Johnnie, to the biffy every day. Walt soon dispatched the bear and brought us a very large amount of fat. My mom and dad decided to render it on the cookstove in the kitchen. This was a two- or three-day process, and by the time it was finished, the house was filled with the stench of rendering fat that lingered until the following spring. Lye was added to a portion of the fat and was made into laundry soap. It was very hard on the clothes, but they sure got clean. A large portion of the fat became lard for pies and what was left became oil to season and waterproof boots. The lard was a tremendous success and made an excellent pie crust. Every time boots were oiled and put into the warming oven to soak in, the smell would permeate the house once again, and that oil lasted for about five years!

"One summer some of our guests took great delight in feeding a young bear cub who became very unafraid of people very quickly and made quite a pest of himself. We named him Yogi and he would sit or lay down outside the cabins for hours and wait for someone to feed him. His favorite was Butterfinger candy bars and he would follow guests to our store where they would purchase them for him. As time passed Yogi became a bit aggressive in his begging and my dad, fearful that someone would get hurt, wasted no time in dispatching Yogi. No way would we kids eat our 'tame bear,' so my mom disguised it with barbecue sauce and called it beef. It was simply delicious and after that almost all of our bear meat was prepared that way.

"Another bear was very considerate when he broke into one of our cabins. The guests were out fishing, leaving the cabin empty with tantalizing smells wafting out the windows. The bear gently removed the screen and went in and helped himself to the contents of the refrigerator. He took a bite of an apple and replaced it on the shelf, ate a pound of butter, set a dozen eggs on the floor without breaking any of them and ate a loaf of bread, a dozen hot dogs and a pork roast. He left the same way he entered but didn't replace the screen!" To no reader's surprise, Sharlene has a couple of excellent bear recipes for us.

Sharlene's son Greg and his wife Barb took over Heston's Lodge in 1989. During the summer of 2000, some of Greg's cousins (who spent their summers at the lodge while growing up) and their families came for a visit. One of the cousin's childhood memories was an eye-opener. Barb relates the story.

"As part of their stay, we decided that a picnic at Little Rock Falls was in order. Gunflint Lake flows into Magnetic Lake, which in turn becomes the Pine River. Little Rock Falls, where lake meets river, is an entry point for the BWCAW and a favorite day-trip destination.

"The family packed a lunch, grabbed swimsuits and boarded the boats for the trip. It was a glorious day for a picnic, quintessentially July, with plenty of sunshine, warm temperatures and few mosquitoes.

"At the falls, cousin Cheryl turned to Greg and remarked at the beauty of the falls, and marveled that it was so near to the lodge. Greg was surprised to hear Cheryl say this, as though she were a newcomer to the area. After all, she had spent the summers of her youth here at the same time that he had. He asked, 'But haven't you been here before?' To which Cheryl replied, 'No, we had to clean cabins and watch the store. You boys got to take the boats out to fish and explore!'"

During her years at Heston's Lodge, Barb Gecas has learned what it takes to be a resort woman.

"As many folks know, a resort keeper wears several hats. One day she may be a housekeeper, the next day a cook. At any time, she might be called upon to help with repair jobs, experience not a prerequisite.

"One sub-zero day, cabin guests stopped in to report that the bathroom plumbing was backed up. Greg prepared to go over and work on the problem, and he asked me to be his assistant.

Plumbing jobs around here are the least favorite, and to be completely prepared for the worst, I put on plenty of old clothes.

"Sure enough, this problem was not to be solved by merely the plunger. Soon we were retrieving tools and a snake, in order to go into the space below the cabin to clean out the sewer pipe. Greg and I both crawled in, belly down on dirt and gravel to begin the necessary task.

Barb Gecas and Sharlene

"At one point, he asked me to go 'upstairs' to the bathroom to try plunging again. Some of the guests were still in the cabin while we worked, so I politely knocked on the door before entering. I stuck my head in the door and called, 'Plumber!' The ladies laughed, and I went on to my task. Soon the problem was repaired, plumbing functions were restored, and all that remained was the clean-up.

"I went back to the lodge to change clothes and retrieve my cleaning supplies. Returning to the cabin, I again knocked, then stuck my head in the door to announce my return. 'Cleaning lady!'

"So the question, 'What qualities make for a perfect resort woman?' has probably as many different answers as there are resorts and lakes in the whole state. A short list can include the obvious things, like a willingness to work hard, a liking for working with people, knowing how to be a good hostess and having the ability to be flexible. I guess that I can claim to have those capabilities. I can also say with certainty that by no means does that make me perfect for this! Like many others who have been in my shoes, I think that we all are doing the very best that we can with the job, for the love of the place and the well-being of our families.

"I suppose that at times, to an outsider looking closely, a resort woman is somewhat of a marvel. This lifestyle is very public, especially if the lodge also serves as the family home. When we had our third child, we hung a sign on the door that said simply 'Closed today. Having a baby.' The guests due in later that day asked a neighbor if it was really true. She assured them that I indeed was in town, having delivered a daughter that afternoon. Another neighbor relates to me that she recalls coming to visit me here at the lodge the next afternoon, and the new little one was asleep in a bassinet. The two resident toddler boys took off running out the back door, and I was instantly up and running after them to check on their destination. She was so amazed that I was able to do that one day after delivery. I told her that I was simply doing what I had to do. And so it is true of every resort woman or mother. Any mom has several balls to juggle in the air at one time. A resort woman/mom seems to have a few more up there.

"A resort woman is able to simultaneously answer guests' questions, do laundry, prepare dinner and know the whereabouts of her small children. What makes all of this possible are things like washers and dryers with timers, slow-cookers for the meals and squeaky door springs that indicate if a child is headed outside. I used to purposely not oil the hinges, and I trained my hearing to listen for that sound. It meant that a little boy was disappearing out the door.

"The kids knew when they were inside, that if I was busy with a customer, they were to interrupt me for only two reasons: smoke or blood. I taught them to let me know that they needed to talk to me by laying a hand on my forearm. This signaled to me that when I was able, I would turn my attention to their question. One August day several years ago, my daughter Addie did this. I continued to talk with the guest at the counter, but I also could hear sounds from the bathroom that indicated the immediate need for first-aid. I quickly turned to her and said, 'Is this about blood?' She nodded vigorously. My son Robert had sliced open the side of his face on a low-hanging branch. Fortunately, his dad was with him. I realized that Addie had taken the training a little too seriously.

"Sometimes, in the midst of scrubbing a floor or washing yet another window, I'll reflect on how I got to this point in my life. There must have been something about me that gave Greg the confidence to ask me to marry him, some subconscious force at work that told him that I would be a good partner in the family business. If not that, then perhaps it was the words of his mother. Several months into our relationship, when the discussion of a possible marriage was coming up, Sharlene said to Greg, 'If you don't marry her, I'll kill you.'"

Did you know . . .

Since Peggy did not drive, she would often ski the three miles from her place to the main Trail to get her mail. The Kerfoots would see her tracks in new snow when taking their boys to the bus the next day.

About halfway between Heston's and the Trail lived Ade and Helen Hoover. Helen would become well known in the 1960s with the publication of her book, *The Gift of the Deer*. Several other books followed, but this was her most popular.

During the 1970s Lucille Gallagher sold the island in Magnetic where she and her husband had summered since the 1920s. For the next few summers Mama Gallagher (as she was known to all) rented a large cabin at Heston's so she could continue to summer on Gunflint Lake.

Barb Gecas is one of the most accomplished weavers on the Gunflint Trail. One wonders when she finds time to do it.

BAR-B-Q BEAR

This is Peggy's well loved family favorite.

3–4 lb. rump roast of bear
2 T bear lard
1 onion, chopped
3 cloves garlic, minced
salt and pepper to taste
1 cup cooking wine or sherry

2 8-oz. cans tomato sauce
½ cup brown sugar
½ cup cider vinegar
1½ T cornstarch, dissolved in ¼ cup cold water
½–¾ tsp. salt
½ tsp. pepper

Brown roast on all sides in an ovenproof pot using the bear lard. Add onion, garlic, salt and pepper. When brown, add cooking wine or sherry and cover.

Bake in oven at 325° for 2½ hours or until meat thermometer registers 170°. Remove roast from pan and slice thinly.

Meanwhile in roasting pan, add tomato sauce, brown sugar, cider vinegar, cornstarch mixture, salt and pepper. Cook, stirring constantly, until thickened. Add meat and cook on low for 15 minutes. Serve over mashed potatoes, rice or buns.

PIE CRUST made with BEAR LARD

There is a bear hunting season in Minnesota. Hopefully one of the successful hunters or their spouse will have the courage to try this recipe. Also don't forget that Nancy Patten from Okontoe says bear grease is the best for frying donuts.

2 cups all-purpose flour
1 tsp. salt
¾ cup bear lard
6 T ice cold water

Mix flour and salt together. Then add lard and blend with a pastry blender until mixture is crumbly. Add water slowly while mixing with a fork until pastry holds together. Shape into a ball and refrigerate for 30 minutes, wrapped in waxed paper. Makes enough for two pies.

GRAMMA PEGGY'S CINNAMON ROLLS   HERITAGE

Barb has shared with us a couple of recipes, one from Peggy and one of her own.

1 package dry yeast
2 T sugar
2 T lukewarm water
1 egg
1 cup lukewarm milk

1½ tsp. salt
3–3½ cups all-purpose flour, divided
2 T shortening, melted
brown or white sugar, and some cinnamon

Soften yeast with sugar in 2 tablespoons lukewarm water. Beat the egg and add the milk. Then combine the milk mixture with the yeast-sugar mixture, salt, half the flour and mix thoroughly. Add the melted shortening and beat well. Add balance of flour, or enough to make a soft dough. Turn out on a floured board. Knead until smooth and elastic without sticking to board. Place in a well-greased bowl. Grease top of dough. Cover. Let rise until double in bulk. Knead down, and then let rise for 45 minutes.

Roll dough about ½" thick. Brush rolled dough with melted butter and sprinkle with a generous amount of brown sugar and cinnamon, which have been mixed together. You can vary the amount of cinnamon to suit your own taste, but usually 1 cup of brown sugar and 1 tablespoon of cinnamon is the accepted amount. White sugar may also be used. Roll dough carefully, beginning at wide side and working away from you. Carefully seal by pinching edges of roll together. Cut roll in 1" slices. Cover the bottom of greased pan with cooled syrup (see below) and place slices, cut side down, in pan. Do not crowd them or they will pop up in the middle. Don't cut too thick, either, because then it takes too long to bake them and the syrup may burn. Bake in a preheated oven, 375°, for 20–25 minutes. When removed from the oven, let stand in pan for about 5 minutes. Then invert on cake cooler. The reason it's a good idea to let them stand about 5 minutes is to give the sticky syrup a chance to thicken. You may use muffin cups if you prefer, but they make dish-washing more of a chore.

SYRUP for CINNAMON ROLLS

1 cup light brown sugar
¼ cup butter or margarine

2 T corn syrup
¼ cup water

Cook ingredients until sugar has completely dissolved, stirring most of the time. Cool before placing cut dough in syrup. For something extra special, put a few chopped pecans on top of syrup before placing the sliced dough on top of the syrup mixture.

Cross River Lodge

The original name, Borderland Lodge, was given by Charlie Johnson. It reflects the fact that the Minnesota-Canadian border runs through Gunflint Lake. This is the only location on the Gunflint Trail where you can see the Canadian side of a border lake from the road.

What is today known as Cross River Lodge (and before that, Moosehorn Lodge) was started before the Gunflint Trail reached Gunflint Lake. With no road access, Charlie Johnson, a well-known Grand Marais businessman, would hike the 50 miles from Grand Marais carrying a 70-pound pack to explore the area. The return trip the next day was easy because he didn't have the pack to carry.

Charlie bought property on the Canadian shore of Gunflint, which he sold to his friend, Jake Preus, who was then Minnesota's governor. Since Governor Preus was going to build a cabin there, Charlie decided to build a cabin nearby at the present location of Cross River. The year was 1922.

It soon became obvious that Charlie Johnson could not spend as much time as he wished with his wife and son on Gunflint Lake. Anna stayed at the lake all week with their son, Lloyd, and Charlie would come up on weekends. In order to have some company for Anna during the summer, Charlie built several rental cabins and a main lodge building. He named the resort Borderland Lodge.

"It was built basically by my dad and a bunch of crews that he picked up at the jail and made a deal with them that if they let them loose, he'd give them a job out of town there for a while."

Charlie and Anna's son, Lloyd K. Johnson, told how his father built the main lodge, during an interview with the Cook County Historical Society. "It was built basically by my dad and a bunch of crews that he picked up at the jail and made a deal with them that if they let them loose, he'd give them a job out of town there for a while." Charlie was enough of a politician to get the men released to his custody from the Grand Marais jail. He paid them, kept them working at Gunflint Lake, and kept them out of trouble. Everybody was happy.

Lloyd went on to describe the lodge building, "My father had all of the main room done in cedar bark and birch bark and it was very attractive. We had all rustic furniture."

Eventually Anna and Charlie Johnson sold the resort to Warner Swanson. Benny Ambrose and his wife Val ran the resort for several years while Swanson owned it. In 1954 he sold the business to Dave and Ann Clark.

Ann Clark later recalled, "Life was easier at Borderland. We occasionally served dinners but all the cabins were equipped for housekeeping." Their son, Marty Clark, remembers coming up with his father to open the lodge the first spring they owned it. The two men slept on cots in the main lodge. There were squirrels running around inside the lodge. Marty sat in the lodge one night and shot six squirrels.

In 1962 Vern and Agnes Behsman bought Borderland Lodge. Aggie was known for her baking. By 1969 the Behsmans were ready to sell the resort. LaVonne Groth recalls how she and her husband, Gene, bought Borderland. "Gene and I honeymooned at End of Trail with Al Hedstrom and managed to go back at least once a year for a few days to fish and to get away from the telephone—no phones in the cabins. We most always had a guide, although sometimes we just fished by ourselves. George Plummer was often our guide and in the fall of '69 he said, 'You two should just move up here. There is a resort on

The Johnsons at Borderland Lodge

Gunflint Lake for sale called Borderland.' Our friends, Dick and Marie Pulse, were with us on that trip and even though I rarely missed a chance to fish no matter what the weather, the next day was cold and rainy so the guys went by themselves. Marie and I went to look over Borderland. I stood on that peninsula and looked out over Gunflint Lake and I remember asking Aggie Behsman, 'What direction is that?' She said, 'South.' That did it. I fell in love with it. We became resort owners and left the corporate life behind."

The first winter was a learning experience. "That first winter, with new snowmobiles, was a busy and fun time. I did learn that there was quite a difference between an occasional 20 below in Iowa and 40 to 58 below on the trail. I remember having frost on my new light switch one morning and wondering if it was safe to turn it on.

"Also, the squirrels, my nemesis in the old lodge. There was a hole in the birch bark ceiling of the old lodge right over where my check-in counter for guests was located. I remember checking in a couple from Chicago. She was dressed in a black suit complete with white gloves when a squirrel decided to introduce her to the woods and showered the counter with 'stuff' of mice and squirrels from over the decades. Bless her heart, she took it in stride and I hardly recognized her an hour later in her old fishing garb. However, I was mortified at the time.

"Old Moose, as we called him, hung over the old stone fireplace (I hope he is still there). It was a favorite sitting place for a squirrel in the wintertime if he brought something to eat with him, or if he decided he needed some minerals he would chew on the antlers. I kept a broom handy and we had many a chase."

LaVonne also learned to deal with cooking for guests. "Aggie did a lot of baking. I decided there was no way I could follow in her footsteps so we served 'home baked bread' not 'homemade.' I served very basic things that I was comfortable with fixing. The most overwhelming thing was either Sue Kerfoot or Marie Mark calling me to say that Bob Cardinal from Sexton would be here to take my yearly order. How in the world was I supposed to know what, let alone how much to order for a once-a-year delivery, when I had no idea what I was going to serve, let alone how many people I would be cooking for? Aggie was in Florida—no help there."

It wasn't long before LaVonne and Gene were starting to make improvements at the resort. "The fall of '70 after Labor Day, when the tourists had gone home, we started to build 'warm' living quarters on the east end of the old Lodge. It also included a kitchen and dining room for our future American plan guests and others who chose to eat with us. The fall of '71 found us tearing down, with much misgivings, the old Lodge to make way for the new one designed by Les Vickers' son-in-law who was an architect from Madison, Wisconsin. The old Lodge was such a work of art, but it was beyond repair and sitting in the only location that was practical for the Lodge."

Like all new residents on the Trail, LaVonne had to learn new driving techniques. "I was driving home from town one day, coming down that slight incline just before The Pines. Lindy Mark was with me in our Ford Econoline van and we had picked up our big Magnavox Entertainment Center that was not fastened down and sitting on the metal floor. Here came two big moose, one on the road and the other still on the side. I had to make a split-second decision of slamming on the brakes

Part of the building crew at Borderland

and having that big entertainment center slamming into our flimsy seat or going between them. I chose the latter. I remember glancing at Lindy with her eyes as big as saucers and informing me 'You always stop for moose!' 'Yes, I know—buuuut.'"

In 1975 LaVonne and Gene Groth sold Borderland Lodge to Jim and Nancy Thompson. Nancy tells the story of their first days.

"Jim and I and our three children, Jim Jr., Eric and Jean, moved up to Borderland Lodge the end of August, 1975, just in time for Jean to start her sophomore year in high school. Our sons were students at the University of Minnesota. This was a true move into the past for us. Life on the Gunflint Trail and in Cook County became a matter of survival for the Thompsons those first years.

"On our first morning Gene Groth gave us the local paper with the startling news that the school board had canceled bus service to the upper Trail. We were plunged into battle with the school board. Then we learned the county board had abandoned the bridge that provided the only access to our property. Several days later when we signed our future away purchasing the business, we learned there was a dispute with a neighbor and one of our cabins was about half on disputed land. The local druggist couldn't fill one of my prescriptions because it was an antiquated medicine no doctor ever used anymore. We were totally numb—a blessing that after such a major lifestyle change, the eight-party telephone line, three-day mail delivery, no radio reception until 1 a.m., only Thunder Bay television, constant

Charlie Cook

power outages, lettuce that frequently froze in the refrigerator, forest fires and chimney fires, one dilemma after another. We might have thrown in the towel except for the wonderful reception of our guests and the help and friendship of our neighbors.

"Our first Christmas we had an open house inviting everyone on the Trail we had met and a few we had not. The main reason we had our first party was to become acquainted with our neighbors. We had moved up just before Labor Day and had little time to become part of the community. About the only people I knew were Vince with the propane delivery, Bill the game warden, Earl from the Forest Service, George and Charlie, and, of course, Al the man who came for dinner. Who knew last names? Jim had gotten to know the Danielson family and I had met Lois during our episode with the school board. I cannot remember when we met Sue Kerfoot but we met Robert Kerfoot when Sue was in the hospital having Lee. Virginia and Jack Williams had brought him over for lunch! We needed some sort of holiday celebration this first year away from all family and friends. Thus a party.

"We were so pleased that everyone came who was around for the season. Nobody ever helped or contributed to our parties. These were strictly Thompson affairs. Jean and I did the baking, cooking, etc. Jim and the boys took care of the tree and, most of all, the plowing and shoveling and wood splitting for the fireplace. We had a great deal of snow that fall and Jim had all he could do to keep the road open with his tractor and blade. Justine wanted to know what he was going to do as it got narrower.

"People came in wool pants, flannel shirts, pac boots and parkas. Outer garments were thrown in heaps by the front door. Jean wailed at me in the kitchen, 'We were so overdressed in our long skirts and dress pumps!' It was a great success and we enjoyed meeting our neighbors. In no time we too traveled in the winter in our Sorels just like everyone else."

Thinking back on the friendships formed during their years at Borderland, Nancy says, "I shall never forget my best friend of all, Charlie Cook. His knowledge of things past, his gentle wisdom and comical advice gave depth and color to our life. His warning about the dangers presented by the lake during freeze up and spring thaw became our way of thinking in making many decisions. His advice was one he always followed. 'Let Georgie go first.' More than once we would look at each other and say, 'Let Georgie go first.' After seventeen years it was time for us to leave Borderland Lodge."

For several years Jim and Nancy's son, Eric, along with his wife, Jane, ran the resort. In 1999, they decided it was time to move on. Several of the cabins were sold off to private parties. The main lodge and a couple cabins were purchased by Dave and Paula Beattie. With fewer units to rent, they changed the resort into a bed and breakfast and renamed it Moosehorn Lodge.

Part of Paula's background was working as an interior decorator. In keeping with the tradition of bed and breakfasts, the main rooms and rental units are highly decorated. Paula tells the story of what happened while she was working on the main lodge.

"I decided to work with what we had, resulting in a combination of masculine and feminine, Victorian and Northwoods. While we were pulling this all together, we lived in one of the cabins. I started painting everything I could get my hands on white.

"One day, when my husband was in town, I was painting the kitchen when I heard a noise. There was something moving around in either the dining or living room. Being a 'city girl,' my imagination was working overtime. There was furniture stacked everywhere in the center of the rooms, because we were working on the walls, so I couldn't see a lot.

"I peeked around the corner into the dining room and saw nothing. I inched my way toward the living room. The noise of something wildly moving around was getting louder, and then I saw it: a DUCK! It was flying around the room crashing into the windows, which is pretty much the whole front of the lodge. I was relieved, but then I had to get him out. I opened the front door and assumed he would leave. Not so! Fortunately Dave came home and got him out. Over the years since, I have seen a lot of animals inside and outside of our Lodge, but I always remember my first experience."

In 2009 John and Rose Schloot bought from Paula Beattie and changed the name to Cross River Lodge. John had worked at Borderland Lodge while in school.

Twenty-Four-Hour Cole Slaw

On busy days a bowl of this recipe in the refrigerator saved LaVonne from having to make another salad for her dinner guests.

1 medium head of cabbage, shredded
A bit of red cabbage for color
1 small onion, chopped
1 carrot, chopped
one-quarter to half a green pepper
salt and pepper to taste

DRESSING:
1½ cups sugar
¾ cup oil
¾ cup vinegar
⅛ tsp. celery seed

Combine the vegetables with salt and pepper and set aside. Simmer the dressing ingredients until clear. Pour hot mixture over vegetables as follows: add one-third of the dressing and mix. Repeat until all is used. Cover well and refrigerate for 24 hours. Keeps well.

Anna Johnson's Breakfast Recipe

Lloyd K. Johnson's cousin, Doris Popham, remembers the following recipe from Anna Johnson.

wild rice
onions, sliced thin

eggs
butter

Cook the wild rice. Separately saute the onions in butter. Remove the onions and scramble the eggs until soft. Fold in the wild rice and onions and serve on heated plates. In a variation of this recipe, Anna would substitute a small can of creamed corn for the wild rice.

Poppy Seed Cake

LaVonne sent in this recipe.

1 package Duncan Heinz yellow cake mix
1 package instant vanilla pudding
4 eggs

½ cup oil
1 cup water
¼ cup poppy seed

Combine all the ingredients and beat for 4 minutes. Pour into a pan that has been greased and well coated with sugar and cinnamon. Bake at 350° for 50 minutes. Cool for 15 minutes and turn out on wire rack.

UGLY DUCKLING PUDDING CAKE

Paula says that this crumbly-looking cake turns absolutely beautiful at the first succulent bite.

1 package (2-layer size) yellow cake mix
1 package (4-serving size) lemon flavor
instant pudding and pie filling
1 16-oz. can fruit cocktail including syrup
1 cup coconut

4 eggs
¼ cup oil
½ cup brown sugar
½ cup chopped nuts

Blend all ingredients except brown sugar and nuts in a large mixing bowl. Beat 4 minutes at medium speed with an electric mixer. Pour into greased and floured 9x13" pan. Sprinkle with brown sugar and nuts. Bake at 325° for 45 minutes or until the cake springs back when lightly pressed and pulls away from the sides of the pan. Do not underbake. Cool in pan 15 minutes. Spoon hot Butter Glaze over warm cake. Serve warm or cool with whipped topping if desired.

Butter Glaze: Combine ½ cup butter, ½ cup granulated sugar and ½ cup evaporated milk in a saucepan. Bring to a boil and boil 2 minutes. Stir in 1⅓ cups coconut.

CRANBERRY CARAMEL DATE BARS

Paula says that the easiest way to chop whole pitted dates is to use a sharp knife sprayed with a non-stick spray or to snip them with a kitchen scissors. Each date should be cut into 6–8 pieces. To keep them fresh after opening, store the dates in a sealed container in the refrigerator.

1 cup cranberries
½ cup plus 2 T granulated sugar
2⅓ cups all-purpose flour, divided
2 cups oatmeal
½ cup packed light brown sugar

½ tsp. baking soda
1 cup margarine or butter, melted
1½ cups dates, chopped
¾ cup chopped walnuts, toasted
1 cup caramel ice cream topping

Heat oven to 350°. In a bowl, combine cranberries and 2 tablespoons granulated sugar. In a separate bowl, combine remaining ½ cup granulated sugar, 2 cups flour, oatmeal, brown sugar and baking soda. Add margarine; mix well. Reserve 1 cup crumb mixture; press remainder firmly on bottom of 13x9" pan. Bake 15 minutes. Sprinkle dates, walnuts and cranberry mixture over crust. Mix caramel topping and remaining ⅓ cup flour; spoon over fruit and walnuts. Top with reserved crumb mixture. Bake 20 minutes or until lightly brown. Cool. Cut into bars.

Tuscarora Lodge and Canoe Outfitters

As at most resorts on the Gunflint Trail, Tuscarora's guests were originally fishermen but most of them journeyed into the lakes of the Boundary Waters for world-class lake trout fishing. One portage between Tuscarora and the Boundary Waters was a mile and a quarter, up and down hills. In spite of the difficulties of getting to Tuscarora, Harry Anderson knew that great fishing would bring guests.

Tuscarora Lodge was started by Mr. and Mrs. Harry Anderson on Round Lake sometime before 1935. Not much is known about the Andersons. The *Cook County News Herald* mentions Harry Anderson as helping the CCC boys put out a lightening fire on Peter Lake on July 26, 1935.

Harry was also mentioned in an article entitled "Inherit Money and Land After Two Years Legal Battle" in the *Cook County News Herald*. The short article said: "After two years of involved legal manipulations, Mrs. A. B. Cook, Joe Blackjack and Ed Burnside, finally came into possession of about $1500 in money and about 800 acres of land.

"Unceasing efforts of Harry Anderson, manager and owner of Tuscarora Lodge and J. Henry Eliasen, County Attorney cleared up the will formerly left by Mrs. Spruce and Mrs. Tamarack."

The three people inheriting were well known Native Americans living on the Canadian side of Gunflint Lake. Justine Kerfoot used to talk about Mrs. Spruce and Mrs. Tamarack coming over to Gunflint Lodge and living there during the summer in a tepee. Billy Conners, another local Native American, would come over in the evenings and play a drum while the two women danced. Justine felt that the passing of people like this left a great void in life on the Trail.

In 1946 Harry Anderson sold Tuscarora Lodge to Frank and Agnes Fuller from Chicago. The Fullers had been married in 1936. Frank wrote, "I married Agnes Connelly in June, 1936. She was a beautiful red head and Irish as Patty's pup. Both her parents were born in Ireland." After serving in the Navy in the South Pacific during World War II, Frank came back to Chicago with the urge to move. His daughter Nancy Fuller McRae has Frank's written account of this move and his years at Tuscarora. Here is what he wrote:

"So, you would like to own a resort. So did I, and in 1946 my wife Agnes and I with another couple bought Tuscarora Lodge and resort. Fifty miles north of Grand Marais, Minnesota. Fifty miles of dirt road, curves, hills and holes. With some luck you could make Grand Marais in two hours. In fact, our first few guests said upon arriving (those that could still talk), 'You didn't tell us about the road.' So we started off on the wrong foot with them. From then on, in answering inquiries we tried to warn people, but words could not describe that road.

"Whether you call it a 'resort' or 'lodge' it was just a fishing camp and we made no bones about it. At least we did have some of the best fishing in Northeastern Minnesota. Lake Trout, Walleye, Northern Pike. We had six cabins and a lodge, plus an outpost on Tuscarora Lake with two cabins, each cabin could sleep 8 not counting the mice. Here's how it all began . . .

"I talked to Agnes, telling her I would like to get away from the city [Chicago] and she agreed. We had saved a bit of money, so I said, 'Let's look at a farm or a fishing camp.' She told me we could keep working and see what might come up.

_____

"No running water, but there was a very good well and out-houses. Now, you take the women and my friend who always had indoor plumbing—this was a shock. As for me, no sweat. The high school I attended in Upland, Indiana, had outdoor privies. Sometimes it pays to be an old country boy."

"We were pal-ing around with another couple and we were very good friends. They were looking to make a move, too. He was just out of the Army. So during the winter we went to the Sports Show with our friends and met a man by the name of Anderson who owned Tuscarora Lodge on the Gunflint Trail in northern Minnesota. He was interested in selling and so we talked. I was full of questions regarding the length of the season, about the fishing and what kind of fish. The main camp was on Round Bear Lake, and he had an outpost on Tuscarora Lake.

"After the show, he invited us all up to visit the camp. This was in the winter, so we took a few days off and drove to Grand Marais and boy, was it cold! The trip up the Gunflint Trail almost changed our minds.

"Well, after lots of chuck holes and such we arrived at the camp. It was covered in better than two feet of snow. I walked around with Anderson to all the cabins and the lodge. There were six cabins. Two of them would only sleep two people and the others slept four or five. I will tell you now, never inspect a resort in the winter. The price Anderson asked was $10,000. We left and drove back to Chicago and on the way we talked things over.

"After much discussion of the pros and cons, we decided to purchase the resort. We sent Mr. Anderson the down payment of $1,000. So it amounted to $500 apiece. I talked to a friend who owned a resort outside of Ely, Minnesota. I had fished out of his camp a couple of times and he gave me some very good advice. We greenhorns needed all the help we could get.

"In late April the four of us packed up and drove to the resort. Mr. Anderson was there and stayed awhile to give us a hand and boy, did we need it. We had a small shack to sleep in, two double bunks, a dresser and room to hang our clothes. No running water, but there was a very good well and outhouses. Now, you take the women and my friend who always had indoor plumbing–this was a shock. As for me, no sweat. The high school I attended in Upland, Indiana, had outdoor privies. Sometimes it pays to be an old country boy."

As with almost all new resort owners, Fullers learned a lot during the first year.

"The first year was crazy. As close as we were to our partners when we were in Chicago, things changed in the North Country. Things were just not working out for them. They were just not the outdoor type, which cast no reflection on them, having lived in Chicago all their lives. But Agnes and I loved every minute of the wilderness—the views, the eagles, beautiful sunsets and even the bears (though Agnes didn't go for the bears too much).

Old Tuscarora brochure

"It was soon clear they wanted out, so we sat down and talked things over. Agnes and I decided to buy them out. This happened in early September. After paying them off, we were damn near broke. They packed up and left and there we were—with no wheels and 50 miles from town. I got a ride into Grand Marais and floated a loan, enough to pay Anderson his first payment and enough to buy a Ford truck. We still had a few guests in camp and had some inquiries for deer hunting, but we thought we had better head for Chicago and find work as we could make more working there than we would make off the deer hunters.

"Closed camp in October, then off to Chicago. Agnes was a file clerk and had no trouble getting a job. I went to work for the Pennsylvania Railroad loading boxcars. I thought I was in good shape, but that job was a killer. I hung on and soon could keep up with the best of them. We were trying to save money for I knew it would take about $500 to open up in the spring. We decided to have American plan and housekeeping cabins and to make more room in the lodge. To do that, I would have to take off the railing, enclose the front porch and re-roof it. I could also see that we needed another cabin. Thank goodness we had a 15-ft. freezer, which would hold a good supply of meat, and we found out you could keep bread some time by freezing it.

"So it does cost money just to open and you always hope you have lots of advance reservations. You needed gas for motors plus the light generator—and what a generator. Every night about dark, one of the guides and I would start cranking. Take turns and crank some more. Once it started you had lights, but beware if someone in a cabin had an electric fry pan or toaster. Then the lights would dim and the motor would slow down. I'd run like hell around camp from cabin to cabin till I found the one.

Ages seven and eight, they hadn't fished much alone, but they had proven their ability to survive on the dock after a swim test (falling in fully clothed and making it successfully to shore).

"At night, most of our guests would come up to the Lodge. It was not very big: four booths plus a small counter. Back of the counter, we had a cooler for pop and 3.2 beer and on the wall we sold fishing tackle, bug dope, etc. There were no strangers here—you were so close to one another you had to get acquainted. Through the years, we collected our share of stories and tall tales . . . we always enjoyed the evenings even though at times we were very tired due to the fact that we were up every morning at 5 a.m. At times Agnes and I took turns staying up with the guests.

"Another nice thing about that generator–the tank would only hold so much gas, so about 11:30 p.m. out went the lights. The guests would say, 'Well, we can take a hint—time to go to bed.' I told them, 'Before you come to the lodge at night, be sure to bring a flashlight.' Otherwise I would have to show them to their cabin and keep an eye out for bears."

Bears were a constant source of interest to the guests and a constant source of work for the owners. "Our guests just loved to see one. Me, I thought they were a pain in the butt. I guess I had cleaned up too many garbage cans they had dumped over. Agnes wanted no part of them. A couple of times she would be cooking and a bear would stick his nose against the screen door. She would yell for someone to get the gun and shoot that bear. If I were close by, I would take my old '97 Winchester shotgun and load it with Number 8 shot. Yell like hell at the bear and he or she would take off running. At about 40 or 50 feet, I'd let go at the rear end. When those Number 8's hit, the bear really flew.

"At that time there was no law against shooting bears, but I wasn't interested in hunting them. In my 18 years at the resort I never killed a bear, though our guide Jim killed one that made a pest of itself and Agnes said to get rid of it. We skinned it out. It was my first time and I was not too crazy about the job. The skinned-out paws were just like human hands. We tacked the hide to the guide's cabin and salted it. Now and then we would scrape off the fat. The hair stayed on and it turned out to be a halfway-decent hide, much to our surprise. We hung the hide in the fork of a tree in front of the lodge where everybody could get a look at it."

Right after World War II there was pressure on all the Trail resorts to add indoor plumbing. As Frank says, the process was started by Doc Remple at Northwoods Lodge on Poplar Lake.

"We blamed our troubles on Doc Remple for he was the first to modernize a resort on the Gunflint Trail, though we could see the writing on the wall. We received a great number of inquiries, with people wanting to know if we were modernized. They weren't as interested in hot and cold running water as they were in indoor toilets. I had done some plumbing in the Navy, but not enough. I was just an amateur, but Agnes and I decided to modernize.

"That winter, we went to Chicago and found jobs. Agnes said, 'I am now working to buy toilets.' There wasn't a lazy bone in her body and I promised her as soon as we got the note paid off, there'd be no more working in the winters and we would employ more help so she could take it easy. She told me she would still do the cooking—she was a very good cook.

The Mark girls at Tuscarora

"It took about two years to install toilets and showers and hot water heaters. Our sleeping quarters and office were the last to be modernized. After all, the customer comes first."

Frank and Agnes learned that in remote areas, the neighbors all work together.

"When you are 50 miles from the nearest town and 5 miles from your nearest neighbor, neighbors become very important. And when greenhorns buy a resort there is so much to learn. Thanks to Bill and Justine Kerfoot—they were always there when I needed some answers regarding the operation of a resort. Even though we were all fighting for business, when someone needed help everybody gave a hand. When the lodge burned at Gunflint the resort owners and a number of summer homeowners spent a few days helping build a new lodge. That makes the world go around.

"Our friends and neighbors included: [spellings may be wrong] Warner and Ann Swanson of Borderland Lodge, Bill and Justine Kerfoot of Gunflint Lodge. Myrl and Peggy Heston of Border Camp Lodge, Mert and Ed Cavanaugh of Bearskin Lodge, George Stapleton and his wife at Loon Lake Lodge, Doc Remple and his wife on Poplar Lake and the folks at Golden Eagle Lodge, Russell and Eva Blankenburg of Seagull Lodge, Mr. and Mrs. Ralph Griffis of Chick-Wauk Lodge, Mr. and Mrs. Bud Kratoska, Mr. and Mrs. Dave Clark and good old Al Graykowski."

In the fall of 1960 Frank and Alice Fuller sold Tuscarora Lodge to Jerry and Marie Mark. Along with a dog, the Marks brought their three school-age daughters: Pip, Deb and Lindy. For the first time the school district provided daily bus service down the Gunflint Trail to school in Grand Marais. This ride, of course, was a little bit different from your average school bus route. Marie remembers those rides:

"The trip started with a van driven by Clarke Dailey from Seagull Resort, to Trail Center where he met Pat McDonnell from Hungry Jack Lake who then transported his children and the upper trail kids to town. When Joe Denham moved to Saganaga, he became 'the' bus driver all through the Mark girls' grade school and high school years. This consisted of a daily trip of 50 miles to school and 50 miles home each school day. Joe worked as a mechanic in the school garage between the two trips.

"At that time the trail was paved from Grand Marais to Hedstrom Lumber yard, then gravel to the Tuscarora Rd. In the spring the gravel road had to be planked to get it past overflowing creeks and washout holes in the road, like Timber Creek, etc. One spring Timber Creek washed the entire road away. We had to drive 30 miles down to the creek to pick up the girls. Even though the county trucks were busy restoring the roadbed, the only way home that night was for the girls to walk a plank thrown across the raging creek.

"In the winter the bus broke trail many times, and also had to contend with icy roads and snowy whiteouts. If the weather was 45° below zero, the bus wouldn't go to town. Moose, deer, lynx and sometimes timber wolves were a regular sight, along with bear in the spring and fall.

Pip and Deb Mark with their grandmother

"Joe said he would retire when the last of the Mark girls graduated from high school. On Lindy's, our youngest, last day of school the girls had a parting gift for Joe. When we went out to meet the bus on that last day, it seemed to be pulling in slower than usual. To our surprise Lindy was driving the bus and Joe was sitting in a back seat—not exactly what Cook County School District would like to hear."

Having three girls rather than three boys made life a little different around Tuscarora. The girls could do all the chores demanded at the resort but they put their own twist on the work. For example, in the spring the girls often shoveled the roof of the lodge building. It was a common job in those years. When the job was finished, the Mark girls added a little extra. After putting a towel down, the warm roof made a great place to sunbathe long before the rest of the snow had melted!

During the years the Mark family ran Tuscarora, Marie was the cook for their guests, staff and family. The girls all helped their mother but it was with their mother's recipes. Marie was known by one and all for her big smile and wonderful meals.

Andy, Sue, Shelby and Daniel Ahrendt moved to Tuscarora in 2004. Sue and Andy's dream of owning a Gunflint Trail outfitter was sparked at Wilderness Canoe Base on Seagull Lake. They had

Sue and Andy Ahrendt with their children, Dan and Shelby

been campers as youth and met on staff in the early 1980s. They were married and began a family in the Minneapolis area, but consistently returned to the BWCAW. Each time they left, they experienced homesickness for the water and the woods. Finally, the time was right and they purchased Tuscarora from Kerry Leeds.

They had a fantastic first season in 2004. "Our kids have been on canoe trips since they were in diapers, but we wondered if they would find the transition difficult. Not so. On one of the first days of the summer Daniel spent the day on the dock with his good friend Joe (whose family was on staff). Ages seven and eight, they hadn't fished much alone, but they had proven their ability to survive on the dock after a swim test (falling in fully clothed and making it successfully to shore). They were thrilled to catch a good sized smallmouth bass from under the dock. They managed to land it and get it on the stringer before it flopped back into the water. Shelby and the other kids joined them and they spent the entire afternoon with a net. By evening they re-caught their bass, removed the stringer, had Mom snap a photo and returned it to the lake." Needless to say, Shelby and Daniel are as much at home at Tuscarora as Sue and Andy.

Did you know . . .

About one block in from the Gunflint Trail on the Tuscarora Road is a pond. In June as the aquatic grasses start to grow, this is one of the most reliable places to see moose feeding in the evenings.

Tuscarora Lodge and Canoe Outfitters is in the enviable position of being the only business or home on Round Lake.

Frank Fuller used to have outpost cabins on Tuscarora Lake for his guests. One time he took a couple from the Twin Cities to the cabins. The wife put on a hair net before retiring for the night. She woke up in the middle of the night with a mouse stuck in her hair net!

For many years the lake trout season did not close in the late winter and spring. It was well known that the best lake trout fishing was about one week after the ice went out. Marie and Jerry Mark used to send "Ice Out" cards to their canoeing guests letting them know it was time to fish lake trout in open water.

Breast of Chicken Magnifique

According to Marie this great recipe can be made the day before and reheated.

4 whole chicken breasts,
    boned and split (8 halves)
¼ lb. butter
2 cups fresh mushrooms
2 cups cream of chicken soup

1 clove minced garlic
a generous dash of thyme
⅛ tsp. crushed rosemary
⅔ cup milk

Brown the chicken breasts in butter. Remove from pan and set aside. Brown the mushrooms. Stir in soup, garlic, seasonings and milk. Add the chicken. Place in a casserole dish and bake covered at 325° for one hour or until tender. Serve with half wild rice mixture.

Egg Dumplings

This recipe of Mrs. Anderson's came down from the 1950 printing of North Shore Cookery.

1 egg
3 T milk
⅔ cup flour

1 tsp. baking powder
¼ tsp. salt
1 T sugar

Mix in order given and drop by teaspoon into boiling milk and boil for 15 minutes, covered. Serve at once as a one-dish meal. Makes delicious light lunch or evening meal.

Popovers

Sue's popovers are a great alternative for bread at dinner.

2 eggs
1 cup milk

1 cup flour
¼ tsp. salt

Preheat oven to 375°. Grease 12 muffin cups. Beat eggs and milk. Add flour and salt and whisk until reasonably well blended. Fill muffin cups two-thirds full. Bake 30 minutes without opening the oven. Yield: 12 popovers.

APPLE PIE CAKE

This is the only recipe of Agnes's to come down to us, but it's a great one.

¼ cup butter
1 cup sugar
1 egg
¼ tsp. salt
1 tsp. nutmeg
1 tsp. cinnamon
1 tsp. baking soda
2 T hot water
1 tsp. vanilla
1 cup flour
½ cup chopped walnuts
2½ cups diced apples (do not peel)

Stir all the ingredients together and place in a well greased pie plate. Bake at 375° for 45 minutes. Serve with whipped cream or a rum sauce.

RUM SAUCE

This was Agnes's sauce for the Apple Pie Cake.

½ cup butter
½ cup cream
½ cup white sugar
½ cup brown sugar
2 T rum extract

Mix together and let come to a boil. Cool. Heat before serving and add the rum extract. Pour the rum sauce over each piece of cake. Agnes notes that regular rum will not work with this recipe.

—Memories of—
Seagull Resort

When Russell Blankenburg first came to Seagull Lake, the road ended there. The lake had no homes or inhabitants. The only way to get to Saganaga Lake was to go down the river from Seagull. And all of this was happening in the late 1920s. It wasn't that long ago!

One of the outstanding physical characteristics of Seagull Lake is the natural sand beach at the east end close to where the Gunflint Trail originally came to the lake. Russell Blankenburg found out that the Speilman Estate owned this property. He contacted them about buying forty acres around the sand beach. They only wanted to sell the entire holding, which included a few hundred acres and two miles of shoreline on Seagull. Unfortunately much of this shoreline was still recover-

Seagull Resort

ing from a 1918 fire. Russell had no choice but to buy the entire piece of property. Eventually the trees grew up and he sold the shoreline to homeowners, keeping the sand beach for Seagull Resort.

The first resort on Seagull Lake was Seagull Resort, started by Russell Blankenburg immediately after he sold Gunflint Lodge to the Spunners. After his marriage, he and his wife, Eve, operated the lodge for many years.

> "Eve had a trick that would drive Russell crazy. She was able to accurately predict when they would have bear trouble at the resort."

In later years Eve told some stories about her experiences cooking at Seagull Resort. As was common at the time, dessert at Seagull was a choice of freshly baked pie. Guests often had trouble deciding which kind of pie to have for dessert. One guest solved this problem in a novel way. When he came in from fishing, he would go into the kitchen where the pies were cooling for the evening meal. Then he would stick his finger into each pie to taste it. At dinner he always knew which pie to order. Although Eve knew what he was doing, all she did was chuckle about it.

Janna Webster, author of *Ki-osh-kons: People, Places, and Stories of Sea Gull Lake*, has another good story about the Blankenburg's days at Seagull Resort. "Eve had a trick that would drive Russell crazy. She was able to accurately predict when they would have bear trouble at the resort. She would occasionally announce, 'We are going to have a bear tonight.' It just about did Russell in that Eve could do this. Eve never did tell him that her clairvoyance was due to the fact that, without fail, they would get a visiting bear any time she cooked a ham."

In 1958 Clarke and Jean Dailey bought Seagull Resort from the Blankenburgs. They became one of the first owners to stay open all winter. After Clarke and Jean separated, Jean ran the resort for several years before selling in 1966. During those winters she drove the school bus to Poplar Lake, meeting Pat McDonnell of Gateway Lodge who drove the rest of the way to town. Jean tells about driving the bus.

"It was quite a task to drive the Trail in the winter. Of course, it was not paved at that time. Many mornings I had to get up early to put an electric heater under the motor to get the bus going. It was often like driving in a tunnel as the snow was so deeply piled on the sides of the road. On one trip I hit a deer that jumped in front of the bus. I had to drive to Gunflint Lodge to get Bruce Kerfoot to come out to shoot it."

Clarke and Jean Dailey

Jean remembers other challenges to winter living on the Trail. "We saw some of the most beautiful sunsets over the lake and great northern lights during the winter. Some of our guests used to ask, 'What do you do in the winter?' It took all our time and energy just to keep everything going. One time the water pipe coming into the cabin burst and I had to quick go down to the pump house to shut off the main line. I was soaking wet when I went out because I had been sprayed with water. By the time I had shut down the water and got back inside, I could hardly move since my clothes were frozen stiff. Because the pipes could not be buried very deep due to the rocky terrain, they sometimes froze, so I devised a way to thaw them by connecting a hose to the relief valve on a large pressure cooker that I heated on a camp stove. I kept pushing the hose into the frozen pipe. The steam gradually melted the frozen pipe. We generally tried to keep water running slowly in the pipes."

Eventually Jean Dailey sold Seagull Resort to Ward and Margarite Ingersoll in 1965. They ran the resort until 1971 when they sold to Al and Lois Danielson.

As with many resorts, this was a family operation. At various times they had two daughters, four sons, one son-in-law, one daughter-in-law and one mother-in-law working at the resort.

Lois tells about the many changes they made to the facilities. "Our first improvement was the addition of another cabin. Then we turned the old lodge into living quarters for family. We built a large addition to the snack bar, creating a nice area for evening dining and relaxing. Next came our four-unit motel, the moving of several buildings from within the Boundary Waters over the ice, and turning them into laundry facilities and an addition to one of the family cabins. I cringe to remember that the last portion of one of the buildings was pulled over the ice just the day before the ice broke up and our son was operating the machine that pulled it. Our last project was a building to enable us to do outboard motor sales and repairs with sleeping quarters upstairs for workers other than family."

Lois has some very good memories of that meal when the residents of the Gunflint Trail entertained a party of legislators for a traditional fish fry at the resort. "My biggest regret is the time we had senators and congressmen from several states visit Seagull Resort prior to the legislation regarding boat and motor usage in the BWCAW. After feeding them a delicious fish dinner, they were waiting for the float planes to take them back to Ely. I overheard one of them say (sorry, I have forgotten his name) 'That's the best fish I've eaten in my life, but I hope they don't think it's going to change our minds on the BWCAW issue.' I had such an urge to 'bump' him off the dock into the lake; and I didn't do it! After all these years, I still wish I had."

In 1978 Al Danielson died of a heart attack. Lois sold the resort to Lynn Paulrud and Dave Canfield. They operated it for a couple of years before selling out to the federal government.

The location of Seagull Resort is now called the Blankenburg Public Landing. It provides public access for boats to Seagull Lake. The sand beach that Russell Blankenburg bought so many years ago is now used by the public as part of the Blankenburg Public Landing.

If you go over to the boat launch, the Forest Service has placed a small plaque remembering Russell and Eve Blankenburg, both of whom will long be remembered by the residents and summer home-owners on the Gunflint Trail. Starting in 1925 with the land Gunflint Lodge stands on, Russell Blankenburg bought and sold property on Gunflint, Seagull, Loon and Saganaga Lakes. Over the years he would go in and start a business on one piece of land. After getting it going, Russell would sell the business. After all, it was worth more with a business on it than as just vacant land. Then he would sell lots (never less than 250 feet) on either side of the business to private parties. In the early years the resort or outfitters would be a plus for the sale since the new owners could get their mail there or use the telephone or buy groceries. During all these sales, while Russell discussed business and financing, Eve chitchatted and served pie and coffee. They were quite a sales team! During their lives, they were responsible for the start of Gunflint Lodge, Seagull Resort, Seagull Outfitters, Portage Outfitters, End of the Trail Lodge, Tip of the Trail Outfitters and Saganaga Outfitters. Who knows how many homes were built on property that they sold.

Seagull Fish Chowder

Jean Dailey always had some leftover fish to make this tasty soup.

4–5 strips of bacon
1 onion, chopped
1–2 fillets (depending on size) of cooked and boned fish
2 potatoes, cooked and diced
1 cup stewed tomatoes
5 or 6 cups of milk
salt and pepper
red pepper (optional)
soda crackers

Chop and fry bacon; pour off some of the fat. Cook onion in remaining fat, then add fish, potatoes, tomatoes and milk.

Simmer to blend the flavors. Add salt and pepper to taste and a shake of red pepper if desired. Thicken with crushed soda crackers before serving. The amounts of ingredients can be altered depending on taste and the number of people to be served.

Tijuana Tidbit Trash

With lots of children, Lois always needed snacks like this around the house.

½ cup light corn syrup
½ cup butter
½ cup brown sugar
1 tsp. cinnamon
1 T chili powder

¼ tsp. red pepper
3 cups Crispix
1 bag of popped microwave popcorn
6 cups broken tortilla chips
1 12-oz. can of mixed nuts

Bring corn syrup, butter, brown sugar, cinnamon, chili powder and red pepper to a boil, stirring often. Mix the Crispix, popcorn, chips and nuts in a large roasting pan. Pour the syrup mixture over the dry ingredients and toss or mix lightly. Bake at 200° for 1 hour, stirring several times. This stores well in a covered container for several weeks.

Soy Sauce Roast

Soy sauce and ginger add an interesting twist to this recipe from Lois.

4 lb. bread-and-butter cut beef roast
1 clove of garlic
¼ cup soy sauce

½ tsp. dry ginger
2 sliced onions
¼ cup water

Brown the roast on both sides. Pour a sauce made from all the other ingredients over the roast. Cook slowly at 200° for 2½ hours. Turn several times during cooking. Slice and serve hot.

French Dressing

This recipe of Eve's has come down to us from her days cooking at Seagull

1 cup Mazola oil
1 cup vinegar
1 cup tomato soup (undiluted)
½ cup sugar
1 tsp. dry mustard

1 small onion, grated
1½ tsp. Worcestershire sauce
3 tsp. salt
½ tsp. pepper

Combine all the ingredients in a jar and shake well.

Pumpkin Bread

Jean always saved this recipe for fall.

3½ cups flour
3 cups sugar
1½ T soda
1½ tsp. salt
1 T cinnamon

1 tsp. nutmeg
4 eggs
1 cup salad oil
⅔ cup water
2 cups canned pumpkin (1 15-oz. can)

Sift flour, sugar, soda, salt, cinnamon and nutmeg. In another bowl, beat eggs, oil, water and pumpkin. Add wet ingredients to dry ingredients. Stir until smooth. Pour into greased pans (half full). Bake at 350° about 1 hour. Cool before removing from pans. Makes several loaves. For a variation you can add nuts or ½ cup powdered rose hips to the dry ingredients.

— Memories of — **Seagull Outfitters**

The original public landing for Seagull Lake was located over the creek and just south of the present Blankenburg Public Landing. On that location Russell and Eve Blankenburg started the first Seagull Outfitters. The Blankenburgs ran the outfitters until 1965 when they sold the business to Stan and Grace Smith. Their daughter, Robin Du Chien, tells about her parents' background and life on the Gunflint Trail:

"My mother and father, Stanley and Grace Smith, moved to the Gunflint Trail in 1937 with two small children. They lived in a small log cabin next to the Gunflint Tower (located on what is now the Kekakabic Trail). To get to the cabin they had to park on the Gunflint Trail and walk up a path for one mile, most of the time carrying supplies and both children. Once while walking up to the tower, my Mother came face to face with a bear. They stared at each other for a while before the bear turned and ran.

"Gunflint Tower was an octagon-shaped metal box set 85' up in the air. This tower was for spotting forest fires. In the center of the room was a fire finder. A fire finder was a map with a rotating eyepiece that the spotter would look through at the smoke and it would tell the coordinates of the fire. The coordinates were then radioed in to the Forest Ranger and he would go put it out. My mother was the spotter and my father was the Forest Ranger.

"In 1940 my parents moved into a house where the current Seagull Guard Station is. They spent the next 23 years working for the US Forest Service. A heart attack in 1963 forced my dad to take an early retirement from the USFS. My brother, Russell, took over Dad's position as Forester in charge of the Seagull Guard Station.

"In 1965 they bought Seagull Canoe Outfitters from Russell and Eve Blankenburg. It consisted of a canoe outfitting business, small campground, and a lunch counter where my Mom served up to 50 people at a time. My parents were very hard working people, as most of the Gunflint Trail people are, working from the time they got up in the morning until they went to bed at night.

"Once a local plane couldn't power down and came right up into the parking lot in front of the building. Fortunately no one got hurt, but it caused quite a commotion. Dad and a number of other people pushed the airplane back into the water.

"Another time, the Hamm's Beer people came up to the end of the Gunflint to shoot a commercial. Dad and I got to paddle a canoe for some of the filming. I don't think any of that footage ever made it into the commercial, but it was fun.

"Sometimes even the 'rich and famous' showed up at our business. My dad took Elizabeth Congdon, from Duluth, on a boat ride to the other end of Seagull Lake and back.

"Sundays were always my favorite day. My brother, Carl, would fly his airplane up to Seagull and deliver our Sunday paper. Not in the usual way, but all wrapped up and thrown out of the airplane to land, hopefully, in the parking lot. I remember chasing it into the lake, the river, up the driveway, or in the parking lot."

"In 1970 they sold the Canoe Outfitters to Janet Hanson and moved into Grand Marais to run the Municipal Campground. They remained at the Campground until 1982.

"The Gunflint Trail was always in their minds and hearts, so when the Forest Service needed a caretaker for the End of The Trail Lodge, back to the end of the trail they went. They stayed there the summers of 1983 and 1984. The Government had bought the Lodge and all of the cabins but one had been removed."

When Janet Hanson bought Seagull Outfitters from Stan and Grace Smith in 1969, she and Justine Kerfoot had just ended their 25-year partnership at Gunflint Northwoods Outfitters. Janet was an experienced canoe outfitter and businesswoman. She wanted to put a new outfitting building at Seagull and knew exactly what kind of building she wanted. In a 1981 interview with the Cook County Historical Society, Janet tells how she and three old timers got the job done.

"I hired three men to build a new building. I wanted that building completed so that it was ready for operation the following spring. I asked Stan Smith about working and he said that he could get a couple of others. He brought down Claus Olson, who was 73, and old Arnie Olson who was 75 or something; Stan was 69. So, I had these old timers who worked for me for $2.50 an hour.

"I had fun with those three old timers. At first, they did not know how to build a building in a swamp. The site was a filled-in area with no solid base for putting posts down below the frost line. It's all water under that swamp. I talked to the Arrowhead Electric and they suggested 32-foot creosoted telephone poles laid flat with the building on top of them.

"They dug holes 8 inches deep and made pads about three-foot square, one for each post. I think there were probably 15 of those pads. They poured the concrete and then built right on top of them. That darn building hasn't moved; the frost would heave up one corner maybe an inch or two and then it would settle right down on the concrete pad. At the end of the second week the men had started to frame in the building and were really just going lickety-split. I was pleased at how fast those three carpenters could produce.

"I did all the planning; all of the buying and paid for all the materials, and I just paid them for their labor. There were a lot of things they knew that I didn't know but there were a few things that I had to learn that they didn't know how to do. I didn't know that they had never built a two-story building. So, they built a one-story building and then they started all over again and built another story on top of it. They used twice as many 2x8s and 2x6s as they needed. That building is never going to fall down because it is so beautifully constructed.

"Friday came and that was payday. At that point I said, 'Now I want you guys to come in the kitchen when you get through this afternoon; I'm going to give you hell.' They really were worried about this woman. They said, 'Is she another Eve Blankenburg?' Eve would always yell at everybody. They got into the kitchen and there in the middle of the kitchen table was a quart of whiskey and glasses for them and their paychecks. Those carpenters said, 'Is this what you mean by giving us hell?' From then on, every two weeks, that was the procedure. Those men would do anything in the world for me until it came to figuring out how to do the sanctuary arches.

"When it came to putting the roof on over an open span, 30-foot wide, they did not know how to build one without partitions and without a floor under it to support the roof. I had to go to a preacher who knew a little about building sanctuary arches because every church has an open sanctuary. It had to be possible somehow. After I told the men how to build the trusses for that sanctuary arch, Arnie and Stan wouldn't believe me, and Arnie said, 'I'm going off. I'm not going to get caught in that.' But the other Olson was more interested in working. He lived up there on Seagull River so he came down one day and laid out one of those sanctuary arches, the truss for it. He looked at it when he got all through and he said, 'You wait awhile.'

"He went up and found Arnie and Stan and he brought them down. He showed it to them. Then they were convinced and they went ahead and they made them all. Then they told me, 'Now tomorrow morning we need ten people here; we're going to put those all up at once.' I called around and the End of the Trail sent me somebody, Chik-Wauk sent me a man, Archie Sr. came down, and the Forestry man came up, that was young Russell Smith. I was on the end of the pulley with one of the men. Arnie Olson, who was a sailor during the first World War and used to being up high was way up on the peak. Each one of these heavy arches was raised up on a gin pole that had to be 36 feet tall because the peak was 32 feet. They were lifted with a block and tackle. Each truss was carried to the foot of the pole, put on the block and tackle and hauled up then swung around the pole. Two men would slide it right down the sides of the building into place. Arnie was up on top nailing a board to each to hold them 16 inches apart. By 11 o'clock we were all done. We had a big party, believe me.

"Finally the roof boards, 4x8' sheets of plywood, were nailed down and covered with tarpaper on it and they looked at that darn thing. By that time it was the end of November and the snow was coming. They said, 'We'll do the roofing in the spring.' I said, 'Fine, that's alright. It will winter that way okay.'"

As might be imagined, Janet did not spend a lot of time cooking. Like her old partner, Justine Kerfoot, Janet's talents lay in other directions.

Janet sold her outfitting business to Bob and Nancy Wendt in 1973. The Wendts were from the Chicago area and had three children. They juggled jobs at home and summers on Seagull for four seasons and then the business went back to Janet Hanson in 1976. The following year she sold it to Lynn Paulrud and David Canfield. They in turn sold it to the government as part of the 1978 Wilderness Bill.

Today there is still a Seagull Outfitters on Seagull Lake but at a different location. This second business started life as Portage Outfitters and was owned by Russell and Eve Blankenburg. The Blankenburgs sold to Earl Darst who later sold to Debbie Mark. Debbie now runs the outfitters with its new name, Seagull Canoe Outfitters.

Did you know . . .

An added bonus for Seagull Outfitters and Seagull Resort owners are the sunsets each night. City dwellers often lose sunsets (and sunrises) in all the buildings around them. Here the sunsets are in full view for all to see.

Janet Hanson got much of her knowledge of the canoe country from her guests. One party would tell her about something special to see on their route or a great campsite or a good fishing hole. Janet never forgot and would tell later parties about these special places.

— Memories of —
Wildwood Lodge

In *Ki-osh-kons: People, Places and Stories of Sea Gull Lake*, Janna Webster tells how Andy Mayo and Martha Bauman came to the lake the first time. They stopped at Jimmy Dunn's to introduce themselves. Later someone asked Jimmy who they were and he said "Andy and Sue Mayo." From then on Martha Bauman was known as Sue.

Two resorts were located on the west end of the lake. Andy and Sue Mayo started, owned and operated Wildwood Lodge. Sue Mayo expertly cooked all the guest meals on a wood-fired stove. Janna tells one of Sue's favorite ways of making new guests feel welcome.

"Many of Wildwood's guests returned year after year but when a new guest sat down in the lodge for his first breakfast he was treated to Sue's 'flannel cakes.' Sue would pour a bit of pancake batter on the grill then surreptitiously place a circle of cotton flannel on the batter. This was covered with more batter and cooked to golden perfection. The return guests tried to contain their laughter as the unsuspecting new guy tried to cut into the steaming pile of cakes."

Martha Bauman and Andy Mayo
with guest

In 1939 Sue Mayo wrote an article for the *Cook County News Herald* about the dedication of their outdoor fireplace. This is how Sue told the story:

"Monday we had a little ceremony at the building of an outdoor fireplace which was so impressive. I thought you would like to know about it. In the morning the guests gathered the stones, the men bringing the large ones. They were put in place, making a fireplace eight feet wide by six feet high. A place was left in one wing where we buried a sealed tin in cement with the names of all the guests present—twenty-two in number. We also put a copy of the prayer for the ascent of the spirit in this tin, and several coins with the year 1939 on them.

Mr. John R. R. Miles and wife and guests were with us, Mr. Miles, acting as master of ceremonies. Reverend David R. Haupt, rector of St. Luke's Episcopal Church of Hastings, Minnesota, composed the lovely prayer, which was given at the lighting of the fire. After the dedication the guests assembled in the dining room where they were served luncheon.

A Prayer for the Ascent of the Spirit

God of great Nature's goodly out-of-doors,
By Whose skilled hands all lovely things are made;
To Thee we dedicate the stones here laid,
To guide and shield whatever fire roars
In vibrant rhythm from this rocky floor
Or only burns in cheery, kindly blaze,
Symbolic of the hospitable ways
Of host and hostess of this rugged shore.

As every kind of fire, large or small,
When weather's wet with rain or skies are fair,
Sends up the incense of its heart to where
Thou reignest Who dost rightly govern all,
So may the hearts of all who here shall be
Through life and death—ascend, dear God, to Thee!"

When Wildwood Lodge sold out, their main lodge building was taken apart by Bob Cushman and towed down Seagull Lake. There Bob and his wife, Marge, reassembled the lodge to become the main lodge and dining room for Sea Island Lodge. Bob said he exhausted a new motor with all the towing.

The totem pole from Wildwood Lodge was bought by Justine Kerfoot. It has stood in the parking lot of Gunflint Lodge ever since. In fact, time and weather have started to take their toll on the totem pole. Robert Kerfoot just had it repainted and moved into the front room of the main lodge. No one, however, knows if the sealed tin was ever removed from the fireplace ring. In fact, no one is really sure where that fireplace ring was on the property.

Sue's Wildwood Lodge Pancakes

Cliff and Hilda Waters, longtime Trail residents, gave Janna the recipe for Sue's pancakes.

1 egg (separated) per cup of flour
sweetener, sugar or use honey for better browning
shortening
dash of salt

Mix flour, sugar, salt and egg yolks. Stir in melted shortening. Whip egg whites until frothy and gently fold into flour mixture. Fry on griddle.

Did you know . . .

Resorts such as Wildwood Lodge with no road access occasionally needed tractors to help with building projects. These heavy pieces of machinery were brought over during the winter on the ice. Logging trucks even ran on solid ice during the winter. It is said that the trucks were always going uphill because the weight of the logs pushed the ice down at the back of the truck.

— Memories of —
Windigo Point

Jimmy Dunn was one of a number of men who first came up to this area as guides and later operated their own businesses. Some of the other men were Charley Boostrom at Clearwater Lodge, Dave Clark from Rockwood Lodge, Rolf Skrien at Way of the Wilderness Outfitters and Benny Ambrose on Ottertrack Lake.

Janna Webster's book also tells the story of Jimmy Dunn who started Windigo Point. Another glimpse into Jimmy's life comes from a diary he kept in 1935. Most of the entries are short and terse, and almost always give the weather. They also show that the west end of Seagull was a busy place even in the winter. Jimmy was a great friend of the Mayos at Wildwood and they exchanged visits regularly. Groups of Civilian Conservation Corps boys would stop by overnight on their way into the wilderness. Charley Boostrom would spend a night with his dog team. Francis Watters was another good friend who exchanged visits with Jimmy. Life was filled with the daily chores of baking, washing clothes, cleaning, shoveling and getting firewood. There is just enough in the diary to make the reader wish for a lot more information about life on Seagull Lake.

"Dunn had purchased a new speed boat that had won the outboard motor boat races on Pike Lake. The boat was capable of going 33 mph and making the six-mile trip from Windigo Point to the Seagull public landing in just 12 minutes."

The other resort at the west end of Seagull Lake was Windigo Point. Janna Webster gave this outline of the start of Windigo Point and its originator, Jimmy Dunn.

"Jim Dunn came to the Arrowhead region of Minnesota in 1913. He logged and trapped for a few years before becoming a guide in the mid-Gunflint Trail area. In 1926 he purchased land on Seagull Lake and started building a small resort, which would open in 1929. He built a house, three rental cabins, a boathouse and an ice house. For the first summer Windigo Point was open, Dunn had purchased a new speed boat that had won the outboard motor boat races on Pike Lake. The boat was capable of going 33 mph and making the six-mile trip from Windigo Point to the Seagull public landing in just 12 minutes.

"Dunn was a small, wiry Scotsman who was able to wear a pair of ladies size 6½ knee-high leader boots left by a guest. He was a very capable canoe and fishing guide, a master storyteller and a craftsman. Dunn made most of the furniture for his cabins as well as some items for the Tibbetts cabin.

"Most of the guests at Windigo Point were canoeists or fishermen, although Dunn did entertain a few families and honeymooners. In the 1930s he served as canoe guide for a group of young men who turned out to be the Ohio State University basketball team. Some time later when the OSU team beat the University of Minnesota, all the players signed the game ball and sent it to Dunn. That ball became one of his prize possessions.

"Another guest of Dunn's was responsible for naming a Seagull island. One Mrs. Terry was out for a day of fishing when she hooked a large lake trout. Dunn circled a small island several times as Mrs. Terry struggled to land the fish. When the trophy trout was finally in the boat, the lady asked to be put ashore as in all the excitement she had wet her pants. To this day the island is known as Terry's Island.

Jimmy Dunn

"As with most other residents of the lake, Dunn had no road access to his home and resort. All supplies had to be transported across water or ice and, depending upon the weather and conditions, it could be a treacherous journey. Guide, Ray Nelson, and Dunn drove a Model A Ford from the landing down to Windigo Point on four inches of ice. They had taken some precautions though; they had cut long spruce poles and tied one under each bumper in case a wheel dropped through the ice."

In 1947 Harry and Genevieve Brown bought Windigo Lodge from the estate of Jimmy Dunn. In 1949, two years after they bought Windigo Point, Genevieve started keeping a diary of their days on Seagull. She continued that diary for all the summers they spent on the Gunflint Trail. The Seagull portion of her diary is particularly interesting because it paints a small picture of the life on a resort at that time. The diary shows a mixture of resort business, family business, lake activities and weather.

Weather comments usually reflected on various activities at the resort. It was a cold day in June but the kids still went swimming. It was a beautiful drying day or it was cloudy and the clothes had to hang out for three days. Windy days meant it was difficult to get back and forth to the landing on the east end of Seagull where the road was.

Through the years Genevieve also recorded events in their family life. Three of their children had summer birthdays and the diary notes parties, gifts, and cakes. July 28, 1949, notes that it was "Gail's Second Birthday. Had wiener roast on rock Dock. The Dietz's furnished wieners and joined us. Gail pleased with birthday cake and chocolate candy bar which she hovered over for herself. She received "Blue Jeans" from Winnie, Cub Laundry Bag, Candy bars, Picture Books from Mrs. Tibs. [Mary Tibbetts Roberts], paddle from Sue, $.25 from Runyon from Springfield, Ill., and 10 cents for each of the others." That same year Genevieve noted that, "Carol washed her own hair for the first time. 4 p.m. Bud took her to Carlson's and Lil cut off her pigtails!"

Jimmy Dunn

The boys, Bruce and Jerry, were older and helped with chores around camp. They made trips to the landing taking guests, picking up groceries or hauling barrels of gas. They helped paint boats and cleaned the boathouse with their father. In 1953 Genevieve first notes that Bruce guided some fishermen. There was also time for the boys to explore the area with their father. On August 17, 1949, Genevieve states, "Bud, Bruce and Jerry started out with the aluminum canoe and motor for an overnight trip."

Harry Brown's projects around the camp were noted. He regularly guided guests on fishing trips. Rain or shine, at all hours of the day, hauling guests and supplies to and from the landing was another constant job of Harry's. Painting and varnishing in their home and the cabins was done every year. In the fall of 1951, he moved the boathouse. Genevieve says, "Began boathouse moving. Took it down log by log, marked the logs and rebuilt about 30 ft. farther back from water."

Genevieve also told about her activities. Every year she planted flowers around the resort. Weekly washing, its size and the weather were duly noted. June 19 was the first wash in 1953. She recorded, "First washing of the season—14 sheets, 70 socks, four sheet blankets, etc., etc.—beautiful drying day." June 19 was also the "first bread baking of the season. Rolls, bread and cinnamon buns." Spring cleaning of their home and all the cabins was a regular job. Ironing was done in the evenings. Meals at home were varied with wiener roasts and fish fries. July 31, 1952, was a typical dinner, "Had fish fry on rock dock. 18 present. Menu: fish, baked potatoes, cole slaw, cake, coffee followed with marshmallow roast.

For several years the entire family took an August trip to Port Arthur and Fort William (now Thunder Bay). They would also make weekend trips to Seagull when the resort was closed. On January 1, 1953, Genevieve wrote, "Spent New Years' Eve and Day (also extra day) with Rolfe and Gail, Bruce, Jerry, Carol, Harry and Gen in the group. Drove over ice in car. Difficult driving down at night because of driving snowfall, ice clear of snow so that part of the going was good—truly a 'Winter Wonderland.' Sue and Andy stopped in on their way to Wildwood. Harry and Bruce helped Andy put up ice. We all ate over at Wildwood."

Of course, the reason for the family's summer at Seagull was to run the resort. In addition to all the maintenance and repairs, they spent a lot of time entertaining their guests. Hikes, berry picking trips and fishing trips helped show the guests the area. Many evenings were spent with the guests making popcorn or ice cream, showing movies, or eating some of Genevieve's baked goods. Many guests returned year after year and Genevieve tells about each of their trips.

Today the Seagull Lake of those years seems quite isolated, but the Browns were active participants in the life on the lake and on the Gunflint Trail. Their closest neighbors were Mark and Mary Tibbetts who owned a summer home and Sue and Andy Mayo who operated Wildwood Lodge. Genevieve records their adventures, such as the July 17, 1949, entry, "Mrs. Tibbetts experience of swimming from the island to her place to get boat so as to go out and recover canoe which floated away from the island as four of them were picking berries! Two plunges that day!" Sometimes the resort guests and the lake neighbors all socialized together such as on July 26, 1952, "Marshmallow roast in evening. Mary Tibbetts and Peter, the German boy and Mr. Tibbetts joined us. The Becks, Rathjes, Bill Beck and Peter furnished violin music. Beautiful evening – stayed around fire until 11 p.m." Neighbors interacted on a regular basis to help each other. Genevieve would put up Mary Tibbetts's hair in pin curls and Andy Mayo would help put a new roof on the Brown's lodge.

In its quiet, low-keyed style, Genevieve Brown's diary records a life that many of us will never experience. Sure, there was lots of work to do but there was also time to enjoy guests, neighbors and the lake. Many of the modern "necessities" such as TV and shopping malls were not available, but they didn't seem to miss them. The radio brought in news of the outside world and the mail brought the Sears order with new clothes. Sometimes we might all like to turn back the clock.

In 1957, the Browns sold the property to the Izaak Walton League.

Did you know . . .

Genevieve's diaries remind us that the most reliable source of clothing in the Northwoods was still the Sears catalog. She wrote about ordering clothes for her children and when the shipment arrived. This kind of shopping happened up and down the Gunflint Trail.

During World War II both Wildwood Lodge and Windigo Lodge were closed. Andy Mayo and Jimmy Dunn went west to work in war production plants. Jimmy then came down with cancer and was never able to return to the lodge.

Boundary Waters Adventures

Cindy and Tony Faras are two of the newest resort owners on the Trail. Cindy relates a little about their move up here:

"Both Tony and I had a dream of returning to the Northwoods and getting involved in the resort business. As a kid I grew up in the 'sticks,' and as far back as I can remember I dreamed of living in a log cabin in the woods. Little did I know that I'd leave the urban lifestyle in Minneapolis as a hair designer, trade in my scissors for a chainsaw, and crawl through the window of that dream. My husband, Tony, owned a cabin on Seagull Lake and we both visited the Gunflint Area for years. We decided to make it our home."

Cindy and Tony had the opportunity to own a resort in 1992 when several resorts became available for purchase. "After serious consideration, Tony and I decided that rather than purchasing an existing resort, we would develop our own business. Thus, Boundary Waters Adventures!

"Our business is unique in providing our guests with private cabins on individual parcels of property. With this in mind we purchased property on Saganaga and Seagull lakes and built a new log cabin and renovated several existing cabins to rent. For five years, every day was some kind of adventure. Clearing land, hauling, tearing down, sanding, painting and septic systems brought us to our senses.

"After five years we now own one of the most unique rental cabins on Seagull Lake. The little log cabin was built in 1934 by Bill and Margarite Henton. We bought it from their son, Jim. By the time we purchased it in 1995 it was old and in need of some TLC. The cabin became our baby and was restored to the charming, warm cabin it was meant to be. It rents May through September. To keep its history, we still call it The Henton Cabin.

"Over the years we have had many adventures beyond the renovating and renting of cabins. On a warm summer day a friend and I hiked out of Jap Lake. In the middle of the tough two-mile portage, we came across a camper in cardiac arrest. Another time in April, Tony and I rescued our neighbor and our dog, who had fallen through the ice on Seagull Lake. In addition we have had snow-ins, blowdowns and fire threats.

"These adventures were both interesting and challenging, but life up here is worth the effort. One only needs to smell the woods, the earth, our home, or hear the call of the first loon returning in the spring. These can leave you breathless. They are the daily reminders of the magnificent things of our Creator."

BORSCHT (BEET STEW)

Americans normally think of Borscht as just beet and cabbage soup. This recipe is much more complex and adds additional flavors to the combination.

1½ lbs. stew meat
flour
2 cans beef broth
3 tsp. salt
1 tsp. pepper
1 large onion, diced
2 cloves garlic, minced
2 to 3 tsp. dill

1 tsp. allspice
⅓ cup red wine vinegar
2 cans (15 oz.) beets plus their liquid
   or 6 medium cooked beets
3 medium quartered potatoes
1 small head cabbage, sliced
sour cream

Flour and brown the meat in a Dutch oven. Add the rest of the ingredients except beets, potatoes, cabbage and sour cream. Cover and simmer until beef is tender, about 1½–2 hours. Add beets, potatoes and cabbage. Cook until potatoes are tender. Serve in big bowls with a big dollop of sour cream on top and crunchy French bread on the side.

CHICKEN CACCIATORE

Artichoke hearts add new flavors to this traditional Italian recipe.

6 chicken breasts, skinned and boned
flour
1 large can diced tomatoes
½ lb. sliced mushrooms
4 cloves minced garlic
1½ tsp. salt
½–1 tsp. oregano
2 small jars marinated artichoke hearts, drained and chopped (save the liquid)
¾ cup dry sherry

Flour chicken and brown in oil in frying pan. Place chicken in a 9x13" glass baking dish. Place tomatoes and mushrooms around the chicken. Blend garlic and spices and pour over chicken. Bake 60 minutes at 350°. Add chopped artichokes and sherry. Bake 10 more minutes. Serve over ravioli or risotto, with a fresh green salad with feta cheese and olives.

MOM'S REFRIGERATOR PICKLES

In rural areas, gardening and canning your own produce have always been popular.

7 cucumbers, sliced
2 cups sugar
2 T salt
1 cup green pepper, diced

1 cup onion, diced
1 cup white vinegar
1 T celery seed

Combine all ingredients. Refrigerate for 3 weeks before eating.

LOG CABIN CHOCOLATE CAKE

Cindy says: "This great recipe is from my great-grandmother. I can still hear her say in her Swedish accent, 'I came to this country in nineteen-o-two.' She was 101 years old when she died. I love this cake so much that I served it at my wedding."

2⅔ cups flour
2 cups sugar
⅔ cups cocoa
2 tsp. baking soda
1 tsp. salt

2 eggs
2 cups cold coffee
1 cup oil
2 tsp. vanilla

Combine all ingredients in a mixing bowl and beat at high speed about 2–3 minutes. Pour into a 9x13" pan and bake at 350° for 35 minutes.

WHITE TOPPING for LOG CABIN CHOCOLATE CAKE

5 T flour
1 cup milk
1 cup butter

1 cup sugar
1 tsp. vanilla

Cook flour and milk in a saucepan until thick. Cool. Cream butter and sugar and vanilla. Beat in flour and milk mixture one tablespoon at a time until thick and fluffy.

Seagull Canoe Outfitters and Cabins

When Russell Blankenburg began filling in the lowland where this outfitters stands, his neighbors wondered what was going on. Russell soon sold to Earl Darst, and Portage Outfitters was started. The local joke was that it would all sink back into the lake and so the outfitters was sometimes called Underwater Outfitters. Well, Russell had the last laugh as the business is still standing on firm land.

Right off the Gunflint Trail, just before Island Road, is Seagull Canoe Outfitters and Cabins. The owner, Deb Mark, is a second-generation Gunflint Trail owner. Her family started at Tuscarora Lodge. Deb has taken some time to tell of her own memories of growing up on the Trail and how she ended up owning a canoe outfitters.

Deb Mark

"My recollections about the start of Portage Outfitters by Russell and Eve Blankenburg come from Bob and Marge Cushman who used to own Sea Island Lodge. Both Bob and Marge used to tell me how the land was simply a swamp and how the Blankenburgs just kept hauling dirt for fill. Of course Bob, being in the dirt business, would know all about this. I do know that it was sold to four gentlemen from Louisville, one of which I believe was Earl Darst.

"I have a very vivid memory of the day my family moved to the Gunflint Trail. My mom, my sister Lin and I were in the station wagon pulling a boat trailer stacked with 3 boats. My dad and my other sister Pip, along with our black lab Peabody, were in the truck loaded with our belongings. My folks had decided it was time to leave the resort business in Grand Rapids, MN, as it was becoming too populated, and move to the Gunflint Trail. We pulled up in front of the old brick schoolhouse in Grand Marais to register for classes. I was in 2nd grade.

"My folks had bought Tuscarora Lodge and Outfitters on Round Lake from Frank and Agnes Fuller. Frank spent some time with us that first summer showing my folks the ropes around the resort. In addition to that he used to 'race' each of us girls to the dock. I think he was trying to maintain his youth. Surprisingly he even outraced us some days. He would take us fishing and tell stories of his life on the Trail. It was the beginning of a lifelong friendship with Frank until the day he passed on. I can still hear his laugh and feel his zest for life. Even after moving to Minneapolis his heart was still in the woods.

"My grandmother would take us overnight camping down to Ham Lake. My two sisters, my grandmother and I would all get into one 18' aluminum canoe. Pip and I would portage that canoe together to Ham Lake. At 10 and 12 years old that was quite a feat."

"I quickly became enthralled with my life as a kid on the Gunflint Trail. My special moments were choosing which fishing hole to go to after school. It all depended on the wind that day as it does yet today. I had one spot that I would hike to and fish from a rock. My favorite fishing outing, though, was to hop in a canoe and sit in the bow seat facing the stern and paddle out into Round Lake to my 'secret' hole. The special thing about this spot was being able to watch a walleye, perch, bass or pike take my bait. I would never tire of that and it started a lifelong love of fishing for me. In addition to that, my grandmother would take us overnight camping down to Ham Lake. My two sisters, my grandmother and I would all get into one 18' aluminum canoe. Pip and I would portage that canoe together to Ham Lake. At 10 and 12 years old that was quite a feat.

"We used to ride the school bus 50 miles each way to school and back in Grand Marais. When my folks were busy with the resort and couldn't get away to drive the mile out to the bus we had to walk home. We oftentimes took the power line home from the Cross River as it would shorten our hike. I recall scurrying up the hill in our dresses to take the shortcut home. Neighborhood kids were few and far between in those days. My two sisters and I developed a very strong bond as we had nobody but ourselves. That bond remains today. I recall many evenings spent in the old lodge drawing fishing flies together. As we got older we used to go out into the pickup truck at night and tune into WLS radio out of Chicago.

"An older woman by the name of Kelly moved with my family from Grand Rapids, MN, to the Gunflint Trail. Kelly was like a grandmother to us. My sisters and I lived with Kelly in a little one room cabin in the woods about a block from the main lodge at Tuscarora. The lodge was not large enough for the whole family. Many days I remember walking on the path to the lodge with my

Deb Mark at Seagull Outfitter's dock

nose in a book and coming upon either Bruno or Dirty Pierre. They were the two black bears that hung out around the resort like pets. In the winter we moved to a rental cabin where we could all be together as a family. Kelly would go back to her family in Grand Rapids for the winter. We had no running water in the winter growing up as a kid. I had long hair at the time and used to carry two buckets of water from the lake, one to wash and one to rinse my hair.

"My sisters and I became the cabin cleaning crew once we got a little older. We had seven cabins to clean each Saturday and three bunkhouses. I don't recall exactly how old we were but I do remember taking a nap in the bunkhouses as we were getting pretty tired at that point. Growing up in the resort business also involved helping my folks in the spring and fall before getting on the school bus. My job was to fry the bacon each morning. I had two griddles of bacon frying before hopping on the bus. Joe Denham, the bus driver at the time, used to tease me about wearing my 'baco-bits

View of the lake from Seagull Outfitters

perfume.' As we got a little older we had full-time summer jobs at the resort. My job was to run the trading post and collect the customer money. I remember nodding off now and then to be awakened by a guest walking in the door. Those were some long hours for a kid.

"Our winters were spent ice skating out on the lake. I always thought it was so special to see the rocks under the ice when in reality we were skating on some pretty thin ice. We would take our snowmobiles and go trout fishing over at Tuscarora Lake and oftentimes push our machines back up the steep portage out of Tuscarora.

"I decided to get a job in a city and see what that was all about. I ended up taking the city bus to work and it didn't take me too long to wonder what I was doing in that environment. I longed for the lakes and woods of the north country."

"Resort business started flourishing on the Gunflint back in those days and I remember my folks putting money away to take us on long winter vacations. Our first trip was three weeks in Mexico as a family taking the buses all through the little villages. After coming from a sheltered life on the Gunflint that was quite a change to ride the same buses with the chickens on top. Pip, Lin and I would always fight over who had to ride on the bus seat with someone we didn't know. It began a lifelong passion for travel.

"After going off to college for four years I decided to get a job in a city and see what that was all about. I ended up taking the city bus to work and it didn't take me too long to wonder what I was doing in that environment. I longed for the lakes and woods of the north country. I spent some time working in Colorado in the winters and on the Trail in the summers. That was the best of all worlds until one day I decided it was time to settle down. I bought Portage Seagull Outfitters on Seagull Lake and changed the name to Seagull Outfitters.

Deb Mark

"My life as a kid on the Gunflint shaped my life down the road as an owner on the Gunflint. I was accustomed at an early age to the long hours, strong work ethic, dealing with customers and working for oneself. The transition from the kid of resort owners to a resort owner myself was smooth for me.

"I have owned Seagull Outfitters for 18 years now and it is a way of life for me. I love my job and the many interesting and appreciative customers that I meet from all over the world. Life on the Trail has changed immensely from the days of carrying water to wash one's hair and every-other-day mail delivery, to the real world of the Internet and satellite TV. Canoes have become lighter and faster. Gone are the days of marketing the business at trade shows. The fires on the Gunflint and the Blowdown of 1999 have changed the landscape forever. Some of my favorite spots along the trail look so different now. But then life is all about change. The Northwoods is in my blood and my heart is here. It is home to me. I grew up surrounded by these same lakes, trees, loons and wildlife. I couldn't imagine doing anything else. I feel privileged to be here."

MAGGIE'S CRAZY CHOCOLATE CAKE

This recipe is from Deb's grandmother, Maggie.

3 cups flour
2 cups sugar
6 T cocoa
2 tsp. baking soda
1 tsp. salt
¾ cup oil
2 T vinegar
2 tsp. vanilla
2 cups cold water

Mix all ingredients and pour into ungreased 9x13" cake pan. Bake at 350° for 30–40 minutes.

Did you know . . .

As a person stands on the dock of Seagull Outfitters and looks out, there is no hint of the numerous islands to pass and large lake to cross as you paddle west to the far shore of Seagull. A quick look at a map shows how little you see of this magnificent lake.

— Memories of —
Sea Island Lodge

At the end of Island Road is another longtime Seagull Lake resort. It started out life as Diamond Willow Lodge. When Bob and Marge Cushman bought it, they renamed it Sea Island Lodge. Marge was well known for her wonderful meals while everyone knew that Bob could fix anything.

Sea Island Lodge began its business career as a dream of Bob Cushman's. It became a reality as he and Marge and their three kids jumped into a land purchase in 1955. They escaped the corporate world by buying Diamond Willow Lodge on the northeast shore of Seagull Lake. At that time there was no road into the property and the previous owners came across the lake from the public landing either by boat or on the ice.

Bob Cushman with the 25th wedding anniversary gift that he gave to Marge

There were about four cabins on the property that had been built by Richard "Rosie" Rosecrantz and his assorted partners. The plan was for Diamond Willow Lodge to have rental cabins and a main lodge and handcrafted furniture made out of diamond willow. Apparently making ends meet for this group was a bit of a financial problem and in the end a man named Luther Hester had sole possession of the property and sold it to the Cushmans.

First order of business was putting a road in for easier access. Bob Cushman was in his element in this venture where you had to just go ahead and do it yourself and figure out how to make it work. It is possible that this wasn't exactly what Marge had in mind as a career move, but she came nonetheless and pitched in hard. She rode a pull-grader, drove the assorted trucks to try and get the assorted "cats" unstuck, in the meantime raised three kids and wondered just where the money was going to come from season to season. It is probably a very good thing that she had no idea what she was getting into!

In 1956 the log lodge building from Wildwood Lodge at the far end of Seagull was being auctioned off. This was a result of the Wilderness Act that incorporated the western end of Seagull into the wilderness and necessitated the removal of several resorts and cabins. Bob and Marge were the high bidders (at $500) and now owned a wonderful log building at the wrong end of a long lake. The physical effort to move it was astounding but the foresight and dreams of what they might do with it certainly were more than enough to carry them through.

It was fairly well established at its new site by 1958 and Marge opened her dining room in 1960. This was more her forte and with her talent as a cook it didn't take long for the good food reputation to take hold. She was and still is a marvelous hostess and always enjoys entertaining. Running a resort, of course, is a lot more than entertaining . . . laundry, cleaning, fixing pipes, putting up firewood, bookkeeping, hiring help, painting, and maybe taking care of your family on the side.

The Cushmans were good at it though. Every year they would tear down a cabin and replace it with a new one. Cush did most of this in the winter and Marge would move into town so the kids could go to school. Marge taught home economics in the Grand Marais School for a while. She also took in sewing trying to stretch those few dollars early on. They hired college kids like so many of the Trail resorts to help in the summer.

Workers at Sea Island became part of the family right off the bat. That included both the good and bad parts of being close. As the walls weren't too tight in the back part of the lodge, where the two bedrooms housed the help in one and Bob and Marge in the other, some-times an answer to a question or a comment would come wafting across from an unseen listener. Cushman's son Bobby had a solution to this. When he was a teenager he built an 8x10' shack out back to live in that Marge referred to as the Sulk House.

Marge taught her employees a lot—things they didn't even think about knowing, like how to run a wringer washer and a mangle. It was often said that working for "mother" Marge ought to be a prerequisite for a marriage license. But after twenty years and a million memories Marge and Bob decided it was time to sell.

Kathy and Mike Lande were the next and last owners of Sea Island Lodge. Kathy shares the story of their beginning as resorters.

Bob and Marge Cushman

"In 1978 my husband Mike and I bought Sea Island Lodge from the Cushmans. They had started phasing out in the late sixties by selling off the individual cabins and then continuing to rent them to tourists when the owners were not using them. We purchased just the lodge building and a little land behind it on Cupid Lake. It worked out well for us, as the initial investment wasn't as large as a multi-cabin resort would have been. Also it was small enough that it didn't take both of us to be here all the time, leaving Mike to pursue his building business.

> "The other was to close the dining room on Wednesday nights in September and go out on a picnic, rain or shine. Rain was the norm, and we have some wonderful memories of rain-soaked hotdog buns and camp cups of very diluted wine."

"Seagull is a spectacular lake to live on. I guess the work mattered very little as long as we could live here. I can't think of a better place to raise a couple of kids. Long days and every day, but time off for good behavior in the winter. I think there is always a tendency to push family priorities too far back in the summer, but we did have two things we tried hard to do. One was to go down the lake on Sunday afternoons for an hour or two. We explored pretty much every nook and cranny on this lake at one time or another. The other was to close the dining room on Wednesday nights in September and go out on a picnic, rain or shine. Rain was the norm and we have some wonderful memories of rain-soaked hotdog buns and camp cups of very diluted wine. We won't include the recipes for these but there is no way we would trade any of it for a gourmet meal.

"It was fun to share the area with old and new guests and rewarding to watch their appreciation for the woods expand with their stay. We made many friends over the years from all walks of life in both the clientele and in the hired help. It would be nice to think we taught them one or two things, but perhaps just exposing them to what nature has to offer was the best. At the very least we learned a lot along the way. And then after twenty plus years it was time for us to be done." Kathy and Mike still live in their home behind what used to be the main lodge.

Reassembling the lodge from Wildwood at Sea Island's property

Did you know . . .

Observant paddlers at the far west end of Seagull will notice that this designated "wilderness" has had some human intervention. A couple of small bushes of white roses, some lilacs, a patch of garlic chives, a few daffodils and an out-of-place oak tree all tell the tale of a property owner from earlier times trying to make the woods look like "home."

One of Rosie Rosencrantz's partners wrote a romance novel centered on the Gunflint Trail. Carlton Williams's book was printed in 1941 and was called *Trailer Doctor*. Two of the residents mentioned are Russell and Eve Blankenburg.

Marge's Rolls

Here are a couple of Kath's favorite recipes. Even if you've never eaten at Sea Island, you'll find that your mouth starts to water just reading the recipes.

    1 cup hot water
    ⅓ cup white sugar
    ⅓ cup melted butter
    1 tsp. salt
    1 cup cool water
    2 T yeast
    5 cups flour, divided
    1 egg

Stir hot water, sugar, butter and salt together in large mixing bowl. Add cool water and yeast and stir until dissolved. Stir in 2½ cups flour. Add egg and beat well. Stir in another 2½ cups flour. Turn out onto a floured surface and knead lightly until soft and elastic. Put back in bowl and let rise until doubled. Form into desired shapes and put on greased cookie sheets. Let rise until doubled again, about one hour. Bake at 350° for 10–12 minutes. While warm, brush with a light glaze of powdered sugar and water. Serve fresh, as they don't keep well.

Onion Pie

HERITAGE

    saltine crackers
    1 stick of butter or margarine
    1 medium onion, sliced
    2 eggs
    1 cup milk (about)
    salt and pepper to taste
    1½ cups cheddar cheese, shredded

Crush enough saltine crackers to cover the bottom and sides of an 8" pie pan. In a skillet, melt a stick of butter or margarine and pour most of it over the cracker crumbs. Stir melted butter into the crumbs with a fork and press into sides and bottom of pan to make the crust. Saute onion in remaining butter in a skillet until translucent. Put onions into crust. Mix eggs, milk, salt and pepper together. Pour over onions. Top pie with shredded cheese. Bake in a 350° oven until brown on top and set, about 30 minutes.

Wilderness Canoe Base

Wilderness Canoe Base was the brainchild of Pastor Ham Muus. He and his wife Pearl were part of the formation of the North Minneapolis Plymouth Christian Youth Center. While understanding that their work in the inner city was important, they felt that a canoe camp in the Boundary Waters could be an important outreach program for the young people and families that utilized the Youth Center.

Ham Muus tells the story of his dream: "For almost five decades, Wilderness Canoe Base has served youth and families through extensive Boundary Waters adventures. Wilderness has at its core the commitment to spiritual direction."

The goal of the Plymouth Christian Youth Center's Boundary Waters outreach program was to provide positive experiences for needy youth through camping. In the summer of 1954, Pearl and Ham first talked with Russell and Eve Blankenburg about acquiring some land on Seagull Lake for the establishment of a canoe camp base. They agreed that Fishhook Island in the northeastern part of Seagull Lake would be suitable. Handshakes sealed the deal in 1956.

Pearl had grown up on a western Minnesota dairy farm. After she and Ham married, she enjoyed spending time on Lake Superior's North Shore at their family cabin. She remembers the first years at Wilderness Canoe Base.

"The trips up the Gunflint to work and serve at Wilderness were always special. It seemed like another country with more beauty, a little more character, and certainly more adventure. The rich history and natural wonders put me back in touch with feelings of peace and respect I had known while growing up on a farm. A fresh dimension!

"I stayed down on the North Shore the first summer (1957) with our three-year-old. Somehow it seemed the male staff at that time had all they could do to survive, handle campers and carve out an existence with nothing but the old green army tent for starters.

"Let me tell you my first island visit! Ham's mom and dad, aunt, Nathan and myself prepared mountains of sandwiches, cooked chicken, brought chocolate cake and bread. We knew conditions were extremely difficult with over 20 days of rain. At least this wouldn't make extra work; we would picnic with the mosquitoes! Our lunch was the big meal of the month for hungry guys who had been working hard. Their appreciation and welcome was typical of Wilderness spirit."

The extremely rugged living of 1957 gradually gave way to more workable conditions. In the late summer of 1958, log cabins from Seagull Lake's Miles Island were dismantled and reassembled on Fishhook Island. A cabin with one room to sleep in and a half-screen cabin for cooking became summer home for Pearl, Ham and their three very young children: Nathan, Jeffrey and Solveig. Pearl's Morningside cabin became a central hospitality and meeting place. Of Pearl, Ham says, "Her profound sense of hospitality and her ability to cope in difficult situations made her invaluable throughout the beginning decade of Wilderness outreach."

Pearl adds, "Ham and I tried to create an atmosphere of hospitality where everyone was welcome. We worked at that. We tried to have staff to our quarters most evenings to get to know each other. Popcorn and the fondue pot offered a little variety with time to talk about our world and ministry at Wilderness.

"Mary Ekstrom and Dianne Anderson lived with us and participated as daughter/staffers. We baked, did laundry with the gas machine in the woods, hosted staffers, their parents and visitors alike. The sounds, smells, sights being in God's creation made all efforts of Seagull Lake hospitality exciting and important." Pearl valued her relationships with their neighbors on Seagull, and particularly enjoyed the saunas with Hilma Bergstrom and Eve Blankenburg.

Following the first season of operation in 1957, Ham and Pearl determined that a cook/food service person was a necessity. The camp was growing and the need for a more efficient meal plan in camp and on the trails was obvious. They found the perfect person in Beulah Lukason, a student at the University of Minnesota, St. Paul, and a member of the Clovia House.

Beulah has some memories to share from Wilderness Canoe Base. "Many of the guides and counselors who began at Wilderness had little experience in handling food, especially preparing Trail meals. I often was called upon to offer very basic assistance such as how much water to add to oatmeal or macaroni, how long to cook, etc. The variables of the open fires and weather were factors. Some staffers became very efficient in making lefse or pizza crust rolled on a canoe bottom. Some became expert pie bakers with reflector ovens using fresh gooseberries or blueberries. A few, of course, specialized in backpack stews! It was lots of fun to be able to teach the basics of cooking plus cleanliness around the 'kitchen' and how to improvise.

"We had an especially busy month of July during my first season. In addition to groups from the city, Red Wing and County Probation, we had two work camp volunteer groups. Pastor Ham came to me in early August to say that our Open House guests might number 200 or so. I almost panicked. We were dependent upon our cooler at Blankenburg's Landing since our own ice house was running low. We had no electricity on the island, you know. For some reason, I decided to serve glorified rice plus some "Beulah Bread," sliced salami, cheese, carrot sticks and a pan cake. I had never made any rice dish in that quantity. What an adventure it was! As the rice cooked, I filled every kettle in the kitchen, called for the large pots from the trail cook kits, and prayed for the best. Eve Blankenburg helped organize our cooked rice supply at the mainland cooler.

"On the chosen Open House Sunday, I called on all available staff and early guest volunteers to stir up the mountains of glorified rice and crushed pineapple and whipped cream. We literally served the 5000 after the worship service, with enough left to satisfy any rice desire for the balance of the summer. Happily, guests and campers all politely said, 'the best I've ever eaten.' I slept soundly that night!"

The winter of 1959 saw the Wilderness Canoe Base team dismantling and moving of log cabins from within the Boundary Waters Canoe Area. Ham recalls, "The logistics for this were mind boggling and included feeding and caring for over 60 volunteers over a month of bitterly cold weather. Pearl, Beulah Lukason and others kept the operation going."

Ham and Pearl felt that another important meal for the campers was the reception meal they shared upon their return to Wilderness Canoe Base from their adventures. Ham remembers, "We felt this was especially important as a sign of recognition for their accomplishments and as a symbol of Wilderness hospitality. We would always bake loaf upon loaf of "Beulah Bread" (as it came to be known) with homemade jams and jellies. The central entree was most often baked apples and roasted turkey with mashed potatoes and giblet gravy. The often famished campers were pleased and surprised."

Did you know . . .

Wilderness Canoe Base's two islands are connected by a beautiful bridge. First-time canoeists paddling by are always startled to see the bridge.

The chapel at Wilderness Canoe Base is frequently the setting for weddings of counselors and campers who meet here.

BEULAH BREAD

Hundreds of campers every year would go home remembering this all-time camp favorite.

½ cup warm water (not hot, about 110–115°)
2 pkgs. active dry yeast
1¾ cups lukewarm milk, water or potato water
3 T sugar
2½ tsp. salt
2 T soft shortening
7–7½ cups flour

Measure warm water into a mixing bowl. Add yeast and stir to dissolve. Stir in milk, sugar, salt, shortening and half of the flour. Mix with spoon until smooth. Add enough remaining flour to handle easily. Mix with hand, squeezing dough between fingers. Knead dough until smooth and elastic and no longer sticks to board or countertop. Round up in greased bowl. Turn to bring greased side up. Cover with damp cloth.

Let rise in warm place (85°) until double (about 1½ hours). When dough is doubled, punch down. Let rise again till almost double (about 30 minutes). Divide dough into 2 portions. Shape each loaf, let rise and bake. Preheat oven to 400°. Bake loaves 25–30 minutes until golden brown and loaves sound hollow when lightly tapped with fingers.

MORNINGSIDE SNACK MIX

With a camp full of counselors and kids, it is no wonder that this snack vanishes.

2 cups stix pretzels
3 cups Corn Chex
3 cups Wheat Chex
3 cups Crispix
2 cups peanuts

6 T melted butter
1 T Worcestershire sauce
¾ tsp. garlic salt
¾ tsp. seasoned salt

Mix the pretzels, cereals and nuts in large roasting pan. Cover with melted butter mixed with seasonings. Bake at 250° for 45 minutes, stirring every 15 minutes. Yields roughly 12–14 cups of great snacking.

COME-ON-IN CARAMEL CORN

Pearl and Ham's home was a magnet for their counselors. The aroma from this recipe just drew in anyone who could smell it.

6–7 cups popped corn
2 cups brown sugar
½ cup butter or margarine
pinch of salt
½ cup corn syrup
1 tsp. baking soda

Place the popped corn in a large buttered pan. Boil the brown sugar, butter, salt and corn syrup. After boiling, add baking soda. Stir well. Pour mixture over popped corn and bake for 30 minutes at 325°, stirring occasionally.

LOG CABIN CRISP BUTTER-SUGAR COOKIES

Pearl's recipe from home was a big success in the Northwoods.

3 cups flour
1 tsp. salt
1 tsp. baking soda
1 tsp. baking powder
1 cup butter
2 eggs
1½ cups sugar
½ tsp. vanilla
½ tsp. almond flavoring

Sift flour, salt, baking soda and baking powder. Mix with butter as for pie crust. Beat eggs. Add sugar to eggs and beat well. Combine ingredients and add vanilla and almond flavoring. Refrigerate overnight. Then roll to desired thickness, cut out, and bake at 350° for 8 minutes.

When short on time: roll into small balls and flatten with a glass dipped in sugar.

Memories of —
Chik-Wauk Lodge

Bea Griffis wrote about their life before they bought Chik-Wauk. "Ralph traveled with a construction company, Grinnell and Daughterty Co. for 12 years, and we had lived in five states, ending up in Taconite Harbor building that power plant for shipping the taconite from the Iron Range." After all those years of traveling, staying in one place must have been a pleasure.

Chik-Wauk Lodge, which means Jack of the Pines in Ojibwe, was built during the 1930s by Ed Nunstedt and his son, Art. Ed's granddaughter, Nancy Nunstedt Bargen, told the story of building the lodge in a 1999 interview with the Cook County Historical Society.

"The first lodge was log. And before they ever had one paying guest, they had all the dishes out on the floor and all the excelsior (wood shavings used as packing material) and the dog knocked over the kerosene lamp and the building caught on fire. The whole thing burnt. Grandpa said, 'Well, now you rebuild.'

> "The first lodge was log. And before they ever had one paying guest . . . the dog knocked over the kerosene lamp and the building caught on fire. The whole thing burnt."

"Only this time they built it out of granite. They got barges and they took granite down from the different islands on Saganaga. So the construction of the lodge is really quite remarkable. They had stone masons up from Duluth at that time because during the Depression they really just worked for room and board.

"They saved the special amethyst rocks for the fireplace. So on the mantel here you have different colors of large amethyst stones. And there is a double fireplace that is both on the living room side and on the dining room side. They also built the furniture they used. It's very rustic. They used an acetylene torch to burn it so it's very dark and very stocky—a sturdy kind of stocky. Jock Richardson did all the blacksmith work. He made all the light fixtures.

"They had eleven cabins and I believe that seven of them were American plan which at that time meant you had food and lodging included. And then there were four housekeeping cabins. The main cabins,

Old Chik-Wauk Lodge

they were all nicely situated away from the lodge. They were in the woods. They had a bridge across the one bay and that was called the Cabin Across the Bridge. And one on a point and none of these had running water.

Chik-Wauk Lodge

"At Chik-Wauk there were mainly husbands and wives that would come up and have their vacation. My mother, Lydia, used to play the piano and she played ragtime. This was after Prohibition and there were a lot of parties. Jock Richardson was a real entertainer. He could sing lots of songs.

"There were a lot of repeat customers. Mother was really a good part of it because she really was an entertainer. She could play ragtime piano and they would play until all hours of the morning. Governor Youngdahl came up. He told her to stop playing the piano and he got her to get up and dance with him. He sang the 'Missouri Waltz' and they waltzed around."

In 1952 Lydia and Art Nunstedt sold Chik-Wauk Lodge to Phyllis and Carl Noyes and Erma and Herb Brugger for $40,000. After two years the Bruggers bought out the Noyes.

Sharon Noyes Eliasen, daughter of Carl and Phyllis, gives a glimpse of what life was like around the resort.

"Leaving Seagull Lake we came to a fork in the road. On the left was End of the Trail Lodge and on the right was Chik-Wauk Lodge. It was 1952. The roads were unpaved and narrow. There was no lake in sight but we turned right, past an ancient log cabin sinking into the ground. It was the guide shack.

Lydia and Art Nunstedt

"Down the hill we saw buildings and a busy boathouse and dock area. There was an ice house with huge blocks of ice covered with sawdust. It made a cool refuge in the summer. The Crow's Nest, a tiny log cabin above the dock area was a favorite for honeymoons. Across the bay was a lone cabin that belongs to Harry Hummitch, who was reputed to be a hermit!

"Looking higher we saw the only stone lodge on the Trail. It was a square building with a large porch overlooking the narrow ribbon of water leading to mighty Saganaga. It had a double-sided stone fireplace in the center with a dining room on one side and a lounge on the other. There were heavy log beams in the ceiling and furniture made by craftsmen. We saw a piano and a lighted jukebox ready for a party. Because we were high above the lake, the view of the channel of Saganaga Lake was spectacular through the many French windows.

"Adjoining the lounge was a small store and next to the dining room was the large kitchen with a big black range. Breakfast and shore lunch preparations were finished and Lola Drouillard was baking a cake with caramel frosting and a graham cracker pie for dinner. I heard that she presented her husband, Pootie, and Ken Skoog with their own pie after they begged all summer for a piece.

Chik-Wauk Lodge

"Out the screen door of the kitchen we saw a row of utility buildings for laundry and storage and a path lead higher to a wooden water tank. Beyond was a fantastic bridge that took us across the bay to another cabin."

In the 1950s, "two kids from Texas," Bea and Ralph Griffis, came up to Minnesota where Ralph took a job supervising construction for part of the Erie Mining plant on Lake Superior. During their time off they explored the country and discovered the Gunflint Trail with Chik-Wauk Lodge on Saganaga Lake. In 1957 they managed Chik-Wauk with Herb and Erma Brugger. The next year Ralph and Bea purchased the resort. It would be their business and summer home for the next forty-two years. Even after selling out to the federal government, they continued to summer here until age made it impossible.

Interior of Chik-Wauk Lodge

Bea wasn't the cook at the lodge but she remembers the women who were. "We had two talented ladies, who became our friends as well as our helpers. Ida Santa Snell was born in Finland, lived at Hibbing, widowed, and had worked raising her four children. It was a delight to have known her and she was very proficient cooking good meals for our guests and our helpers. Ida came back to help Tilly when the Hamm's commercials were made and Ida and Ralph were in them. She flew to Finland (and bought a new bed with her residuals) to visit relatives. She was with us 12 years.

"Tilly Juth, another widow from the Iron Range (Eveleth), born in Croatia, cooked for the Boy Scout Camp on Lake Vermillion for many years and gave us nine years of excellent help."

Chik-Wauk Lodge complex

When Ralph and Bea Griffis were leaving Chik-Wauk after their last summer there, some neighbors helped them clean out and pack things. One of the items they found was a pair of old wooden water skis. Bea told the story of how she once water-skied from Chik-Wauk to the Cache Bay Ranger Station, a distance of about ten miles. Considering the obstacles of islands and rocks just below the surface of the water, that must have been quite a ride.

In 2010 the Gunflint Trail Historical Society opened the Chik-Wauk Museum and Nature Center in the old main lodge of Chik-Wauk Resort. During the summers this unique building now gives both visitors and residents a taste of the history of this area.

Did you know . . .

Chik-Wauk was well known in this area as the home of the Hamm's Beer commercials featuring Sasha the Bear. One of the more interesting stories is of Sasha riding on the gunwales of a canoe and reaching over to swat the water as the canoe motored forward. Of course, the bear weighed more than the man and the motor in the back of the canoe. This problem was solved by putting sacks of cement in the rear of the canoe on the floor.

SWEDISH POTATO SAUSAGE (POTATISHKORV)

This recipe is from Mrs. Lydia Nunstedt at Chik-Wauk Lodge.

  2 lbs. beef
  2½ lbs. pork
  4½ lbs. raw potatoes
  2 T salt
  1 T pepper
  1 T allspice
  2–3 onions, chopped fine

Grind the meat twice, potatoes once. Mix with seasonings and stuff mixture into casings. Do not fill casings too full because the mixture expands some when boiled. Pierce casings in several places to prevent bursting while cooking. Boil gently one hour. These can be kept in a brine for some time if kept in a cool place.

ROMME GROT

Here is one of Lydia's more interesting recipes.

  1 pt. cream
  1 T flour

Add flour to boiling cream until it is about the thickness of cornstarch pudding. Stir constantly while boiling, and pour off butter as it forms. Thin with milk. Serve with melted butter, sugar and cinnamon.

— Memories of —
End of the Trail Lodge

Many of the early owners on the Gunflint Trail felt it was important for their resort's name to also be the name of the lake the resort was located on. Thus Russell Blankenburg started Saganaga Fishing Camp rather than End of the Trail Lodge. Al Hedstrom would change the name when he bought the resort.

Just past Chik-Wauk on Moose Pond Road is the location of End of the Trail Lodge. The land is now used as a public parking area. In 1931 Russell Blankenburg started Saganaga Fishing Camp. In an interview in 1981, Russell tells the story of buying the land for the new resort.

> "When we wanted to build a road to start a place over there, the land we wanted on Saganaga was owned by John P. Weyerhauser, the grandfather of the Weyerhauser Industry."

"When we wanted to build a road to start a place over there, the land we wanted on Saganaga was owned by John P. Weyerhauser, the grandfather of the Weyerhauser Industry, who lived in Tacoma, Washington.

"I wrote a letter to him about buying this and he answered my letter in long-hand, saying he didn't know anything about the land. He said, 'But if you will go to Cloquet, at the timber industries, there and see Hugo Slenk who is more or less their representative there, whatever he does will be alright with me.'

"One day I started out in daylight from here to go to Cloquet but the roads were so bad at that time, you didn't have the blacktop even along the Shore, that I didn't get there until about 7 o'clock that night, a 12-hour trip, even in favorable weather, without snow. I got there too late and all those offices were closed, so I thought, 'Well, as long as I'm here I'll probably go over to see him at his residence.'

"So, I went in the evening, and I told him what I wanted and I showed him this letter from Mr. Weyerhauser. He said, 'Well, the offices are all closed. I have a key and as long as you are here, I will go over there with you and we'll open up the offices and I'll write you out a Contract for Deed.' So, he did that, just by hand, and I got a Contract for Deed. They had a mile and a

Brochure from the Blankenburgs' days at Saganaga Fishing Camp

quarter along this Bay of Saganaga Lake that came down between the Seagull River on the one side and the Bay of Saganaga on the other.

"I bought that from him more or less for about the scale value of the timber on it. It was a very reasonable price and so I bought that property and then we started to build the End of the Trail Lodge."

In 1940 Al Hedstrom of St. Louis, Missouri, started going up to Saganaga Fishing Camp with some buddies on an annual fishing trip. By 1945 Al knew he wanted to buy the resort from Russell. He and Russell agreed on a price, but Eve wasn't interested in selling.

Al later told about how the sale went through the following year. "In 1946 when we arrived, I walked into the kitchen of the lodge and told Eve that I had come up to buy the resort and she had better make up her mind to sell it to me. Her reply was for me to see Russell. After two or three days, I got Russell to set a price on the resort again, but the price had gone up to $35,000. We stayed at the Jack Pines and rented cabins at the resort. After the end of the week we drove back to St. Louis where I had to talk Mary into selling our grocery stores and buying Saganaga Fishing Camp from the Blankenburgs.

Mary and Al Hedstrom with Cheryl, one of their children

Mary wasn't too well sold on leaving St. Louis and buying a resort in northern Minnesota 57 miles from any town away back in the woods (especially since our second daughter, Cheryl, was less than two months old), but I told her that it was my life's ambition and convinced her it was the thing to do. Since supermarkets were being built and it was plain to see by the way shoppers were flocking to them that the day of the corner grocery was at an end, she agreed. I called Russell on the phone and told him that I was mailing him a check for $1,000 as down payment on the resort, and the agreement was that we would take possession on September 15."

Mary was a working partner in the resort from the beginning. Their daughter, Cheryl, recalls, "Mom took care of the kitchen/dining room, the cabins and the laundry (and the house and us kids). Dad took care of the store, the accounting, reservations and the dock/guides. Mom would do the cooking when we didn't have a cook or on the 1st and 2nd cooks' days off (or any other position that needed to be filled). She and Dad used to work 7 days a week about 16 hours a day, but the rest of us used to get one day off a week. I can remember some of the spring days when most of the guests would leave on a Sunday. We'd wait on them for breakfast and then go out and clean cabins, getting done in time to go down to the lake and soak our feet and then back into the dining room to serve dinner. Hopefully, the labor laws have brought the workday down to something a little easier these days. But we had fun as we worked because a real community built up as we worked, ate and played together so far from town. When Mom didn't have to do the cooking, she would always do whatever needed to be done in the kitchen. But she would get cleaned up and put on a nice outfit at dinner time so that she could mingle with the guests."

Dining area at End of the Trail Lodge

Like all resort wives, Mary had some interesting experiences around camp. The first winter she had a chimney fire. Al was gone and Mary had to get Irv Benson to help put it out. Another time an inebriated guest wandered into the kitchen late at night. The dog didn't wake up, so Mary had to shoo the guest out. One spring Mary was cleaning the outside of two freezers. As she reached between them, she felt an animal that had crawled in there and died sometime during the winter. Mary was so surprised that she jumped back and cracked her ribs in the process.

Bears occasionally visited End of the Trail in the middle of the night. Cheryl told of her mother and the dog's encounter one night. "Our dog Ginger used to run free during the day, but Mom would keep him in after he came for supper. He loved to chase the bear cubs, and one night in the middle of the night she heard him making a commotion and thought he needed to go out. She put him on the leash and let him out the kitchen door. Then she noticed the Mother Bear on the road coming toward him. She knew that he wouldn't stand a chance on the leash so she drug him back in with all her might, slammed the heavy kitchen door and stood with her back against it as the bear landed on the porch!"

In 1965 Al and Mary Hedstrom sold End of the Trail Lodge to Stan and Jewel Stephen and George and Irene Nagode for $125,000. George and Jewel were brother and sister. After several years the Nagodes sold their interest in the business to the Stephens. After Stan died, Jewel ran the resort alone for some years before selling to Nick and Mary Beth Helm. The Helms later sold to the federal government as part of the 1978 BWCAW legislation.

FROSTED APRICOT SALAD

These recipes from End of the Trail Lodge were used by the head cook, Ida Schooley, during the early 1960s.

2 pkgs. orange jello
2 cups boiling water
½ cup apricot juice
1 large can of apricots, drained and mashed
1 large can of crushed pineapple, drained

½ cup sugar
2 heaping T cornstarch
10 large marshmallows
1 cup whipping cream, whipped
Grated American cheese, for
topping

Stir jello and boiling water until well dissolved. Cool slightly. Add the apricot juice and let it stand until thick like syrup. Stir in the mashed apricots and crushed pineapple. Stir now-and-then so the fruit will be mixed all the way through the jello. When it is firm, mix ½ cup sugar and 2 heaping tablespoons cornstarch. Add this mixture to the juice drained off the pineapple. Cook until transparent, then add marshmallows, but don't let it cook hard. Stir until the marshmallows are all dissolved in the liquid. Cool until it starts to set. Beat at high speed. Fold in the whipped cream, reserving some to frost the top. Top with grated American cheese.

RYE BREAD

These recipes from End of the Trail Lodge were used by the head cook, Ida Schooley, during the early 1960s.

2 cakes yeast (takes more yeast to raise the syrups)
3 cup warm water
3 T sugar
½ cup molasses
½ cup honey
2 T dill seed
3 T caraway seed

1 cup rye flour
White flour, enough to make a firm
bread dough (but not real hard)
2 T salt
1 cup shortening

Soften the yeast in lukewarm water and sugar. When real bubbly, stir in the molasses, honey, and the seeds (I soak the seeds in a cup of water, even heat it quite a little if seeds seem hard—and they usually are). Then mix in the rye flour and white flour and salt. Mix and knead on breadboard until it is firm, but not hard. Let it rest 15 minutes on board, then put in greased bowl. Mix the shortening into the dough. Cover and let rise. When double, punch down. Let rise the second time until real light. Make into loaves and bake in a slow oven (350°) for one hour.

— Memories of — **Superior North Canoe Outfitters**

Al Hedstrom later related how Charlie got started at Saganaga Marina. "Charlie loved the country and wanted to start a marina across the bay from the Lodge and asked me to sell him 150 feet of lake frontage. When I told him I would give it to him, he insisted on paying for it, so I sold it to him for $5 a front foot. He ran the marina for several years and sold it the year before we sold the resort in 1965."

Years later Cheryl Hedstrom Dailey recalled the start of the marina. "Charlie had been in the refrigeration business in St. Louis so was good at fixing things. He saw a need for a place to store boats and a repair shop for motors. They built the Marina with two apartments over the storage/workshop area. Their friends would come and stay in the second apartment or, I think, on occasion they would rent it out."

The new owners at the Marina were Ginny and Joe Denham. Their daughter, Sharon Denham Selness, tells how her parents were introduced to the Gunflint Trail. "My husband, Bob Selness, introduced my mom and dad to the Boundary Waters. Bob and his dad had fished on Lake Saganaga since Bob was a young boy. In 1958 they brought my dad Joe and brother David to Saganaga on a fishing trip. My dad was totally enthralled with the beauty of the water and the wilderness. Two years later Ginny and Joe bought a cabin on Gull Lake from Willard Waters and they vacationed there for a summer.

Joe Denham with three of the Skrien children from Way of the Wilderness

"Joe heard that Charlie Niedergerke wanted to sell his outboard motor repair business on Lake Sag. The business was called Saganaga Marina. Joe and Ginny sold the cabin on Gull Lake and bought the marina from Charlie and Gladys Niedergerke. Joe resigned from his job as a mechanical plant engineer in southern Illinois. They sold everything in Illinois and moved into what is now the Sag Store and Superior North Canoe Outfitters.

"Joe ran an Evinrude dealership and repaired outboard motors and drove the school bus for the school district in the winter. After a few years Ginny assisted the chef at End of The Trail Lodge."

When Marie and Jerry Mark sold Tuscarora Lodge and Canoe Outfitters to the Leeds family in the late 1970s, they were not ready to leave the Trail. Marie writes, "We looked for something a little less labor intensive and purchased Saganaga Marina from Ginny and Joe. We gave it a face-lift and some remodeling and converted into Sag Store. Then we added boats, motors and a couple of apartments above. Four years later we started working on an outfitting building, bunkhouses, etc., and started Superior North Outfitters." The Marks eventually sold Superior North to Anita and Earl Cypher. The 2009 Ham Lake Fire burned the outfitters, and the Cyphers were forced to close down.

EGG DUMPLINGS or NOODLES

This recipe is a favorite of Ginny Denham's family.

3 eggs	3 eggshells of water
1 tsp. baking powder	flour

Beat together the eggs, baking powder and water. Add enough flour until the dough pulls away from the sides of the bowl. Ginny always stewed a whole chicken and then dropped dollops of the dough into the simmering chicken broth.

For noodles, add a little more flour and roll out on a floured board. Cut into trim strips and dry overnight in a paper bag.

— Memories of — Tip of the Trail Outfitters

Just beyond Superior North Outfitters is the public landing. The large building next to the landing used to house Tip of the Trail Outfitters and more recently Top of the Trail Canoe Outfitters. Russell and Eve Blankenburg founded Tip of the Trail Outfitters. They later sold to Sue and Bill Douglas, who built the buildings and ran a successful business before taking advantage of the buyout provision of the 1978 BWCAW act. Their log home on the hill was built largely by the two of them. Sue could scribe logs with a chain saw as well as Bill could. She always worked with her hair in place, eye makeup on and joy in her heart. She didn't have much time for cooking. After Sue and Bill sold, the federal government leased the land for a short time to a new business called Top of the Trail Canoe Outfitters. When the lease ran out, it was not renewed.

Voyageur Canoe Outfitters

Driving up the hill past the public landing, the next place encountered is Voyageur Canoe Outfitters.

Don and Opal Enzenauer

Sue Prom said, "In April of 1993 Mike and I made a trip up the Gunflint Trail that would forever change our lives. We were going to check out an ad we saw in the Minneapolis *Star Tribune*: 'Resort of a lifetime on the Gunflint Trail.' We originally wanted to own a canoe outfitting business, but thought with a resort at the end of the Gunflint Trail, we could make it into a canoe outfitting business. So there we were driving up the Trail with snow still in the ditches on our way to Voyageur to meet the real estate agent.

"Upon our arrival at Voyageur, I wondered why we had just driven six hours to get to a muddy parking lot with three rundown trailer houses and a little building with no toilet! An outhouse caught my eye and I was ready to turn around and go home to St. Cloud, Minnesota. We were greeted by an extremely large and friendly man, Don Enzenauer.

"Don was wearing a blaze orange hunting cap and huge bib overalls. A very friendly man, but not what we expected for a business owner on the Gunflint Trail. Don brought us into his 'store,' which was a cement block basement with a couple of shelves and an old cash register. He went on to tell us about how he started the business from scratch in 1961, first by buying the land, then the trailers, a few boats and canoes and eventually building bunkhouses across the river, and did we want to go see them?

"I wasn't very impressed with this side of the river and wasn't very eager to trudge across a supposedly frozen river in April, but away we went anyway. And that trip across the Seagull River is what forever changed our lives.

"Wow, this place had potential. Six cute bunkhouse/cabins awaited us in a beautifully wooded area only accessible by boat or canoe, or in our case, by foot. I was impressed, Mike was ecstatic and we knew this is what we wanted.

"The realtor told us another couple was going to come and check the place out the next day. This bothered us since we negotiated on an outfitting business in Ely for over seven months and didn't end up as the owners. But everything happens for a reason, so we needed to wait and consider our options.

"Well, as luck had it, Don Enzenauer took a liking to us 'kids' from central Minnesota and less than a month later we were driving up the Gunflint Trail again, but this time for good. We were now the proud owners of Voyageur Canoe Outfitters at the end of the Gunflint Trail.

"For the first five years we lived here, there was no indoor plumbing. We had an outhouse that we used year-round. Sometimes I miss getting up in the middle of the night and being able to gaze at the stars or see the northern lights. I don't, however, miss trudging out in the snow when it is 20 below zero.

"Unfortunately, Don's wife Opal passed away before we ever had the chance to meet her. Don had moved up here by himself and was a bit lonely so he wanted to find a wife. There aren't too many options to find love up here, so Don found himself a mail order bride. When he and Opal met, they decided they could live as husband and wife together at the end of the Gunflint Trail.

"Pat Shunn, a neighbor, recalls Opal being the one to teach her how to bake delicious home-made bread. Maybe the reason why Opal's bread was so good was because she rendered her own lard. When we were cleaning out the freezers one time I saw some jars of white stuff. I didn't know what it was until Don told me they would have a pig butchered at Don's relative's farm down in Owatonna and then bring the fat back to make their own lard for cooking.

"Pat Shunn also recalls a story of Opal's outhouse adventure. One winter night Opal went to use the outhouse and fell down in the snow. It was over two hours before Don awoke and realized she was missing. She wasn't seriously hurt, and it wasn't that cold out, but after that incident, Don made her wake him up every time she needed to go out to the outhouse in the middle of the night.

"Don and Opal are both gone now but their memories live on. Don's trophy walleye hangs on the wall of the lodge and when you smell bread baking, you can't help but think of Opal.

"A lot has changed at Voyageur Canoe Outfitters since we purchased it in April of 1993. We have built a lodge, expanded the outfitting business, and expanded our family by having two children, Abby and Josh. A lot remains the same too: the beautiful Seagull River and the friendly faces of neighbors new and old."

AUNT BEA'S SOUR CREAM and RAISIN PIE

Sue says: "I thought that you might enjoy this recipe from my Aunt Bea. It is one of our favorites."

1 cup raisins
1 cup water
1 cup sugar
2 T flour
8 oz. sour cream
3 eggs, beaten
1 9" pie crust
whipped topping

Simmer raisins in water until plump and the water is almost all absorbed. Stir in sugar and flour. Remove from heat and cool until lukewarm.

Stir in sour cream and eggs. Return to heat and cook slowly, stirring constantly until thickened. Pour into baked, cooled pie shell. Let cool to room temperature and then refrigerate. Serve with a generous portion of whipped topping.

Did you know . . .

Sue Prom is one of the budding new writers on the Gunflint Trail. Like Justine Kerfoot before her, she often writes stories for the *Cook County News Herald*.

—Memories of—
Saganaga Outfitters

Years before the Germains bought Saganaga Outfitters, Don had worked for Harry Brown at Windigo Point. He would often wander over to the Blankenburgs to visit and Eve would put him to work. It seemed natural for them to buy the outfitters when it came up for sale. Don was still actively working in the Twin Cities so Carole learned to run the outfitters.

Past Northpoint Outfitters on the narrow side road is what appears to be a small opening in the woods. This was the location of Saganaga Outfitters, the last business started on the Gunflint Trail by Russell and Eve Blankenburg. In 1972 they sold the business to Don and Carole Germain. Don had worked for Harry and Genevieve Brown at Windigo Point on Seagull Lake during the forties. He fell in love with the country during those summers. The Germains would run the outfitters for the next 15 years until it was sold to the U.S. Forest Service.

Main lodge building at Saganaga Outfitters

The Germain family

Carole remembers the Blankenburgs well. "Russell and Eve were special friends. Russell was well cared for by Eve in his year of declining health. Eve would bake a cake or muffins and bring him to Sag to sit at the picnic table to enjoy the fresh air and the area that he truly loved. I would make a pot of coffee and we all enjoyed afternoon visits with Russell and Eve. He was cold even in his heavy Mackinaw jacket and cap with earflaps. He really enjoyed the attention our daughter Candace gave him, as she would wrap a blanket around his shoulders. He would tell stories about his early life and of his years in this country. I regret I didn't write them down. He would tire easily so Eve would take him home, but we looked forward to the next day of his Sag coffee and cake. We did not realize he was failing rapidly. They were wonderful people."

One of the most difficult times during their years at Saganaga Outfitters was 1976. The possibility of a forest fire engulfing home and business always exists in wilderness areas, but the summer of 1976 was a dry one and the threat of a forest fire was on everyone's minds. A small fire had been stopped on the Magnetic Rock Trail early in the summer. In August the Roy Lake Fire broke out just west of Saganaga Outfitters. Carole relates her experience with the fire.

Candace Germain

"Smoke had been hanging heavy in the air and people were moving out on the lake. Three of our staff went out to the narrows to see if they could help. The fire was already large. By the time we called the Guard Station, the fire had been reported and firefighters were on the way to help. We were eating supper when Bruce Kerfoot entered the lodge telling us that there was a possibility we would be in danger. We would have one half hour to evacuate. In two minutes we determined what we would take and who was to do certain things. We left the supper dishes on the table and packed. I took care of the business things, others gathered food, tents, camping equipment, chain saw with gas and oil, axes, saws, our dog Ranger, things we felt we would need to be comfortable until we knew the outcome.

Carole Germain

"The one person designated to float the two boats panicked so Candace motored the boats out from shore, anchored them well, jumped in and swam back to shore. We left Saganaga Outfitters with a very empty feeling. Would we return to ashes or dirty dishes? Many feelings swelled within each of us. Ranger laid his head on my leg as we drove down the narrow road, joining others heading out. We drove only as far as the Seagull Guard Station. A local ranger recognized our van and asked us to pull over to the shoulder. Later we learned we would be going back to our base so it could be used to house the firefighters around the clock. It was an overwhelming feeling of happiness and gratefulness to arrive back at the base, to see the lodge and a table with dirty dishes. Doing dishes at 1 a.m. was a happy and joyous task. The smoke in the air made for tense times, but with firefighters sleeping at base we felt safe. The Command Center would call me to wake up specific crews so they would be ready for the bus transporting them to a nearby resort for meals. Boats would take them to the fire areas. We sincerely appreciated their fine spirit and commitment to their work."

BLUEBERRY MUFFINS

HERITAGE

Like all the women on the Trail, Carole has some great recipes to share with us.

- 1¾ cups flour
- ⅓ cup sugar
- 2 tsp. baking powder
- ¼ tsp. salt
- 1 beaten egg
- ¾ cup milk
- ¼ cup cooking oil
- ¾–1 cup fresh or frozen blueberries

Mix flour, sugar, baking powder and salt. Make a well in the mixture. Combine egg, milk and oil. Add all at once to the flour mixture. Stir until just moistened. The batter will be lumpy. Add blueberries. Stir gently. Fill greased muffin cups two-thirds full. Bake at 400° for 20 minutes or until lightly golden. To make these muffins even more delicious, serve them warm!

LEMON BARS

During busy times, people living at the end of the Trail just don't get to town very often. Lemons are a fresh fruit that keeps well and can be used to add that special flavor that only comes from fresh juices.

- ½ cup powdered sugar
- 2 cup flour
- 1 cup margarine or butter
- 4 eggs
- 2 cups granulated sugar
- 1 tsp. baking powder
- ¼ tsp. salt
- 2 tsp. grated lemon peel
- ¼ cup fresh lemon juice
- powdered sugar

Preheat oven to 350°. In a small bowl, combine the powdered sugar and flour. Cut the butter into the flour mixture until it is crumbly. Press the mixture evenly in the bottom of an ungreased 9x13" pan. Bake for 15 minutes.

In a medium bowl, beat together eggs, granulated sugar, baking powder, salt, lemon peel and lemon juice until fluffy. Pour over hot crust. Bake 20–25 minutes or until no imprint remains when touched lightly in the center. While still hot, sift powdered sugar over the top. Cool in pan. Refrigerate 4 hours or overnight before cutting. It is important that the bars be well chilled before cutting. Store in the refrigerator.

— Memories of — **Northpoint Outfitters**

Just past the former location of Saganaga Outfitters, the narrow private road makes a sharp right turn. Continuing straight ahead before the turn would take you to the former location of Northpoint Outfitters.

In 1974 Fred and Pat Zopff of St. Louis, Missouri, started Northpoint Outfitters. Fred was one of the first businessmen to get a private phone line so he could continue conducting business in St. Louis without leaving the woods. The Zopffs would always have a big 4th of July party for their neighbors.

Main outfitting building at Northpoint Outfitters

Northpoint Outfitters is another business that was offered to the government after the 1978 BWCAW bill was passed. Their location on the river opening into Saganaga Lake was ideal; however, with the ban on large motor tow boats to get across such a large lake, they decided to opt for the buyout. The buildings were sold at auction by the Forest Service and the land is vacant now.

One of their employees, Sandra Wolfe, remembers Fred saying he wanted his workers to have as much fun as the guests and they usually did.

Fred's son, Eric, remembers, "Once I packed a trip for some city folks and I forgot to pack the utensils. Mom, Dad and Daughter were ready to pack it in and return to base. But the eight-year-old son had a pocket knife and carved his own utensils. This inspired the rest of the family and they stayed out the whole seven days using hand carved utensils! An inspiration to all city folks, by golly. They were happy we left out the utensils and even thanked us for doing that. They experienced the real meaning of survival in the wilderness for the first time."

— Memories of — **North Country Trading Post**

Passing the parking lot for the BWCAW entry point at the campground, the first building you see is the former North Country Trading Post store. It was owned and operated by Cliff and Hilda Waters.

Hilda tells about their life here.

"We started the store in 1955. Cal Rutstrum and Cliff built the first building and we operated out of that for a couple of years. Then Cliff and Cal started the larger building, which Cliff finished and we ran the store there for 20 years. We rented from Cal for about three years, then bought the property. The store was known as Way of the Wilderness at first. When we bought the property, we changed the name to North Country Trading Post to avoid confusion with Way of the Wilderness Canoe Outfitters. We sold the business to Bud Darling in 1980."

Cliff, Barbara and Hilda Waters

North Country Trading Post

Way of the Wilderness Canoe Outfitters

In 1957 canoes rented for $3.00 a day and complete outfitting was $5.75 per person per day. In those years motors could be used anywhere in the BWCAW. Later on, motors were limited to a certain horsepower and there were designated motor routes. Finally motors were banned in all the lakes except certain larger lakes on the perimeter of the BWCAW and border lakes.

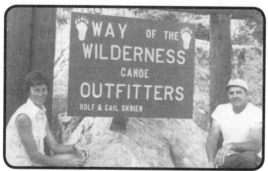

Gail and Rolf Skrien

At first canned goods and bottles were allowed in the BWCAW. They were disposed of by filling them with water and sinking them in the deeper part of the lake. Canoe outfitters used a variety of canned meats, canned bacon, ham, hot dogs, hamburgers and Spam. Next there was a Forest Service program to pack out what you packed in. Numbered plastic garbage bags were issued with travel permits. Finally in 1971 a total ban on bottles and cans was legislated and remains in effect today. The outfitters had to make changes in their menus and food. Dehydrated foods became popular and were lightweight to carry. Fresh meat was sent along for the first day or two. Campers learned to increase their use of fish.

Gail related some events from their early days on the Trail. "During the late 1950s and the 1960s we had many social gatherings at our outfitting building on Friday evenings. Russell Smith from Seagull Guard Station would bring Forest Service movies to show on the outside of our building. Folks came from the Trail's End Campground as well as summer cabin owners and neighbors. Afterwards coffee and refreshments were served. Many times neighbors and friends would gather for potlucks or fish fries.

"We had five children: Sandy, Stuart, Stanton, Susan and Sally. They all had chores to do. Packsacks had to be cleaned out and canoes had to be kept scrubbed. They spent their spare time trying to catch turtles, crawdads, pollywogs or dragonflies. Picking strawberries, raspberries and blueberries was a big part of the daily routine, as was swimming, canoeing and fishing.

"Building and operating Way of the Wilderness Canoe Outfitters was a very fulfilling way of life for ourselves and our children. We had a good repeat business and met many interesting people. We cherish every one of our memories of those years. We sold to Bud and Ruth Darling in 1976."

During her first summer on the Trail, Gail worked for Al Hedstrom at End of the Trail Lodge. Gail said that when she first came up here from Colorado she couldn't get over all the lakes. Toward the end of the summer Rolf asked her to go fishing one day. Gail thought he was a little surprised when she told him that she would rather run the motor than fish. So Gail ran the motor and Rolf fished. They brought in a limit of fish. Not only was this Gail's first date with her future husband, it was her first date with a lifelong love of fishing.

Gail's daughter Sandy recalls fishing with her mother. "One of the fondest memories I have of my mom and I together takes place at the Seagull River. Not surprising since we lived on a bay of the river for most of my early childhood. I was quite young, probably under 5, and the unusual thing about this memory is that it is just of my mom and me. No brothers, no sisters and no Dad. I guess that's why I cherish it—we were alone together.

"We walked up through the Trails End Campground with our fishing poles to Campsite #13, then walked down the path through the woods to the big rock right where the river narrows in the bay below the main part of the rapids. This was a spot we came to many, many times, but this evening was special. I don't remember the details of the fishing. I was probably watching birds or playing in the water. But what I remember is that we caught a ton of fish. Walleyes, I would guess. Mom cut off a branch from a bush and strung up the fish by the gills so we could carry them home.

"What a sight we made walking through the campground with our branch full of fish! People stopped us to ask us how we caught all those fish. Mom acted like it was nothing. This spot on the river remains one of my favorite places whether it is winter or summer, full of people or during the off season, high water or low. It's always an interesting place."

Sandy also recalls that her mother taught her at a very early age to assume stewardship for the land around her. "She helped me connect with the land by teaching me about the small things around me. When I was only five, she helped me record the wildflowers as they bloomed that summer."

Like many other people on the Trail, Gail loved to pick berries. Sandy remembers those berry picking excursions. "We spent many hours of many days picking berries. If I remember right, it was strawberries first. We usually picked these along the edge of the road where the sand and sun mixed to produce the best berry crops. The picking of strawberries never excited me too much. It was too hot in the sun and the berries were so small. But the best part was helping Mom make the strawberry jam. She had a big pot, which I think was supposed to be for boiling baby bottles, but she always used it for canning. She taught me the finesse of stirring so the jam wouldn't sugar. I was too small when I was young to fill the glass jars, but I could help with labeling and making sure they all sealed.

"Blueberries were a different challenge. We got to pick those in the woods or on islands. When I was young, I could pick berries for a while, but I was usually attracted to big trees and would leave the bushes to climb as high as I could to get on tree limbs that were as big as a man's leg. Mom, of course, would be disappointed as we stopped picking to explore and play, but as long as we were having fun and not getting hurt, she let us go and she continued to pick until all the containers were full. Then we'd head back home.

"As I got older, I was challenged by Mom to try to keep up to her picking. I remember when I could finally pick as fast as she could. I was so proud to be able to fill my bucket as fast as she. I think I was a teenager at the time. But I never could pick as clean as she could. Even if we took the same amount back home in our buckets, it would always take me longer to pick out the leaves, twigs and unripe berries. And Mom was very picky, only the best for her pies and jams!"

Sandy's sister, Susan, has another story to tell about blueberry picking with her mother. "I was in college and I came home and we started looking at photo albums. And I looked at this picture and we were on some island. And we're tied to trees! I said, 'Mom, this is child abuse. We're tied to the trees.' And she said, 'Well, I just didn't want you to fall in the water. I wanted to get my blueberries picked and I didn't have a lot of time. So that's what I did and you guys were happy! You sat there and ate blueberries.' I don't remember the day because I was too young. But finding the picture was funny."

In April of 1976 the Skriens sold Way of the Wilderness to Ruth and Bud Darling of Chicago. Bud had extensive experience as an administrator of YMCA camps. The North Country Trading Post, an adjacent business, was purchased from Cliff and Hilda Waters in 1980 and added to the operation.

Bud and his sons, Scot and Mark, operated the business through the 1970s and 1980s. Bud's wife, Ruth, who was a Surgical Head Nurse at Rush Presbyterian St. Luke's Hospital in Chicago, commuted for long weekends and vacation time. Bud and Mark manage the business to this day. A third generation of family is now involved as some of Scot's children currently help out.

The business has been forced to adapt and change over the years. The 1976 Roy Lake Fire consumed over 3,400 acres and burned within several hundred yards of Way of the Wilderness. This was Bud's first year in business and he says, "You could have bought the place for about

50 cents during that fire." In 1978 Congress enacted the BWCAW Act, which limited any future growth in use of the area. In 1993 the Superior National Forest Management Plan cut the then-current usage by over 30%. The Sag Corridor Fire in 1997 burned over 12,000 acres just to the north of Way of the Wilderness, and the Blowdown of July 4, 1999, left the operation with no electric power for two weeks.

Ruth and Bud Darling with sons Scot and Mark

In the late 1970s Bud completed a master's degree in Business Administration and obtained a CPA Certificate. Throughout the 1980s he practiced accounting in the Chicago area during the off-season.

In 1990 Bud and Ruth moved to Duluth, bought and restored a historic building downtown, and currently live there in the winter months. Bud maintains a tax accounting practice and Ruth is the Director of Health Care Services at Interim Health Care in Duluth.

Mark opened the Trails End Cafe in 1998 and serves freshly made pizza and what some people say are the best burgers in Minnesota.

Way of the Wilderness is a full service outfitter offering over 100 canoes for rent, Saganaga Lake tow service, six bunkhouse units, hot showers, shuttle service to all Gunflint Trail Entry points, a trading post and Mark's Trails End Cafe.

The Darlings have a unique lifestyle. They blend professional careers in accounting and nursing with the opportunity to live and work in the "greatest place on earth" for over half of each year.

Did you know . . .

The native fish on the Gunflint Trail are Lake Trout and Northern Pike. Walleyes and Smallmouth Bass were planted by the Department of Conservation in the late 1930s in several major lakes.

Raspberries quickly spring up in an area after it has been logged. In these logged over places, there are often several spots where the loggers have raked together the branches and other debris that is trimmed from the trees. These piles are then burned as part of the cleanup process after logging. If you can locate one of these burn piles in the cleared area, that is where you'll find the biggest and best raspberries.

STRAWBERRY ROMAINE SALAD

DRESSING:
1 cup vegetable oil
½ cup red wine vinegar
½ tsp. salt
¾ cup sugar
2 cloves of garlic, crushed
¼ tsp. pepper

SALAD:
1 large head Romaine lettuce
1 head Boston lettuce
1 pint sliced fresh strawberries
1 cup shredded Monterey Jack cheese
½ cup toasted chopped walnuts

Combine all dressing ingredients in a jar and shake vigorously. This may be kept 1 week. Do not refrigerate.

Tear both heads of lettuce into bite-size pieces. Combine lettuce, strawberries, cheese and walnuts in a large salad bowl. Shake dressing well. Pour over salad just before serving and toss gently

NORWEGIAN COFFEE CAKE

In years past when folks stopped in for coffee, there was always an "and" to go with it. This is one of Gail's favorite "ands."

DOUGH:
1 cup sifted flour
½ cup butter or margarine
2 T water

FILLING:
½ cup butter or margarine
1 cup water
1 tsp. almond extract
1 cup sifted flour
3 eggs

ICING:
1 3-oz. package cream cheese
2 T butter
2 T cream
confectioners' sugar
sliced almonds

Dough: Measure flour into mixing bowl. Cut in butter with a pastry blender. Sprinkle water over mixture and mix with a fork. Shape into a ball. Divide in half. Put dough into two 1⅔"-strips, 3" apart on a cookie sheet.

Filling: Combine butter and water in a saucepan. Bring to a rolling boil. Add almond extract and remove from heat. Stir in flour. Mix until smooth. Add eggs, one at a time, beating until smooth after each addition. Spread over dough. Bake at 350° for 55–60 minutes or until the topping is crisp and browned.

Icing: Combine cream cheese, butter and cream with a mixer. Add confectioners' sugar until creamy. Spread over baked coffee cake and sprinkle with almonds.

BUTTER PECAN TURTLE BARS

With a large family of children, Gail knew you could never have enough cookies and bars around.

CRUST:
2 cups flour
1 cup firmly packed brown sugar
½ cup butter, softened

PECAN LAYER:
1 cup whole pecan halves

CARAMEL LAYER:
⅔ cup butter
½ cup firmly packed brown sugar

FROSTING:
1 cup milk chocolate chips

Preheat oven to 350°. In a 3-quart bowl combine the crust ingredients. Mix at medium speed, scraping the sides of the bowl often, for 2–3 minutes or until well mixed and the particles are fine. Pat firmly into an ungreased 13x9x2" pan. Place pecan halves evenly over the unbaked crust.

Prepare the caramel layer by combining the brown sugar and butter in a heavy saucepan. Cook over medium heat, stirring constantly, until the entire surface of the mixture begins to boil. Boil 30 seconds to 1 minute, stirring constantly until it is like a fairly thick syrup. Pour evenly over the pecans and the crust. Bake near the center of the oven for 18–22 minutes or until the entire caramel layer is bubbly and the crust is a light golden brown. Remove from the oven immediately. Sprinkle with 1 cup milk chocolate chips. Allow the chips to melt slightly for 2–3 minutes. Slightly swirl the chips as they melt. Do not entirely spread the chips. Cool completely and cut into bars.

KRUMKAKE

This is a very traditional Scandinavian cookie that just melts in your mouth with powdered sugar and is positively sinful with whipped cream.

4 eggs
1 cup sugar
½ tsp. vanilla or ground cardamom seed

½ cup melted butter
2 T cornstarch
1½ cups flour

Beat eggs slightly. Add sugar to eggs and beat until light. Do not over-beat. Add vanilla. Blend in melted cooled butter, cornstarch and flour. Preheat iron on both sides. Iron is ready for baking when a few drops of water placed on the iron dance around. Drop about a teaspoon of dough on the center of the iron. Cover quickly and turn the iron. Bake until delicately browned. Remove from iron with a spatula or table knife. Roll quickly into a cone shape or like a diploma on a round wood form or wooden spoon. Cool. Fill with whipped cream or sprinkle with powdered sugar before serving.

Chain of Ownership

Aspen Lodge
1930s founded by Annie and Fred Haffner
1971 sold to Ione Tofte and her son Jack
1974 sold to Dan Melander and Dave Westby
currently in private ownership; no longer in operation

Bearskin Lodge
1925 Harley Jackson founds "Camp Jackson"
1929 sold to Mr. and Mrs. A. J. Allen
1944 sold to Mr. and Mrs. Clifford J. Pine
1945 sold to Myrtle and Ed Cavanaugh
1971 sold to Mary Lou and Frank Rizzo
1973 sold to Barb and Dave Tuttle
2001 sold to Heidi and Mike Pazlar
2007 sold to Bob and Sue McCloughan

Boundary Waters Adventures
1992 founded by Cindy and Tony Faras

Big Bear Lodge
around 1934 founded by Dr. Remple
1949 sold to Ann and Ed Ruidl
1965 Old Northwoods Lodge becomes inactive
1995 Yelena and Gale Quistad purchase Old Northwoods Lodge and bring it back into business
2011 sold to Andy and Ida DeLisi

Chik-Wauk Lodge
1931 built by Ed and Art Nunstedt
1952 sold to Phyllis and Carl Noyes and Erma and Herb Brugger
1954 Bruggers take over sole proprietorship
1958 sold to Bea and Ralph Griffis
1980 sold to the federal government; no longer in operation

Clearwater Lodge
1915 founded by Petra and Charley Boostrom
1946 sold to Lavern and Art Schliep
1959 sold to Sharon and Hank Eliason

1964 sold to Lee and Jocko Nelson
1986 sold to Margy Nelson
1995 sold to Marti and Bob Marchino
2003 sold to Peggy and Mike Trace
2011 sold to Adam and Kasey Van Tassell

Cross River Lodge
1922 Charlie Johnson founds Borderland Lodge
sold to Warner Swanson; operated by Val and Benny Ambrose
1954 sold to Ann and Dave Clark
1962 sold to Agnes and Vern Behsman
1969 sold to LaVonne and Gene Groth
1975 sold to Nancy and Jim Thompson
1992 sold to Jane and Eric Thompson
1999 Paula and Dave Beattie purchase the lodge and two cabins
2009 sold to John and Rose Schloot

End of the Trail Lodge
1931 founded as Saganaga Fishing Camp by Eve and Russell Blankenburg
1946 sold to Mary and Al Hedstrom
1965 sold to Jewel and Stan Stephen and Irene and George Nagode
around 1974 sold to Mary Beth and Nick Helm
1978 sold to federal government; no longer in operation

Forest Lodge
about 1946 founded by Grace and Bill Boissenin
1966 sold to Alice and Ray Kulick
buildings now in private ownership; no longer in operation

Golden Eagle Lodge
1945 founded by Howard Bell and Leonard Scruggs
1963 sold to Jack and Joan Underwood
1976 sold to Irene and John Baumann
1995 sold to Teresa and Dan Baumann

Greenwood Lodge

1912 founded by Myron Graves
1913 sold to William Yawkey
1920 sold to Edith and Gilbert Gilbertsen
1943 Edith sells to Mr. C.A. Carlson
1944 sold to Frank Werline and Earl Johnson
1947 sold to Mr. William Sutherland and Mr. and Mrs. Theodore Sutherland
1956 sold to Marie Anhorn and her son Andy
1965 most property and buildings sold to private owners; no longer in operation

Gunflint Lodge

1925 Dora Blankenburg and son, Russell, start Gunflint Lodge
1929 sold to Mae Spunner and daughter, Justine
1968 Bruce and Sue Kerfoot take over management
2000 Robert and Miranda Kerfoot begin running the lodge
2008 Bruce and Sue run the lodge

Gunflint Northwoods Outfitters

1929 Founded by Justine Spunner
1945 Janet Hanson becomes Justine's partner
1969 Justine buys out Janet's half of the partnership
1972 sold to Bruce and Sue Kerfoot
2000 Robert and Miranda Kerfoot take over the business
2008 Bruce and Sue run the business

Gunflint Pines

1978 Ronnie and Dick Smith purchase Gunflint Pines
2001 sold to Shari and Bob Baker

Heston's Lodge

1930s founded by Luke and Al Finn as The Border Camp
1943 sold to Peggy and Myrl Heston
1971 sold to Sharlene Heston LeTourneau
1989 sold to Barb and Greg Gecas

Hungry Jack Lodge

1923 Jesse Gapen and Robert Wegg begin building
1924 Jesse Gapen takes over sole ownership; Gapen family moves to Hungry Jack Lake
1958 sold to Bette and Pat McDonnell
1970 sold to Bonnie Williams and her son, Dick
1972 sold to Jerry Parson
2003 Forrest Parsons takes over the lodge

Hungry Jack Outfitters

1954 founded by Margaret and Harry Nolan as Sunset Point
1983 Sue and Jack McDonnell purchase the resort and change the name to Hungry Jack Outfitters
1991 sold to Nancy and Dave Seaton

Loon Lake Lodge

1927–28 founded by Clara and Jack Dewar
1935 sold to Marie and George Stapleton
1948 sold to Willard Johnson, Ethel and Kermit Johnson and Cliff Hammerberg
mid-1950s brothers Willard and Kermit in sole possession
1985 sold to Terry and Tom Caldwell

Loon's Nest Gift Shop

1970s founded by Lou and Herb White
1999 sold to Darlene and Dennis Katajamaki

North Country Trading Post

1955 founded by Hilda and Cliff Waters
1980 sold to Ruth and Bud Darling, who merged it with Way of the Wilderness Canoe Outfitters

Northpoint Outfitters

1974 founded by Pat and Fred Zopff
1978 sold to the federal government; no longer in operation

Nor'Wester Lodge

early 1930s founded by Alis and Carl Brandt as Balsam Grove Lodge
1967 sold to Luana and Carl Brandt

Okontoe Family Campground
1970s Founded by Dimnock "Dim" Stevens
1971 sold to Willie (Wilma) and Bill Barr
1983 Nancy and Mark Patten take over as directors of Okontoe

Pincushion Bed & Breakfast
1986 founded by Mary and Scott Beattie
sold to Lynn Parish

Poplar Creek Guesthouse Bed & Breakfast
1974 founded by Barbara and Ted Young

Rockwood Lodge
1926 founded by Jennie and Paul Stoltz and Waldemar (Wally) Anderson
1930s Wally sells his share to Jennie and Paul
1946 sold to Ann and Dave Clark
1951 sold to Loretta and Darwin Noyes
1956 sold to Don Lobdell and Rick Whitney
1979 sold to Dana and Tim Austin
1999 sold to Gale and Val Roloff
2003 sold to Lin and Mike Sherfy

Saganaga Outfitters
early 1970s founded by Eve and Russell Blankenburg
1972 sold to Carole and Don Germain
1987 sold to federal government; no longer in operation

Sea Island Lodge
early 1940s founded by Richard "Rosie" Rosencrantz, Luther Hester and partners
1955 sold to Marge and Bob Cushman and renamed Sea Island Lodge
1978 sold to Kathy and Mike Lande
2000 no longer in operation

Seagull Canoe Outfitters and Cabins
founded by Eve and Russell Blankenburg
1970 sold to Earl Darst and partners, who ran it as Portage Outfitters

1980 sold to Lunn Paulrud and Dave Canfield
1986 Deb Mark purchases Portage Outfitters and creates Seagull Canoe Outfitters and Cabins

Seagull Outfitters
early 1960s founded by Eve and Russell Blankenburg
1965 sold to Grace and Stan Smith
1970 sold to Janet Hanson
1973 sold to Bob and Nancy Wendt
1976 Seagull Outfitters goes back to Janet Hanson
1977 sold to Lynn Paulrud and Dave Canfield
1980 sold with Seagull Resort to federal government; no longer in operation

Seagull Resort
1929 Russel Blankenburg starts Seagull Resort
1958 sold to Jean and Clarke Dailey
1965 sold to Margarite and Ward Ingersoll
1971 sold to Lois and Al Danielson
1978 sold to Lynn Paulrud and Dave Canfield
1980 sold to the federal government; no longer in operation

Soderberg Cabins
1945–1947 founded by Elinor and Carl Soderberg
late 1950s sold to Floyd Soderberg
1960s sold to the Liebertzes
no longer in operation

Swanson's Lodge
late 1930s founded by Sybil and Marvin Swanson
late 1940s sold to Mother Bunn and her son, Walt
1980s sold to Linda and Tom Hendrickson
now in private ownership; no longer in operation

Superior North Canoe Outfitters
mid-1950s founded as Saganaga Marina by Gladys and Charlie Niedergerke
1964 sold to Ginny and Joe Denham
1978 Marie and Jerry Mark purchase Marina and create Superior North Canoe Outfitters

1982 sold to Anita and Earl Cypher

2009 Burned in a forest fire and no longer in operation

Trail Center

1938 founded as a logging business by Mayme and Sam Seppala

1940 Sam Seppala drowns, lumber mill closes; property is vacant

1948 Carrie and Bill Flavell purchase the store and cabins

1962 Eva and George Cleaver take over Trail Center

1966 sold to Thelma, Fred and Gay Lynne Liebertz

1984 sold to Bill and Nancy Edwards-France

1986 sold to Sue and Bruce Kerfoot; managed by Nancy Hemstad as Poplar Lake Lodge

1988 sold to Ginny and Larry Backstrom

1995 sold to Sarah Hamilton

Trout Lake Lodge

1938 started by Grace and Bill Boissenin

1946 sold to Charlet and Bud Kratoska

1986 sold to Nancy and Russ Waver

Tuscarora Lodge and Canoe Outfitters

1934 Founded by Mr. and Mrs. Harry Anderson

1946 Sold to Agnes and Frank Fuller

1960 Sold to Marie and Jerry Mark

1976 Marks sell the resort to Jim and Ann Leeds

1978 Marks sell the canoe outfitters to Jim and Ann Leeds

2004 Kerry Leeds sells to Andy and Sue Ahrendt

Ugly Baby Bait Shop

1992 founded as Loon House Gift Shop by Sue and Bruce Kerfoot and Jennifer and Kevin Walsh

1998 sold to Diane and Scott Stahnke

Voyageur Canoe Outfitters

1961 founded by Don Enzenauer

1993 sold to Sue and Mike Prom

Way of the Wilderness Canoe Outfitters

1956 founded by Gail and Rolf Skrien

1976 sold to Ruth and Bud Darling

Wilderness Canoe Base

1956 founded as outreach program for Plymouth Christian Youth Center by Pearl and Ham Muus and partners

Wildwood Lodge

1931 Andy Mayo and Martha Bauman buy property for a resort on Seagull

1950s Wildwood Lodge is closed; no longer in operation

Windigo Lodge

1957 founded by Genevieve and Harry Brown

1960 sold to Ann and Helmer Larsen

1968 sold to Jean and Harold (Ike) Ikola

1970 sold to Charlotte and Vince Eckroot

Windigo Point

1929 Jimmy Dunn founds Windigo Point

1947 sold to Genevieve and Harry Brown

1957 Browns sell the property to the Izaak Walton League; no longer in operation

Contact Information

Aspen Lodge
(no longer in operation)

Bearskin Lodge
124 East Bearskin Road
Grand Marais, MN 55604-3003
800-338-4170
www.bearskin.com

Big Bear Lodge
7969 Northwoods Loop
Grand Marais, MN 55604
218-388-0172
www.bigbearlodgemn.com
info@bigbearlodge.com

Boundary Waters Adventures
239 Seagull Road, Grand Marais, MN 55604
218-388-0128, 800-894-0128
members.aol.com/gunflnt/bwa
gunflnt@aol.com

Chik-Wauk Lodge
(no longer in operation)

Clearwater Lodge
774 Clearwater Road, Gunflint Trail
Grand Marais, MN 55604
800-527-0554, 218-388-2254
www.clearwaterhistoriclodge.com
info@canoebwca.com

Cross River Lodge
196 North Gunflint Lake Road
Grand Marais, MN 55604
866-203-8991, 218-388-2233
www.crossriverlodge.com
info@crossriverlodge.com

End of the Trail Lodge
(no longer in operation)

Forest Lodge
(no longer in operation)

Golden Eagle Lodge
468 Clearwater Road, Grand Marais, MN, 55604
800-346-2203, 218-388-2203
www.golden-eagle.com
seclusion@golden-eagle.com

Greenwood Lodge
(no longer in operation)

Gunflint Lodge
143 South Gunflint Lake, Grand Marais, MN 55604
800-328-3325, 218-388-2294
www.gunflint.com
info@gunflint.com

Gunflint Northwoods Outfitters
143 South Gunflint Lake
Grand Marais, MN 55604
888-226-6346, 218-388-2296
www.gunflintoutfitters.com
bonnie@gunflint.com

Gunflint Pines Resort & Campground
217 South Gunflint Lake Road
Grand Marais, MN 55604
800-533-5814, 218-388-4454
www.gunflintpines.com
info@gunflintpines.com

Gunflint Trail Association
PO Box 205, Grand Marais, MN 55604
800-338-6932
www.gunflint-trail.com
gta@boreal.org;

Gunflint Trail Volunteer Fire Department
468 Clearwater Road, Grand Marais, MN 55604
www.gunflint911.org

Heston's Lodge

579 S. Gunflint Lake, Grand Marais, MN 55604
800-338-7230, 218-388-2243
www.hestons.com
info@hestons.com

Hungry Jack Lodge

372 Hungry Jack Road, Grand Marais, MN 55604
218-388-2265
http://hungryjacklodge.com
info@hungryjacklodge.com

Hungry Jack Outfitters

318 S. Hungry Jack Road,
Grand Marais, MN 55604
800-648-2922
www.hjo.com
info@hjo.com

Loon Lake Lodge

65 Loon Lake Road, Grand Marais, MN 55604
800-552-6351, 218-388-2232
www.visitloonlake.com
info@visitloonlake.com

Loon's Nest Gift Shop

7575 Gunflint Trail, Grand Marais, MN 55604
218-388-9909 (summer), 218-388-9973 (winter)
www.gunflint-trail.com/lngs.html

North Country Trading Post

(merged with Way of the Wilderness)

Northpoint Outfitters

(no longer in operation)

Nor'Wester Lodge & Canoe Outfitters

7778 Gunflint Trail, Grand Marais, MN 55604
800-992-4FUN (4386), 218-388-2252
www.norwesterlodge.com
stay@norwesterlodge.com

Okontoe Family Campground

110 Bow Lake Road, Grand Marais, MN 55604
218-388-9423
www.okontoe.com
okontoe@boreal.org

Pincushion Bed & Breakfast

968 Gunflint Trail, Grand Marais, MN 55604
218-387-2969
www.pincushionbb.com
lparish@comcast.net

Poplar Creek Guesthouse Bed & Breakfast

Boundary Country Trekking
11 Poplar Creek Drive, Grand Marais, MN 55604
800-322-8327, 218-388-4487
www.boundarycountry.com/guesthouse.html
bct@boundarycountry.com

Rockwood Lodge

Rockwood Lodge and Canoe Outfitters
50 Rockwood Road, Gunflint Trail
Grand Marais, MN 55604
800-942-BWCA (2922), 218-388-2242
www.canoeoutfitter.com
info@rockwoodbwca.com

Saganaga Outfitters

(no longer in operation)

Sea Island Lodge

(no longer in operation)

Seagull Canoe Outfitters and Cabins

12208 Gunflint Trail, Grand Marais, MN 55604
218-388-2216
www.seagulloutfitters.com
seagull@seagulloutfitters.com

Seagull Outfitters

(no longer in operation)

Seagull Resort
(no longer in operation)

Soderberg Cabins
(no longer in operation)

Superior North Canoe Outfitters
(no longer in operation)

Swanson's Lodge
(no longer in operation)

Tip of the Trail Outfitters
(no longer in operation)

Trail Center
7611 Gunflint Trail, Grand Marais, MN 55604-2048
218-388-2214
www.trailcenterlodge.com
trailctr@boreal.org

Trout Lake Resort
789 Trout Lake Road, Gunflint Trail
Grand Marais, MN 55604
800-258-7688, 218-387-1330
www.troutlakeresort.com
troutlake@boreal.org

Tuscarora Lodge and Canoe Outfitters
193 Round Lake Road, Grand Marais, MN 55604
800-544-3843, 218-388-2221
www.tuscaroracanoe.com
ahrendts@tuscaroracanoe.com

Ugly Baby Bait & Boats
7587 Gunflint Trail, Grand Marais, MN 55604
218-388-0303

Voyageur Canoe Outfitters
189 Sag Lake Trail, Grand Marais, MN 55604
888-CANOEIT, 218-388-2224
www.canoeit.com
vco@canoeit.com

Way of the Wilderness Canoe Outfitters
Summer address and phone:
12582 Gunflint Trail, Grand Marais, MN 55604
800-346-6625, 218-388-2212
Winter address and phone:
13 W. Superior St., Duluth, MN 55802
800-346-6625, 218-727-8606
www.wayofthewilderness.com
wowcanoe@boreal.org

Wilderness Canoe Base
12477 Gunflint Trail, Grand Marais, MN 55604
218-388-2241
http://campwapo.org/camp/wilderness
paddle@wildernesscanoebase.org

Wildwood Lodge
(no longer in operation)

Windigo Lodge
7890 Gunflint Trail, Grand Marais, MN 55604
800-535-4320, 218-388-2222
www.windigolodge.com
info@windigolodge.com

Windigo Point
(no longer in operation)

Index of Recipes

Nellie Vogan, cook at Heston's Lodge

Index of Businesses

Lucille Burauger, who helped
out at numerous lodges

The Authors

Luana Brandt
Nor'Wester Lodge
(1967–present)

Sue McDonnell
Hungry Jack Outfitters
(1983–1991)

Sharon Eliasen
Clearwater Lodge
(1959–1964)

Margy Nelson
Clearwater Lodge
(1986–1995)

Sue Kerfoot
Gunflint Lodge
(1968–present)

Barb Tuttle
Bearskin Lodge
(1973–2001)

Jo Ann Krause
Retired school teacher,
Grand Marais

Jean Williamson
Windigo Lodge
(1968–1970)

Kathy Lande
Sea Island Lodge
(1978–2000)

Lee Zopff
Clearwater Lodge
(1964–1986)

Bette McDonnell
Hungry Jack Lodge
(1958–1970)

Bibliography
Bethlehem Lutheran Church Women. North Shore Cookery. St. Paul: North Central Publishing, 1977.
Kerfoot, Justine. Gunflint: Reflections on the Trail. Minneapolis: University of Minnesota Press, 1991.
Kerfoot, Justine. Woman of the Boundary Waters: Canoeing, Guiding, Mushing, and Surviving. Reprint, Minneapolis: University of Minnesota Press, 1994.
Raff, Willis H. Pioneers in the Wilderness. Grand Marais: Cook County Historical Society, 1981.
Webster, Janna. Ki-osh-kons: People, Places and Stories of Sea Gull Lake. Janna Webster, 1997.
Cook County News-Herald, Grand Marais.